PATTERNS OF SOCIAL INEQUALITY
Essays for Richard Brown

Longman Sociology Series

Series Editor:
ROBERT G. BURGESS, University of Warwick

Editorial Advisors:
JOE BAILEY, Kingston University
JOAN CHANDLER, Plymouth University
CHRIS RHODES, London Guildhall University

Published Titles:
Social Europe, 2nd Edition
Joe Bailey (ed.)

Disability and Society
Len Barton (ed.)

Frontiers of Identity
Robin Cohen

Women and Career
Julia Evetts

Poverty and Wealth
John Scott

Shaping Women's Work
Juliet Webster

Patterns of Social Inequality
Huw Beynon and Pandeli Glavanis (eds)

Forthcoming Titles:
Gender, Pain and Emotion
Gillian Bendelow

A Question of Knowledge
Richenda Power

LONGMAN SOCIOLOGY SERIES

Patterns of Social Inequality
Essays for Richard Brown

edited by

Huw Beynon and Pandeli Glavanis

LONGMAN
London and New York

Pearson Education Limited
Edinburgh Gate
Harlow
Essex CM20 2JE
England

and Associated Companies throughout the world

*Published in the United States of America
by Pearson Education Inc., New York*

*Visit us on the World Wide Web at:
http://www.awl-he.com*

First published 1999

ISBN 0 582 29263 8

British Library Cataloguing-in-Publication Data

A catalogue record for this book is
available from the British Library

JC
575
P37

Typeset by 35 in 10/11.5pt Times
Printed in Malaysia, PP

CONTENTS

SERIES EDITOR'S PREFACE

The Longman Sociology Series consists of books written specifically for first and second year undergraduate students. Each covers one key area of sociology and aims to complement other materials.

The series is forward looking and attempts to reflect topics that will be included in syllabuses for sociology and social policy. It provides a range of volumes that bring together conceptual and empirical material. In addition, volumes in the series also examine key controversies and debates, drawing on commentaries using conceptual and empirical material from a range of authors.

Each volume in the series, whether authored or edited, covers an area that would be commonly found in sociology and social policy syllabuses. The focus of each volume is on theoretically informed empirical work with policy relatedness.

The volumes are intended for an international audience and therefore comparative material is introduced, where appropriate, in a form that is suitable for first and second year students.

Undergraduate students deserve good quality teaching from active researchers who can inspire them to think about the key issues and challenges in the social sciences in general and sociology in particular. Such teachers make the subject exciting and encourage students to become professional sociologists. In these circumstances, it is very appropriate for these essays to be written in honour of Richard Brown who has taught some of the contributors (including the series editor) and been a supportive colleague to us all. It is hoped that these essays will contribute to sociological debate much in the style of Richard Brown and inspire future generations of students to think about ways in which a sociological understanding of their world can be developed.

Professor Robert G. Burgess
University of Warwick

ACKNOWLEDGEMENTS

We would like to thank Dave O'Carroll and Emma Hughes for their help with the production of the final typed manuscript and the production of the index.

We are also grateful to the following for permission to reproduce copyright material:

British Coal for an advertisement from the *Observer* newspaper 12.1.92 (Figure 4.1); Cardiff Bay for the advertisement (Figure 4.2, Cardiff Bay) and the Office for National Statistics for 1981 and 1991 Census data.

THE CONTRIBUTORS

Sheila Allen was, until September 1998, a Research Professor of Sociology, and Equal Opportunities Adviser in the University of Bradford. Her main areas of research are the sociology of work, ethnic and race relations and the sociology of gender divisions. Her recent publications include 'What is Work for? The Right to Work and the Right to be Idle' in R. K. Brown (ed.) *The Changing Shape of Work*, Basingstoke: Macmillan, and 'Gender Relations and Research on Work' in J. Holmer and J. Karlstad (eds), *Rethinking the Question of Work*, Aldershot: Avebury, 1997.

Huw Beynon is Director of the School of Social Science at Cardiff University. Previously Professor of Sociology at the University of Manchester. He has for many years been concerned with the study of social change and the lives of manual workers.

Robert G. Burgess is Pro-Vice Chancellor, Director of CEDAR (Centre for Educational Development, Appraisal and Research) and Professor of Sociology at the University of Warwick. His main teaching and research interests are in social research methodology; especially qualitative methods and the sociology of education, and the study of schools, classrooms and curricula. He was President of the British Sociological Association (1989–91) and currently Chairs the UK Council for Graduate Education. He chairs the ESRC Training Board and is a member of Council and was a member of the ESRC Research Resources Board.

Margaret M. Curran has worked as a researcher in universities and in central and local government. Her recent work, published by Tyne and Wear Research, includes a review of local quangos and an analysis of 1991 Census data on employment and commuting. Maggie is currently excluded from the labour market by ill health.

John Eldridge is Professor of Sociology at the University of Glasgow. His main research areas have been in industrial sociology and the sociology of the media. He is a founder member of the Glasgow Media Group.

Tony Elger is Senior Lecturer in Sociology at the University of Warwick. Recent publications include *Global Japanization? The Transnational Transformation of the Labour Process*, London: Routledge, 1994 and 'International Competition, Inward Investment and the Restructuring of European Work and Industrial Relations' *European Journal of Industrial Relations*, 1997 (both with Chris Smith).

Frank Ennis is a Lecturer in the Department of Environmental Planning, University of Strathclyde. His doctoral research at the University of Durham was an examination of regional identity in the Northeast of England. His current research interests include development appraisal, the operation of property markets and urban development processes with particular reference to questions related to infrastructure provision. He has co-authored a book on the use of planning agreements *Negotiating Development – Rationales for Development Obligations and Planning Gain.*

Pandeli Glavanis is a Senior Lecturer in Development Studies, and Director of the Centre for the Study of Globalisation, Eurocentrism and Marginality at the University of Manchester. He has lectured and conducted research in the political economy of development, historical and comparative sociology and recently in the area of the social construction of identity. He has published on issues relating to power and inequality in the Middle East, and recently he has focused his research and publications on the emergence of 'Muslim Voices' within Europe.

Theo Nichols is Professor of Sociology at the University of Bristol. He has written extensively on the labour process and related issues. His latest publications include *Work and Occupation in Modern Turkey*, London: Mansell, 1996 (ed. with Erol Kahveci and Nadir Sugur) and *The Sociology of Industrial Injury*, London: Mansell, 1997. He is Editor of *Work, Employment and Society.*

Ian Roberts studied sociology at Durham University after working in the shipbuilding industry. He graduated in 1982 with a first class honours degree. He worked for several years as a contract researcher at Durham University Business School and for a short spell at UMIST. He gained a Ph.D. in 1988 and returned to the Department of Sociology and Social Policy at Durham as a British Academy Post-Doctoral Fellow. He was appointed as a lecturer in Sociology in 1991. He has recently written a book on the Wearside shipbuilding industry; *Craft Class and Control*, Edinburgh University Press.

CHAPTER 1

Introduction

HUW BEYNON AND PANDELI GLAVANIS

We have come together in these pages to write a book which reflects upon the nature of social inequality in contemporary society, something which we feel has been severely neglected in recent times. Our emphasis is upon changes taking place in UK society and this, in part, relates to our concern to produce an account which sits easily with the work of one of Britain's leading sociologists, Richard Brown. Richard retired from his post as professor at the University of Durham in 1995, and these essays mirror his interests and parallel the work which continues to preoccupy his thoughts.

Our concern to restate the importance of social inequality to an adequate sociology might seem a little odd. The study of social stratification has been one of the bench marks of British sociology. 'Class', 'status' and 'social mobility' remain dominant concepts whose study has been marked by a high degree of conceptual and methodological rigour which has rightly been granted international aclaim. However, this dominance has not been unproblematic. In the 1980s and 1990s it provoked attack from sociologists who claimed that its rigorous conceptual framework was more of a straightjacket than a help to our understanding of the dramatic and remarkable processes of change taking place in the contemporary world (see Morgan and Stanley, 1993; Pahl, 1992). In particular it was felt that new complex questions of social differentiation were being raised in relation to issues such as gender, ethnicity and race. Moreover, contemporary society seemed to be creating other equally problematic and marginalised social catagories often associated with age and residence. These changes in the social composition and demography of societies were accentuated by technological changes. Patterns of communication have altered dramatically as a consequence of television and the uses of information technology. Forms of contraception and reproductive technologies have contributed to new forms of sexual identity and household organisation. Furthermore, a century of nationalist movements and labour migrations has produced a complex set of diasporas and novel political and socio-cultural patterns in the 'host' societies (Papastedgiadis, 1998). These were the themes which attracted the attention of cultural studies and sparked the 'culturalist turn' in sociology. It has become increasingly clear that if the study of social inequality is to take up its place as a central part of a sociological agenda, it also needs to address them, not least because they figured dominantly in people's understandings of the ways in which inequalities are ordered, reproduced and experienced in daily life.

In the changed political culture associated with 'Thatcherism' new accounts of society emerged which gave central ground not to class and social stratification but to issues relating to identity and culture. Radical in intent, these new and inspirational analyses reopened society for analysis, and discovered highly complex and intriguing sets of social relationships and understandings. Increasingly in these years a 'class analysis' which stressed material inequalities in society was contrasted and opposed to a variety of analyses which gave primacy to the examination of cultural practices and identity formation in daily life. In contrast to the theories of social stratification, these approaches most frequently relied upon qualitative research methods, drawing their materials from ethnographic studies, and the analysis of text and visual images. Unintentionally, perhaps, these approaches tended to underplay issues of material inequality and the ways in which these affect the conditions of life of particular groups in society.

One of the unfortunate consequences of these developments has been the separation of the study of social stratification (once the mainstream) from more generalised studies of social life. Distinct academic literatures (on class and inequality, culture and identity) developed with increasing degrees of separateness. As a consequence, British sociology approaches the end of the century in a rather schizophrenic state, its high sophistication in both theory and method masking the fault lines that run between its major schools of thought. While this diversity has its strengths, it can also be seen to weaken the discipline's capacity to address adequately many of the problems and issues that present themselves in contemporary society. This is perhaps demonstrated most clearly in relation to the study of work and employment. Here, there might have been a possibility of combining the two frameworks in interesting and novel ways. However stratification theorists have tended to ignore the routines of work in producing their accounts in the changing class system. Their studies have emphasised patterns of income inequality and occupational mobility to the neglect of studies of power and inequality in the workplace. For their part, theorists who have emphasised culturalist approaches have tended to be attracted to accounts that conceptually recast society as 'post-Fordist' or 'post-modern' (see Hall and Jacques, 1989). These conceptions have often relied upon assertions of the changed nature of economic relations, especially in the workplace, and the replacement of 'the worker' by 'the consumer' as the central economic agent in society. In this way leisure and consumption as people's 'central life interest' were seen to have replaced 'work'. This was seen to have occurred in part as a result of technical changes in the workplace. As a consequence studies which have emphasised the creative nature of human capacities in relation to identity-formation have often relied upon notions of a 'flexible' workplace where jobs are becoming increasing open-ended and humane. However very little empirical support has been produced to support these accounts. With few exceptions (see du Gay, 1995) the 'culturalist' accounts of post-modern society *assume* changes in workplaces rather than investigate them.

A society in transition?

UK society at the end of the century remains deeply unequal, and the inequality is patterned along lines that are familiar. The share of income received by the least affluent declined steeply in the 1980s for the first time in 40 years. In the last decade of the twentieth century, the children of unskilled manual working parents had as much chance of getting to university as they had in the first. Income, education and housing still map together well as variables of inequality. It is for this reason that insurance companies, estate agents, credit agencies and others, rely so heavily upon the postal code for guidance in their assessment of risk and reward. In so many ways these issues are reminiscent of an earlier period when social inquiry by Booth, Rowntree and the Webbs focused on the condition of the working and workless poor. In the contemporary period, the writers who have drawn most attention to these conditions have been journalists, not academic sociologists (see e.g. Danziger, 1995; Davies, 1997). Accounts such as these point to the damage done to people and to social relationships as a consequence of social dislocation, poverty and inequality.

Yet within this familiarity there is also change and, with it, the appearance of novel patterns which are not easily understood, or which raise dilemmas and complications not encountered previously, or at least for some while, in the United Kingdom. There are many reasons for this. The established system of employment relations that underpinned the economic relationships within our society has changed considerably. There has been a continuing decline in the proportion of the labour force engaged in manual work. This has been closely associated with the accelerating decline in employment in extractive and manufacturing industry, and the concomitant absolute and relative growth in the size of the service sector. Added to this has been a radical transformation of the public sector as a consequence of political programmes of privatisation and commercialisation of many state-owned industries and services. So intense and rapid have been these changes that sociologists have talked of a new international division of labour (Frobel, Heinrichs and Kraye, 1980) and a new kind of *post-industrial* society (see e.g. Kumar, 1985; 1995).

In the UK, these changes have been linked with the continuing increase in the proportion of women in employment, including married women, and the rapid growth in the number of part-time jobs, the majority of them also filled by women. Alongside this has gone a reversal of the long-term decline in the proportion of those who are self-employed, and the marked and rapid increase in their numbers. Most of these self-employed people, are not *entrepreneurs* in the classic sense: they employ themselves alone. Their rise is associated with continuing, though fluctuating, high levels of unemployment, especially for younger and older workers, and for those without skills and/or qualifications (see Brown, 1997; Reich, 1991). Not surprisingly these developments have contributed to a serious weakening of the power of trade union organisations, and the likelihood that individual workers will have trade union membership and the patterns of collective association which relate to it.

These changes have considerable implications for the ways in which society is ordered and is understood. At the very least they would seem to indicate some significant alteration in the ways in which men and women organise their lives and relate to each other. The increased involvement of women in the formal economy has combined with changes in divorce legislation to alter the overall structure of households and of their internal organisation. Sociological analysis for decades has relied upon the idea of the male household head (and alongside this some normative notion of the nuclear family) as the basis of its analysis of social differentiation. This was especially appropriate to the old industrial regions like the North-East of England where employment (of all grades from unskilled worker to manager and director) was dominated by men, and a 'woman's place' was understood to be in the home. This was the context of most of Richard Brown's empirical researches and where the changes have been seen most dramatically. Here, the shipyards, the steel mills and the coal mines have been replaced by office complexes, call-centres and electrical and light engineering factories. Industries and activities associated with the production and use of computing and information technologies are seen to be the new growth points. Across the burgeoning service sector, women dominate. As a result, the two-income household replaced the established notion of the 'family wage' in the minds of most people. Alongside the no-income household, it required sociologists to contemplate the ways in which social class related to gender in the patterning of power relationships and social inequalities.

These, of course, are not the only changes that accompanied the transformation of the old industrial economies at the end of the twentieth century. The boom years of the post-war period were associated with a severe labour shortage. The employment of married women as part-time workers helped ease this, but alone this was inadequate. The largest supply of new employees (industrial labourers, bus drivers and doctors) came through international migration. Within and between continents the migrant worker has endured as a key – low-paid – element in Western economies. In the USA, Mexicans and Puerto Ricans joined black people – descendants of the freed slaves – in the dirty jobs. In Europe, the southern Mediterranean states provided the labour to fuel the boom years of the 1960s. In Britain it was slightly different, for Britain had had an Empire which had become a Commonwealth. This, on the one hand, gave British business access to a potentially infinite supply of labour, while on the other made them dependent upon labourers who, as Commonwealth citizens, had gained their own political rights. If they came as migrants they, unlike the Mexicans and Turkish, had the right to stay.

Between 1955 and 1967, two-thirds of a million people from India, Pakistan and West Indies arrived in the United Kingdom. As a wave of immigration it fell into three distinct periods. In the 1950s, West Indian migrants dominated. These – male and female – were in the most part manual workers and mostly skilled. In the 1960s things changed. Anticipation of the 1962 Commonwealth Act brought a flood of migrants keen to 'beat the ban'. After the Act itself – and the voucher system it introduced – the focus of migration shifted from the West Indies to the East. It shifted too from manual workers to professional, as Indian and Pakistani teachers, doctors, engineers and scientists took up their 'B vouchers' and moved to the United Kingdom.

Migration therefore was tied closely to the needs of the British economy, a fact that drove one contributor to an annual conference of the Royal Society to point to its 'uncomfortable resemblance to slavery' (Skinner, 1971: 63). The new immigrants were 'drawn to those regions which, in spite of demand for labour, have not been able to attract much net population from other parts of the country'. They went to the towns British people had moved out of. They moved into the 'decreasing urban cores of expanding industrial regions', pulled in by the web of capital's needs. Many of them have now lived in these cities – places like Birmingham, Bristol and London – for over 30 years. They arrived – particularly those from the West Indies – with high hopes and fond feelings for the United Kingdom and the 'English way of life'. Sadly, these were badly shaken by their early experiences of racism and discrimination in the housing and employment markets. In reflecting upon these processes, an editorial in the *Financial Times* in 1973 carried the headline 'We live in a multi-racial country':

Irretrievably? Short of the overthrow of the British constitutional tradition and the installation of an authoritarian regime, the answer must be 'Yes, irretrievably'. The reason is that no British government that respects British law and tradition could honestly legislate for the enforced expulsion from this country of people born here, or people who are British under the law, and are already living here. . . . Thus it must be accepted that significant numbers of people of West Indian and Asian origin are here to stay. Once this fundamental fact is established it should not be very difficult to proceed to the next, which is that these newcomers should be treated as equals within the society of which they are now a part. The fact that so many of them are not so treated, which is amply documented in dozens of learned reports, should alarm us, because it is this that could lead to conflict in the future. (3 October 1973)

These movements of workers were accompanied by movements in capital, as large manufacturing and service corporations began to operate more and more freely as transnational organisations. In the early 1970s, for example, senior executives in the Ford Motor Company were heard to complain the 'we are not Ford Europe – we are Ford half of Europe'. As a consequence the company began to move their factories toward the workers in the south of Europe and not the other way around (see Beynon, 1984). This process was not unique to Ford. Increasingly the world's largest corporations began to operate with a view of their investment strategies that were global in scope (see Barnett and Muller, 1974; Dicken, 1997).

In the context of such major transformative processes associated with complex patterns of migration and industrial and social change, it often seems that such established notions of class are also swept away. Certainly if the concept is to help make sense of current patterns within our society, it will need to go beyond conventional definitions which relate it to occupation or income and other material characteristics alone. This need is exacerbated when we realise that these processes of migration by capital *and* labour have had cultural as well as economic implications. The economies of places became increasingly associated with other parts of the world. These changes impacted upon people's understandings of themselves and of their ways of life. They were further accelerated by technological changes in patterns of communication. Coca-Cola and the logos of Shell and the MacDonald companies became easily recognised throughout the world as global symbols (see Ritzer, 1993). Moreover the eating habits of people in the United Kingdom altered to incorporate international cuisine. So much has this been the case that Harry Redknap, the manager of the West Ham football team, was amusingly described in 1997 as a man who had never eaten a curry! This complex process of cultural change has been well described by Robertson as 'the interpenetration of the universalisation of particularism and the particularisation of universalism' (Robertson, 1992; 1995). It influences our concern with the study of social inequality through its impacts upon people's subjective understandings of their situation and their relationships with each other.

Within stratification theory, the study of the subjective world has most usually been dominated by discussions of class consciousness and of processes of collective solidarity which derive from class position, often expressed through notions of community. In the contemporary world, such accounts need to be transformed by an understanding that gender, race and ethnicity are equally important sources of social differentiation, and that classes are made up of people with complex identities which often run across class lines. A working class composed of migrant workers will be a different one from that made up of skilled indigenous workers organised in a trade union. Equally, the social position and kinds of understandings developed by women manual workers may well be very different from those of men (see e.g. Hunt, 1980;

Porter, 1983; Skeggs, 1997). Nevertheless, to recognise the importance of the social composition (and thereby the *formation* of classes) is not to deny the centrality of life chances (and *class location*) in structuring social inequality. Access to education and differing urban environments and cultures constitute equally significant indicators of social differentiation, social exclusion and marginalisation (see e.g. Massey, 1994). This broader analytical remit for the concept of social class can be gleaned from the writings of E. P. Thompson (Thompson, 1965) and was alluded to by Richard Brown when he emphasised that:

with respect to some areas of social experience religion and region may be further important independent lines of social differentiation. As a result social analysis becomes very much more complex, but hopefully also more adequate. (Abrams and Brown, 1984: 3)

Perhaps it is through this notion of an 'adequate' sociology that some important developments can take place. Certainly there is a worry that accounts which focus purely on the cultural and social realm cannot adequately grasp and account for the changes that are taking place in the world at the present time. Equally certain is the fact that analyses which ignore this area of life will be unconvincing ones.

Social inequalities, work and community

In attempting to understand the complex ways in which UK society is changing, it is helpful to draw attention to the ways in which associated processes of differentiation (gender, ethnicity and class) each and together explain on-going patterns of inequality. These patterns are played out in the economy: through the education system which serves as an allocative mechanism, and the workplace itself. People's understandings of themselves in relation to each other are often influenced by what goes on at work and by the ways in which this iterates with life in the locality beyond the workplace. Commonly understood as 'the community', these localised places have historically given meaning to people's lives and their sense of place within their society. These are the themes which organise this book. The chapters that follow aim to accomplish a dual objective. First, to consider the new characteristics and parameters which map social inequality in contemporary society. Second, to examine carefully the particular ways in which social inequality is still reflected within our society and how sociologists are attempting to account for it. They are written from a variety of perspectives and each of us has developed insights in our own personal and particular ways.

The first three essays consider the three primary elements in the social ontology of collectivity: gender, class and race. Sheila Allen addresses the theme of social inequality through the interrelationship of gender relations and work and the conceptual changes this have provoked. She examines the ideologies of home/household/family in relation to those of work and employment and considers the associated inequalities of condition by reference to a broader analysis of structural persistence and change within our society. Huw Beynon introduces a discussion of class by highlighting the way in which our society and culture continues to be deeply affected by class-based inequalities, while politicians, social scientists and historians have come to abandon the concept as an analytical or political tool for discourse. He stresses the need for a 'class analysis' which enters the everyday world and through an examination of language, rhetoric and life-style constructs accounts of the ways in which complex social processes are textured into class understandings. Pandeli Glavanis considers the persistence of race and race politics as a central characteristic of the way in which different communities construct their individual and collective identities. He shows how this has given rise to a number of different explanations reflecting different paradigms within the discipline. His chapter illustrates how any consideration of inequalities within contemporary British society needs to take account of the 'politics of identity'.

This discussion is followed by four essays each addressing the theme of social inequality with specific reference to the two areas of social reality in which Richard Brown has made his most significant contribution: education and work. Using statistical and ethnographic evidence Robert Burgess highlights the manner in which the educational system in schools, colleges and universities continues to reproduce inequality in contemporary society. The commitment of different governments to establish education as the lynch-pin for economic performance in the next century has made little impact upon established patterns of differentiation. For their part, John Eldridge and Theo Nichols consider the importance of workplaces and the ways in which the study of culture and the labour process have allowed a broader understanding of the ways in which social inequality is both reflected and structured in contemporary society. Common to both these accounts is the view that the study of work requires a wider perspective than the narrow confines of conventional industrial sociology allow.

Nevertheless, detailed emprical accounts of workplaces and what goes on inside them are of great importance. This is especially the case when sociologists seem to be using almost opposite accounts of workplace change as part of their wider analyses of society and social inequality. For some, who emphasise the 'post-Fordist' shift, workplaces are increasingly becoming more flexible, prouctive and humane. For others, and Richard Brown was amongst their number, the changes seemed less benign. His analyses have tended to emphasise the growing insecurities associated with these changes:

managements have emphasised the importance of increasing the 'flexibility' of their workforces, for example by employing at least some of their workers on contracts of employment which are 'non-standard' in the sense that they offer less than full-time employment and/or are not open-ended in duration (e.g. part-time, temporary, and fixed-term contracts). (Brown, 1995: p. 5)

In his view, workers' experience of work during the last two decades has been characterised by growing insecurity and precariousness of employment (unemployment), along with work intensification, and the increasing demands by employers for greater flexibility in employment practices.

Tony Elger steps into this minefield with a careful scrutiny of the empirical evidence related to the labour process in British manufacturing. He concludes that change has been very slow and small-scale. Elger goes on to reflect on these changes with reference to an account of a rapidly changing world economy and its implications for established patterns of social inequality.

Ian Roberts examines the different constructions of working-class communities in the post-war period, and especially the tendency for these accounts to deviate either in the direction of pathology or in the direction of activism. Relying upon his own research, Roberts goes on to challenge the way in which several classic accounts have portrayed the working class, and especially the tendency for such studies to rely upon a 'middle class' perspective in their accounts of working-class communities.

The last two essays by Ennis and Curran extend the discussion of social inequality to the analysis of working class communities. Frank Ennis, through a detailed historical account, considers the sexual division of labour within these communities and highlights the importance of sexual segregation and inequality to any understanding of their developments. Maggie Curran, on the basis of contemporary analyses of the 1980s and 1990s, considers the experience and consequences of long-term unemployment in inner-city areas. She asks us to consider the meaning, for a social analysis of inequality, of the emergence of entire inner-city communities with minimal connection to the world of work.

Taken together, we hope that these chapters serve to honour Richard Brown and his contributions to sociology, as well as making a novel contribution to the ongoing examination of social inequality in a changing world.

CHAPTER 2

Richard Brown and British sociology[1]

IAN ROBERTS

It is sometimes said that sociology has difficulty dealing with the individual. Such a view is of course incorrect, the essence of an acceptable sociology has to be the mutual interaction between individuals and social structures, however variously conceived. There are few better definitions of 'the promise' of sociology than that classically defined by C. Wright Mills (1959) as the interconnection between private troubles and public issues. Such a conceptualisation has always informed the work of Richard Brown who, whether studying substantive issues of work histories and careers or reflecting upon the development of an academic subject, has stressed not only the importance of the interaction between individuals, contexts and the wider mutual interpenetration of structure and agency, but also the play of chance and contingency in the unfolding of history. Thus,

Work histories focus attention on one of the areas of social life where there is an interaction between individual decision and action and social structural opportunity and constraint and where the outcome of such interaction has important consequences for both individual and society. (Brown, 1982: 123–4)

No subject develops in an entirely neat and systematic way; among other things, personal interests (intellectual and material), external influences, and chance see to that. (Brown, 1992: 33)

What I shall seek to do in this interpretation of Richard Brown's work is to turn these insights on to the choices, contingencies and external influences that have exercised an effect upon his sociological career. I hope to show how Richard's career has both contributed to and been expressive of the shape that British sociology took in the post-war period. However, a word of warning needs to be issued at this point. Whilst sociology can deal with issues at the level of the individual especially in charting the choices, decisions and actions that have been made, and the effects that those have had on the construction of career, it has greater difficulty in dealing with the intrinsic personal qualities of individuals. Weber developed the concept of 'charisma' to account for individuals whose qualities are seen to be supernatural, in possession of other powers 'not accessible to everybody' (Weber, 1968: 19). Sociologists are understandably reticent to tread upon a terrain which deals with more mundane moral qualities, and the kinds of influence which comes from exemplification and not dominance. However, you cannot understand the extent of the influence that Richard Brown has exerted upon British sociologists and, more widely, sociology without recognising such a specific quality.

Richard's early career showed many of the features of the dialectic of choice and contingency that he has discussed in his later work. Following three years of alternative national service as a conscientious objector with the Friends Ambulance Unit on international service he subsequently applied to read history at Cambridge. It was at the interview for admission to Cambridge that he first came across the term sociology:

I went for interview for admission to Cambridge and Peter Laslett interviewed me for admission, and he said something like, 'the economic interpretation of history has obviously made quite a difference to historical scholarship in the way in which people think about history'. Did I think that there would be a sociological interpretation of history which might have the same sort of effect? I completely failed to answer the question because I didn't know what sociological interpretation of history might look like, or what sociology was, or what he was going on about, so we moved on to something else. I still got in. I can remember that, this stuck somehow.

Greater familiarity with sociology came in the final year at Cambridge when Richard attended a series of lectures given by the visiting American sociologist George Homans who provided not only an eloquent demolition of functionalism but also discussed industrial sociology. At the same time he read J. A. C. Brown's *The Social Psychology of Industry* (1954) and was very impressed 'by the overt message of the book',

that if only work was organised properly everybody would be satisfied and all could be wonderful and happy and if not it was because it was badly structured and badly managed and so on, that you had conflict; it was a good human relations text. I thought 'that's what I want to be doing, at least that's something that attracts me'.

In furtherance of this interest, after graduating, Richard made a successful application to the LSE in order to study for a one-year certificate in personnel administration. Not only did this provide useful practical placements (a month at Rowntree's, and also Courtaulds' as well as with Marks and Spencer, London Transport and the Employment Exchange at King's Cross), it also provided exposure to the teaching of Nancy Seear and an industrial sociologist, John Smith. On completing the certificate there followed a number of applications to firms for personnel work. However, at this juncture external circumstances intervened. In the wake of Suez, Harold Macmillan argued that the crisis had indicated the 'weakness of our post-war economy'. There was a run on reserves, a loss of exports and, 'by early 1958 it was clear that the economy was in depression' (Pollard, 1969: 475). As Richard recalled,

Unfortunately the summer and autumn of 1958 was a sort of mini-slump, so nobody was recruiting very much, so I went for lots of interviews, discovered how badly most Personnel Managers interviewed and how appalling their paper work was, in the sense that you got a rejection months after you'd been interviewed, they were really very bad, but I didn't get a job.

The first opportunity to present itself at this time came not through the impersonal labour market but as a result of what Grannovetter (1985) has called 'embeddedness', the existence of social networks within the labour market. A project studying the recruitment and employment of married women in Peak Freans biscuit factory in Bermondsey had been under way at the LSE for some time with Pearl Jeffcott employed as the researcher. In this establishment the employment of married women was a new development in the post-war period. The sociology department at the University of Leicester considered that a useful comparative piece of work could be done, looking at the local hosiery industry where the employment of married women had a long history. Richard was appointed as a research officer in 1959, initiating an interest in gender and employment that was to remain a focus throughout his career. The department at that time was composed of three others, Ilya Neustadt, Norbert Elias and John Goldthorpe.

Richard was employed at Leicester as researcher and lecturer until 1966. The department at Leicester seems to provide a null example to what Giddens (1978), himself a member of the department, has described as 'the orthodox consensus' in British sociology in the 1950s and 60s. The orthodox consensus, according to Giddens, was a focus upon the dichotomy between industrial and traditional society and a co-related emphasis upon functionalism and naturalism. Reference to the European tradition was largely mediated through US sociology. However at Leicester at this time there was a very direct link to European social thought:

The interesting thing about Leicester was that Elias knew his Marx, but he was very much in the tradition of Weberian sociology, even though he was quite critical of some of it, particularly the nominalism. . . . Neustadt was rather different . . . he did a doctorate in Belgium (Liège School of Economics) and then did another PhD in London. But he was very well founded in the sort of history of sociological theory, European history of sociological theory and his specialism was Comte. . . . It was quite an interesting situation because I don't think that there was very much . . . reference to functionalism in the teaching there – the core second-year theory course was a Comte, Marx, Durkheim and Weber course really. . . . So Leicester would have defined itself when I got there as certainly not Marxist – there was an importance attached to the expectation there would be conflict in social relations and that that should be analysed, it was structural, it wasn't just a case of people behaving badly to each other, it was basic and probably ineradicable. American speakers used to be asked 'Well, what about conflict? How do you explain conflict?'

Not only was the subject matter at Leicester distinct, but what also made an impact on the recent recruit was the intensity of commitment towards the subject:

There was a sort of missionary ethos to sociology in Leicester; Neustadt and Elias, and I think Goldthorpe to some extent, maybe we all did, but they particularly, I remember thinking at the time it was their religion, they were committed to it in that sort of way and it had a significance and importance which was far beyond earning a living or doing something which was interesting. . . . So that was quite interesting and I suppose in the end quite influential; influential for me but also it had a lot of influence on the students at the time who, something in the air or what have you, suddenly flocked to sociology in large numbers.

The department at Leicester did experience phenomenal growth during this period, going from 5 staff in 1960 to 25 three years later. Other departments of sociology were growing too, although few at quite this rate. Moreover the public profile of sociology was beginning to emerge:

other people began to think sociologists had something to tell us and I did a series of lectures in the school of architecture in Leicester Tech because they thought sociologists had the answer to 'what we should build and where?'

After being appointed as lecturer, Richard's research work at Leicester advanced on three fronts. First was a piece of work which initiated his interest in the concept of career. This involved a survey of junior managers in industry as they gained entry and began to develop their careers. A second project was undertaken with the careers advisory service at the university and involved a survey of student attitudes towards and knowledge of careers in probation and child-care work. Finally came his role as an advisor on a project carried out in the Leicester diocese by young clergy who were developing a survey of rural parishes and wanted professional sociological advice.

Such a growth in the popularity of the subject as well as growth in the numbers of those practising sociology brought with it tensions and problems as well as opportunities. For some, especially those displaying a 'messianic ethos' who had fought to promote the distinctiveness of the subject, there were threats of dilution from those recently arrived from other disciplines. Also threatening was the broader popularity of the subject which others defined as an overarching social science. The response of those practising the subject differed according to the position that they took in relation to the 'threat' of dilution. Moves to professionalise the BSA produced a lively debate (Barnes, 1981) and somewhat of a compromise solution with the setting up of the Conference of University Teachers in Sociology. Richard was admitted through one of its seven gates, that which included anyone who had a teaching position in a recognised sociology department.

Perhaps the strongest theoretical and substantive theme to engage British sociology during this and subsequent periods is that of social inequality. Richard's own work has concentrated on socio-economic and gender inequality. There are both historical and institutional reasons as to why a concern with social inequality should be seen as almost synonymous with the practice of sociology itself. The sources of social theory on which British sociology drew in its early post-Second World War development involved, as we have seen, both the wave of functionalism from the United States with its emphasis on orderly social reproduction and the classical European tradition which, in the work of Marx and Weber in particular, emphasised the inevitability of social conflict. Added to these currents was a more home-grown emphasis and empirical concern with the effects of poverty understood as an issue of social policy. Often enough the political arithmetic that flowed from this approach was informed by values of the non-conformist Christian tradition, as in the work of Seebohm Rowntree.

British sociology did not invent a concern with social inequality then, but can be seen in many ways as inheriting such a terrain. This was especially so in the early years after the Second World War when concerns with pragmatic social policy issues were recast in the light of the threats and uncertainties that the post-war world appeared to offer. Some believed that slump and recession would inevitably follow a short replacement boom as after the First World War. Allied to this, however, was to be the opportunities for change that were afforded in a new international order where the role of national and international institutions in managing the economy was to be accentuated. In Britain the election of a Labour government also added to the air of expectation that change was the order of the day.

If the pessimistic vision of post-war development was to ensue, the question that many social analysts were asking was whether the working class would turn to conflict, as sections did in the wake of the First World War? Or if the more optimistic picture of the post-war world came into being the question was: did Britain have the modern institutions, in particular an education system, to promote the technical skills necessary for development, or were its institutions merely reproducing traditional inequalities and stifling moves towards meritocracy? Either way questions of class inequality in both a political and an apparently pragmatic sense were seen as burning issues. This terrain has proved a particularly well visited site in post-war British sociology, as many of the papers in this volume testify.

What was rather slower to develop as an arena of debate approaching anything like equal importance given to the issue of social class was that of issues of gender inequality. Whereas class inequalities appeared to invoke both immediate institutional and policy issues as well as macro political commitments, issues of gender inequality, despite some impressive individual researches, remained to a large extent 'hidden from history'

(Rowbotham, 1975). It is arguable that, as a newly developing discipline in Britain, sociology initially followed where other social sciences led. Social and economic inequality was largely the substantive terrain on which British sociology developed its disciplinary approaches and identities. Only later were identifiably sociological accounts of other forms of inequality forthcoming. This is true of ethnic and racial inequality as it is for gender inequality. Thus whilst individual sociologists were studying problems within the paradigm of 'race relations' in the late 1950s and early 1960s (Glass, 1960; Patterson, 1963) a specifically wider sociological literature dealing with ethnic and racial inequality emerged from the late 1970s onwards (Gilroy, 1987; Donald and Rattansi, 1992).

Whilst it is difficult to delineate sharply what a specifically sociological approach to inequality involves, one candidate for this distinction that seems to make sense is as an approach which mediates between aspects of structure and agency – the ability to look at issues of inequality not only as defined by pragmatic policy concerns but to seek to relate the experience of those variously situated, positively and negatively privileged, as contributing towards a more complex understanding of forms of inequality. Sociological practice towards the understanding of social inequality has made many individual contributions, ranging from issues of theoretical conceptualisation, to a more rigorous and technically demanding empirical focus, as in John Goldthorpe's work on class analysis (1997). Nevertheless, arguably the central defining quality of the sociological approach is to see those studied (and of course those studying) as implicated both as subjects and objects of an historically evolving reality. There are those within the discipline, including Richard Brown, who would contend that many of the 'realities' of social inequality are still not appreciated by those who see themselves as either not affected or not implicated. As such the study of social inequality remains of central importance. A precursor and necessary accompaniment to changing the world must be an honest attempt to understand it. It was this conviction that shaped Richard's developing approach to social inequality throughout his career.

One institutional tension that accompanied the growth of the subject was connected with the rise in the size of departments of which Leicester was a prime example. The non-formal and very personalised relationships that were possible when only four or five people worked together became increasingly incongruous as the numbers involved increased and, in a process that parallels small-firm growth, strains began to show:

We never had departmental meetings. The first departmental meeting in that department was called when Neustadt was in Sierra Leone doing something for UNESCO. Syd Holloway and I were left in charge and called a departmental meeting. Before and after that there weren't any. In the early days it didn't matter because we all had coffee together so it was all done informally, but by the time you have 25 you can't do it that way. We used to talk about people being in and being out and it seemed time for a change.

Richard made the active choice to leave Leicester and was appointed at the University of Durham in 1966. By this time he was well established as a national figure in industrial sociology in Britain with two respected journal articles making a particular impact. The first, 'Participation, conflict and change in industry – a review of research in industrial sociology at the Department of Social Science, University of Liverpool' was published in *Sociological Review* prior to leaving Leicester. The second, 'Research and consultancy in industrial enterprises – a review of the contribution of the Tavistock Institute of Human Relations to the development of industrial sociology', was published in the first issue of *Sociology* shortly after his arrival in Durham. Both of these articles showed Richard's ability to produce critical and yet constructive appraisals of the work of distinct schools of thought. Moreover his ability to relate both the intricate details and complexity of evolving work and yet position these within the context of wider developments was a skill which he was to develop further into his more recent book, *Understanding Industrial Organisations* (1992).

On the empirical research side Richard began to investigate the shipbuilding industry in a number of projects, the first of which was initiated by Peter Brannen and subsequently involved Jim Cousins and Michael Samphier. The importance of these projects was the way in which the empirical detail was related to an ongoing critique of existent theoretical frameworks. In particular the work challenged the validity of categorical orientations to work and images of society supposedly held by proletarian workers (Lockwood, 1966). In suggesting that 'Patterns of Paradox' were what characterised the social imagery of the workers that they studied, the team in a number of publications (Brown and Brannen, 1970; Brown, 1973; Cousins and Brown, 1975) were doing more than seeking a refinement of Lockwood's ideal types. Rather, they were adding both empirical and theoretical weight to a movement that was seeking a more sophisticated grasp of the interaction of structure and agency. Up until this point most of the calls for such approaches had been made at the level of social theory, not as the combined outcome of the dialectic between theory and empirical research (e.g., Dawe, 1970; Silverman, 1970). Richard recalled the complexity of the task that he had set himself in objecting to the notion of orientations to work as the solution to understanding the perspectives and associated behaviours of workers:

Once you began to look at it there were all sorts of feedback loops. Once you started saying people's work experience as well as their experiences outside work influence their orientations to work then there's room for all the other things to come back in again, technology, management styles, all the rest of it, because it's not a simple one-line causative chain. . . . So it posed problems. . . . The one thing which I tried to develop was the idea of some negotiated order as a way beyond that, which again was trying to say this is taking place in a particular sort of context, but within that context there is room for the actors to work out their own destinies to some extent, or at least to create a particular patterning of social relations.

A number of issues of substantive focus and style had become very clear in Richard's work by this time. The focus upon the importance of a complex relationship between structure and agency would permeate all areas of his research and teaching. Associated with this is his enduring belief that an eclectic and varied approach from several different schools of thought could only be beneficial to the subject as a whole. In this belief he was steadfast that there was unlikely to be any single approach that could successfully account for the full complexity of social life. In the increasingly ideologically loaded context of sociology in the 1970s this meant that at times there were attacks forthcoming on his approach both from the proponents of 'scientific' structuralist Marxism as well as some of the more hysterical proponents of a rabid anti-Marxism. Throughout this time Richard sought to defend a plurality of theoretical approaches to sociology although he was unlikely to give his name to any single one of these. This is exemplified in his attitude towards labour process theory, reinvigorated after the publication of Harry Braverman's *Labor and Monopoly Capital* in 1974. He recognised that at the time the labour process approach potentially offered a very powerful lens through which to view the changing nature of work, but consistently cautioned some of the younger and more enthusiastic devotees, including myself, to beware of the theoretical baggage we might need to take on board in signing up to the whole agenda.

Such a solid, 'feet on the ground' yet critical approach might have ensured Richard's unpopularity with younger and apparently more radical students and teachers of the subject. The opposite was in fact the case. Much of this is explicable in terms of his tolerance, indeed willingness to engage with the most radical of ideas, a trait that has not diminished with age. However, perhaps more convincing are his personal qualities, one of the most notable of which is a total absence of any arrogance or detachment that so often follows in those experiencing even a modicum of success within academia. He has always taken tutorial discussions with first-year undergraduates as seriously as he would discussions with senior colleagues. Those who have particularly benefited from the quality of such relationships with Richard have been the numerous post-graduate students that he has supervised over the years, many of whom are now leading figures in British sociology. This living legacy will continue to strengthen British sociology into the future.

Richard's career at Durham progressed, with promotion to Senior Lecturer (1970), Reader (1974) and, following the untimely death of Philip Abrams, Professor (1982), until he was undeniably a major figure in national and ultimately international sociology. His work for the BSA saw him act in capacities as various as convenor of the industrial sociology study group (1968), member of the executive committee

(1968–72, 1983–9), member of the editorial board of *Sociology* (1978–82) and President of the BSA (1983–5) as well as a number of other duties. From 1986 to 1989 he served as the founder and first editor of *Work, Employment and Society*. In many ways the initial impetus behind *WES* was the substantive breadth of Richard's conception of work and society coupled with his non-dogmatic, non-partisan approach. Its success also owed much to his estimation of the commercial viability of such a venture. He also served in a number of capacities on committees of the Social Science Research Council/Economic and Social Research Council. A number of other prestigious appointments followed such as President of the Sociology and Social Policy section of the British Association for the Advancement of Science (1995), an edited collection following from his arrangement of one day of the section conference of that year (Brown (ed.), 1997).

It may appear with hindsight that Richard's career displays a smooth inevitability which I am sure cannot have been the way that it felt at the time. However, if timing is everything then Richard did arguably appear on the sociological scene at the right time. The long boom of the post-war period did present unparalleled opportunities for the development of a 'new' subject within a university sector that was to expand with relatively generous resources. In the early years at Leicester he was unsure of his future career and occasionally tempted to seek a change and work in personnel management. In later years he had no such doubt about his commitment to a belief in the subject. In the 1980s higher education was operating in a changed context. Ironically, when Richard was having to rise to the challenges and responsibilities of professorship within a climate of financial stringency, he identifies the strength of sociology as a discipline that had truly arrived:

I do have a sense of pride in being part of it, and what has happened. . . . (In the) early 80s there were cuts in the air, I was on a faculty planning committee and we were talking about 'what did we essentially need to have a faculty of Social Sciences?' Sociology, politics and so on, in a way in which 20 years earlier it wouldn't have been. Sociology might have been dispensable, of course it was in one or two universities, but at least here and in other universities in the rest of the country it wasn't.

This period was an uncomfortable one for Richard, having to deal firstly with the cuts and then the pressures that arose from commitment outside of academe, most notable of which was his support for the miners' cause during the strike of 1984–5. During what he recollects as a 'pretty gloomy ten years' one friendship and academic relationship proved of particular importance. Huw Beynon arrived in the department in 1976, having been appointed when Richard was away on holiday. Their relationship became one of the most productive of academic associations and yet this did not present itself directly in many joint publications or projects, Richard explained:

In some ways our styles of writing and presenting material are very different, and I don't think I can do what he does and he probably could do what I do but doesn't want to and so it probably is difficult to pick out influences in a way. . . . And yet the ten years or so he was here (at Durham) we talked a lot and exchanged ideas a lot.

The influence of Huw and indeed, through the more impersonal route of written work, that of Elliot Jaques (1961) and William Baldamus (1961) is perhaps discernible in Richard's developing work upon the employment relationship (1981, 1988). In this work we see very overtly a concern to work out the relationship between structure and agency through the deployment of both theoretical elaboration and empirical exemplification. The Marxian problematic that 'when you employ somebody else you've got an enormous black hole of uncertainty, how do you ensure that the contract is closed?', is pursued through an approach stressing the negotiated order of organisations and the strategic power available to agents as a result of contextualisation within institutions embedded in specific labour markets. This is one aspect of Richard's work that is ongoing:

I'm very happy with that, I don't think I've worked it out yet fully, that's what I retired to do . . . one of the things I retired to do.

Of his own career Richard is fond of referring to a remark that Cromwell once made that 'No man goes so far as he who knows not where he's going'. I think that this is to give too much to contingency and chance in this particular case. The timing may have been right but Richard Brown would not have achieved the level of respect that is so evident within the wider academic community if his work had not been of the highest of standards. More importantly Richard's example has exercised a profound effect upon those of us who have been lucky enough to know him personally. Hopefully some of his unbounded enthusiasm for the subject and open mindedness with respect to ideas and traditions that are not necessarily one's own will have rubbed off. Insofar as this effect is embedded within a wide network of people he has taught and worked with it would be good to think that such agency has in some ways become institutionalised within the dynamics of British sociology itself.

Note

1 All direct quotations from Richard Brown are taken from tape-recorded conversations with the author.

CHAPTER 3

Gender inequality and divisions of labour

SHEILA ALLEN

Over the post Second World War period considerable change has taken place in some social relationships and in the discipline of sociology. This essay considers those which relate to the relationships of gender, their associated divisions of labour and the ways in which these have been perceived and analysed by sociologists. It focuses mainly on the British context. The mobilisation of women's labour in the Second World War, the increase in part-time jobs during and after the war, together with the post-war pressures to return to 'normality' led to constructions of women's economic participation, divisions of labour and domestication which owe more to prevailing ideologies of what ought to be than what actually is. These constructions to a large extent still play a dominant role in research design in, for instance, the questions asked and not asked and the uncritical production and use of official statistics. In the 1990s the concentration by politicians on the family and so-called traditional family values, not only in speeches but in policy formulation, rely heavily on and reinforce the same ideological constructions. Maybe part of the explanation for their strong re-emergence is to be looked for in the restructured economy, with its high levels of unemployment, an increasingly low-paid employed sector, the spread of casualised working conditions, the removal of protective legislation and a weakened trade union movement. Collective provision based on taxation according to income and wealth becomes narrower in scope and less adequate to meet the needs of the majority.

These changes have altered the material base of everyday life and have exacerbated the inequalities of condition on which it is conducted. The individualising of responsibility and the privatising of services assumes the norm is a family structure where fathers keep children, mothers look after them and those needing care for reasons of age and sickness or disability can call on family members to provide it. At the same time finding or creating a job to provide income is 'encouraged' through measures to reduce the amount of and eligibility for benefit, even where full contributions have been made. The agenda of politicians who speak about the failings of individuals, 'irresponsible' parents (single or otherwise) in terms of some lost morality and family values is highly functional in diverting attention from the problems created by restructuring and from informed discussion of economic and social policies which could deal with these changes more adequately.

The need to incorporate the broader political context into analyses of gender inequalities and divisions of labour is obvious, but the need to treat with the utmost caution constructions – of the family, of inequality and of divisions of labour – which are limited in their scope, partial in application and for which the evidence is either lacking or distorting is equally so. My concern in this essay is to address the gendered inequalities in existing divisions of labour and to suggest some ways of researching which are more adequate for explanations of the persistence in the levels and forms of this inequality and for policy formulation. In selecting what to include in this essay I was struck by the current relevance of many of the issues raised by Richard Brown in his paper for the 1974 Annual Conference of the British Sociological Association (Brown, 1976).[1] I argue that despite the extensive literature produced subsequently on women's work and the body of research on gender relations and work, much of this remains unincorporated in social and economic writings.

Contextualising gender

Before turning to these issues I should make clear that my approach to the study of gender relations is based on the many contributions to social theory developed, particularly since the 1970s, by feminists.[2] These have stressed commonalties in women's conditions as well as differences. In both cases some have taken up extreme positions, by either universalising 'women' as a category or stressing differences to a degree that any commonality disappears. Neither can be justified sociologically, though politically they may function to mobilise support, either among women generally or along particularistic divisions, such as those of race, ethnicity or class.[3] The diversity among women is part of the complexity of social relations which requires theorising.[4] But so too are the structures and processes of patriarchy, which impact on all women's lives and on the production of social scientific knowledge.

At the present time, after two decades in which research on women and, to a lesser extent on gender has increased, we have reached a stage where it is not uncommon to find the argument being put that

Class theory is . . . not sufficient to handle all major forms of oppression and exploitation, neither is patriarchy or racism. . . . The only way out . . . is to confront the intransitive and irreducible nature of each major structure of oppression in its own right, while realizing that gender, division of labour and class are constructed simultaneously and reciprocally. (Sayer and Walker, 1992: 40)

What is not clear in such formulations is how having stated that none is reducible to the other, we can then proceed to analyse their mutually constitutive formation. To place them side by side will not do, for this fails to address the central question. To prioritise one in relation to the others carries the danger of returning to (or continuing), the all too familiar analyses of either 'genderless class' or 'classless gender'. This defeats the project. It is in fact meaningless to construct theoretical propositions about one without the other. What is required is a specification of their interconnectedness at different levels of generality. At the most general level it can be argued, quite properly in my view, that class formation and patriarchal relations are integral to the processes of production, distribution and exchange. To understand any particular pattern theoretical propositions about their specific intermeshing are necessary. There is nothing to be gained from approaches which seek a solution by circumventing the centrality of this interconnectedness or by retreating into atheoretical statements which construe the interconnectedness as randomly contingent. That there is room at any level of analysis for competing theories and explanations cannot be gainsaid, but assessing their rival claims is part of the project. One proposition might be that gender inequalities, in terms of the division of labour in post-war Britain, cut across class and racial divisions; and a second is that there is a high probability that the degree of gender inequality, although not the form, varies with class and racialised location. An adequate exploration of these propositions is possible only if the implications of the feminist critique of class theory and the black feminist analyses of racism are taken on board.[5] Much thinking about how this work is to be developed and assimilated into mainstream analyses remains to be done.

Divisions of labour

The division of labour has long been seen as central to the structuring of social relations. For the most part the attention of social scientists has been focused on its relevance to class and status formation (Lockwood, 1986; Parkin, 1978; Rattansi, 1982; Stacey, 1981). Theorising this relation developed almost entirely without serious reference to gender and most empirical investigation adopted assumptions and used measurements which denied its salience (Allen, 1982; Crompton and Mann, 1986). The sexual division of labour was not ignored, but constructed in such a way that it became irrelevant to the explanation of structures of inequality. As an example, Durkheim's treatment of the division of labour between the sexes is instructive, not for its historical value, but for its pervasive influence on sociological constructions well into the third quarter of the twentieth century. It was important in the approaches adopted in industrial sociology and the sociology of work and in creating boundaries between these and the sociology of kinship, family and community. The sexual division of labour is integral to his thesis of social integration where he argues that 'the sexual division of labour is the source of conjugal solidarity. . . . The further we look in the past, the smaller becomes this difference [division of labour] between man and woman. . . . Long ago women retired from warfare and public affairs, and consecrated her entire life to her family. Since then, her role has become even more specialised. Today, among cultivated people, the woman leads a completely different existence from that of man. . . . One of the sexes takes care of the affective functions and the other of intellectual functions'. He has no difficulty in fitting into his argument the observations that some women participate in the same activities as men. He claims 'even in this sphere of action [artistic and literary life], woman carries out her own nature, and her role is very specialized, very different from that of man' (Durkheim, 1960: 56–60). For good measure he adds that if tasks become feminine, men permit this so they can give themselves 'more specially to the pursuit of science'. A division of labour, characteristic of a paticular group at a particular time, was seen as a reflection of the natural differences between men and women and as socially necessary. Though few sociologists would now accept the biological or physiological evidence which underpinned his conception, the significance he attached to this version of the sexual division of labour in making possible and sustaining a modern moral and social order proved extremely durable.

Durkheim's view can be seen as part of the more general post-enlightenment thinking which, in Dorothy Smith's words, 'culturally eclipses' women (Smith, 1978). The consequences are still apparent wherever men are constructed as the universal human subject and the tendency to treat the gendered division of labour as a given, which marks much social theory and consequently empirical research, is one of its strongest supports. The significance and consequences of the pervasiveness and historical longevity of the divisions of labour between men and women remain largely unincorporated in social theory because these divisions are deemed natural, given and necessary (Delphy, 1993).

Challenges to these constructions were mounted long before the 1970s, but they never became part of mainstream theories and still in the 1990s remain marginalised. This is in large part due to the structures of knowledge production, which are in general antipathetic to re-examining domain assumptions and incorporating the intellectual consequences of so doing. It is also due to the enormity of the task of constructing a more encompassing approach to social scientific knowledge.

As a social order the relations between men and women operate to create and to maintain forms of interaction and structures of allocation, of material and cultural resources and of people, whereby within, as well as between, households and kin groups gender inequalities persist. These systems differ across societies in terms of material and cultural content, but they do not appear to differ in terms of hierarchies, whereby men dominate and women are subordinated. The particular formation depends on the type of society and on the extent of economic and social relations between societies.

The division of labour is a core feature of the inequality of condition between men and women and a key concept in rendering less opaque systems of gender relations, and it is to a consideration of these I shall now turn.

Counting women's economic activity: market labour and paid work

In reviewing state policy towards the mobilisation of women during the Second World War Summerfield (1984: 29) argues that policy-makers faced a major dilemma. 'In essence the problem was whether the demands of wartime production for an increased supply of female labour should be allowed to take precedence over the demand for women's labour in the home, or whether intrusion upon women's conventional domestic roles, particularly those of married women, should be avoided'. In her view, 'In trying to resolve the dilemma, policy-makers searched for a compromise between the two spheres of activity, domestic and industrial, such that neither would be profoundly changed' (ibid.). This dilemma for policy-makers demonstrates the dominant value system which constructs women as wives and mothers and takes for granted married women's separation from market labour. The separation of the two spheres and the strongly held notion that women (particularly those who were married) were not conventionally part of the labour force were taken as given in industrial sociology.

A particularly difficult problem in evaluating the changes in divisions of labour between men and women arises from the failure of dominant approaches to take a serious and systematic look at the ways in which the economic activities of women continue to be under-recorded in much the same way as they have been in the past. Even among some feminist scholars the analysis does not take fully into account the very grave shortcomings of the data on which observations about changes in women's relation to market labour are based.

Brown (1976: 27) drew attention to the effort that had been expended in many investigations on 'trying to establish the facts of women's employment, their occupations and conditions' because of the absence of adequate official statistics. Despite attempts to change the methods and assumptions of official statistics gatherers over the intervening 20 years, this problem remains for those analysing women's employment, unemployment and work more generally. There have been United Nations resolutions and recommendations for improvements in the collection of national, regional and international statistics on work (1976, 1980, 1986) and the UN Decade for Women (1975–85) emphasised the need for changes to be made, not simply to give recognition at all levels of statistical accounting to the economic contribution of women, but also to provide improved economic indicators for development planning in both the Third and First Worlds.

Pressure was put on the UN and the ILO to devise ways of accounting for women's work more in tune with the reality of their working lives (see Pietila and Vickers, 1990, for a review of the role of the United Nations). These efforts cover three areas: the recording of employment, especially part-time/temporary activity, paid/income-generating work outside the employment sector, and unpaid work carried out as part of domestic labour. The latter includes servicing work, subsistence and production for the market. Some advances have been made; for example, the Indian Census began to include homeworking labour in 1990, Sri Lanka counts the work of women in subsistence agriculture, and Bangladesh and Thailand have taken steps to enumerate the work of rural women, in cash crops, income-generating work and subsistence activities (Nuss, 1991). In Western economies there has been little advance in the public recording of women's economic activity. Many forms of their work remain invisible. For example, a woman interviewed as part of our homeworking research was also a paid child-minder, had two part-time jobs outside her home, one in a bar and one as a cleaner, as well as looking after her two children. Given the way labour statistics are collected she would be recorded, at best, as a part-time worker, when in fact she was in paid work for well above the average full-time hours. Her paid work, excluding child-minding, took up to 55 hours a week. In addition she carried an unpaid workload (see Allen and Wolkowitz, 1987).

Research on homeworking was very sparse for a period of some 70 years, roughly from the passing of the Trade Boards Act in 1909 until 1980. When we began our project there were some descriptive accounts which detailed abysmal rates of pay, the lack of employment rights and poor, and in some cases, dangerous and unhealthy conditions of work (Bolton, 1975; Brown, 1974; Hope *et al.*, 1976). It was officially regarded as socially and economically marginal and almost totally neglected by social scientists, except as a rapidly declining historical phenomenon (Bythell, 1978). This is not surprising since the taken-for-granted idea that 'The typical and statistically normal state of affairs in an industrial society is that people do not work where they live' (Berger, 1964) considerably narrowed the sociological analysis of work and workers. In our attempt to understand and explain homeworking we had to develop a conceptual approach which acknowledged the capitalist penetration of the household, rejected the home/work split and the technical and legal definitions of self-employment and devise a methodology to investigate homeworking as a method of production integral to capitalist production, rather than something women did in their spare time, by choice or because they were 'trapped' at home with small children.

These approaches were built upon in subsequent projects, one concerned with women in business enterprise and the other with women in mining communities (Allen and Truman, 1992, 1993a; Allen, 1989; Measham and Allen, 1994).[6] In all of them it was necessary to deconstruct dominant ideologies of women, of work, family and household which permeate so much of sociological theory and empirical research.

The systematic marginalisation of homeworking labour, of women's involvement in businesses and their paid work in mining communities raises questions about what counts as work and who is counted. Can we take as given, for instance, that 'Since the Second World War, but particularly in the last fifteen years, there has been a dramatic world wide expansion of women's participation in the waged labour force' (Phizacklea, 1983: 1)? This widely held view needs challenging on two grounds. First this increase may be more apparent than real. Forms of labour recruitment and payment organised through one individual, usually the male head or male elders, obscures the work done by 'family' or community members. This practice still exists in many parts of the world, as the following example from Malaysia indicates:

The total number of 111,728 settlers noted in the official figures actually refers to the male head of settler households who . . . are free to mobilise family members to work . . . the number of people engaged in land scheme production is a lot higher than the number of registered settlers. (bin Salleh, 1991)

Historically labour in plantation economies, in the fenlands of East Anglia, in textile mills of West Yorkshire and many areas of central and eastern Europe were so organised, at least until the Second World War. The work of women and children disappears from economic accounting.

Secondly in the United Kingdom the technicalities of statistical recording and the assumptions on which they rest leave little room for complacency about the volume or rates of increase in women's paid labour. The situation in the inter-war years is a particularly difficult one, but since it is frequently taken as a base line, it plays a crucial role in discussions of post-war changes. In many oral histories, diaries and autobiographical accounts, as well as research projects into women's working lives, there is much evidence to indicate that women were undertaking paid work throughout this period, not only as young and single women, but for much of their lives (Allen, 1989; Glucksmann, 1986; Jewish Women in London Group, 1989). Summerfield points out that 71 per cent of the women aged 18–59 employed in the wartime industries had been in paid work when the war started (1984: 30). The official statistical recording of women's labour during the period was highly restrictive for a variety of reasons. Reliance on Census data and on the counts of the insured population, together with the incentive to secrecy which accompanied the imposition of marriage bars and the consequences of the Anomalies Act, as sound indications of the volume of women's employment, let alone women's paid work, is highly problematic. Consequently some of the propositions about post-war change are open to doubt.

In counting labour it is always important to examine the overall framework in which the exercise is being conducted and the assumptions underlying the selected methods of investigation. I am not arguing that the pre- and post-war patterns of women's employment/paid work are identical, or that there were not industry and regional variations in both periods, but that there were continuities which have tended to be overlooked and the volume of women's paid work has certainly been underestimated. One very important reason for this was the strength of the ideology of the male breadwinner and the woman as actual or potential wife and mother. In the inter-war years high levels of male unemployment, eugenicist concerns with 'healthy' mothers and the power of the cult of domesticating women reinforced such ideological constructions.[7]

While much of the past remains obscure, what of the present? In the 1970s and 1980s many of the assumptions made in industrial sociology were questioned which opened up the possibility of radical reconceptualisations. The debates ranged widely, covering areas not conventionally included in studies of work. Theoretical constructions and methodologies which took men as the norm and women as 'other', or simply left them out, were challenged. Despite some breakthroughs, much of the reconceptualising has not been integrated into mainstream thinking.

The examples of women as workers are endless, even leaving aside that unpaid domestic labour expected of them, as daughters, wives, mothers and sisters.[8] Where their work conforms to the narrow construction of full-time, regular, continuous, work outside the home it is recorded (Crompton and Sanderson, 1990; Dex, 1985; Garnsey, 1978, 1984; Rubery, 1978; Walby, 1988; West, 1982). Part-time work may or may not be, much depends on the level of casualisation, the hours involved and the location of the job. Sub-contracted labour, casualised income-generating activities and much self-employment goes unrecognised and therefore unrecorded.

Much was made in the 1980s of the increasing participation of women in self-employment, but the statistics on which such claims are based present many problems. There is no adequate historical basis for assuming an increase (Allen and Truman, 1993). In Britain the Labour Force Survey and the Inland Revenue adopt different criteria and so regularly produce widely varying estimates of the numbers of self-employed and business owners. A survey conducted in the European Economic Community found the numbers of women who worked independently, or ran their own business, or worked (unsalaried) in their partner's business was higher by some 10 million women than those recorded in official Eurostat figures (EEC, 1987). In Eurostat definitions these were non-salaried, therefore not economically active, so excluded. By asking a large sample of them about their sources of income, the survey showed clearly the deficiencies of official statistics and furthermore reveals the lack of recognition and understanding of the complexities of the structures in which women's work is embedded.

Women's economic activities in mining communities are equally rendered invisible by official counting. In 1986 we included questions on all types of paid work and distinguished between the voluntarily and involuntarily economically inactive. Such simple changes gave a picture of women's economic activity quite different from that produced when the same localities were investigated using the standard Social Change and Economic Life questionnaire in 1987 and by Martin and Roberts (1984).[9] But such questions are only a beginning. Skills in listening and observing are also essential to providing more rounded accounts. For example, in response to questions about work, women would say that they had not worked since having children, or since marrying. When talking about leisure or giving their reasons for not working, they referred to going to the club 'to give a hand' or 'helping' with their partner's business. Such activities as working several shifts a week serving behind the bar, regularly staffing market stalls, or being accountants and secretaries for a partner's business were not regarded as having a job and certainly not a real job by the women themselves, their partners or families. This marginalisation in popular discourse is reflected in the formal methods of data collection. If observation and analyses of conversation were more widely used the data would be significantly improved. As Waring has written, 'if women's work cannot be successfully incorporated into a system which purports to measure all economic activity . . . then it is invalid' (1988: 44). This failure to record women's level of economic participation is both a reflection of ideology and a source of their inequality.

Gender inequality

Social inequality is, according to Beteille, universal and has 'occupied a central position in the discipline of sociology since its inception' (1969: 9). He notes later that inequalities between the sexes appear even in the simplest social structures, but his observation is nowhere taken up in the rest of the book. The study of inequality and equality in post-war Britain coincides roughly with the two approaches that he idenifies, the distributive and the relational. The first is concerned with the ways in which factors such as income, wealth, education and so on are distributed differently in the population and is exemplified by studies of poverty, the distribution of educational and occupational opportunities and inequalities in health care (Abel-Smith and Townsend, 1965; Coates and Silburn, 1970; Titmuss, 1962; Townsend, 1979; Townsend and Davidson; 1982). These studies documented quantitative differences and focused on how measures of poverty could be improved. 'The second refers to the ways in which individuals differentiated by these criteria are related to each other within a system of groups and categories' (Beteille, 1969: 13). Despite Westergaard's claim that 'class is in essence a matter of inequality,

inequality the very stuff of class' (1977: 165) the issues of inequality were in the main addressed only obliquely in class analyses. The focus was rather on the adequacies/inadequacies of Weberian, Parsonian and Marxist theories in explaining post-war structures and debates around the thesis of embourgoisement, the continuation of elites, the 'new' middle class and the rigidities and fluidities of class divisions.[10] The concept of relative deprivation became for a time the panacea for the problems of quantifying and explaining the persistence of inequalities, within and between societies, and the modes of legitimation employed to make them acceptable. This gave rise to a lively debate which brought into the same arena those whose work had centred on poverty and those whose main interest stemmed from analyses of class.[11] It was at its height when the politics of establishing a prices and incomes policy and the role of the state in redistribution were centre stage.

What is remarkable is that little or no attention was given to inequalities arising from gender relations. Atkinson, in an otherwise exemplary critical survey of measures of poverty and income inequality, does not raise any question of gender differentials. Women appear only as wives, and that very rarely, the young and the old are either male or genderless. In concluding that the gaps in our knowledge about inequality were such that no firm statements could be made about its rise or decline, and suggesting a range of issues to improve the conceptualisation of inequality and the collection of statistical information to establish its extent and causes, he neglects to include any reference to gender (1974: 68).[12] It is not until the 1980s that the issue of gender inequalities begins to enter the discussions both of distributional and relational approaches (Green, 1981; Jennett and Stewart, 1987; Robbins *et al.*, 1982) and into debates around theorising and investigating class. By then it is no longer seriously claimed that such inequalities do not exist and the UN calculation 'that women do two-thirds of the world's work, get 10 per cent of the income and own 1 per cent of the assets' is widely quoted (UN, 1980). What is disputed is the significance of gender to class structuring and action.[13]

In arguing that inequalities of opportunities and outcomes have had and should have a subordinate place in stratification analysis, Lockwood makes a strong case for what has been labelled 'conventional' analysis and asks 'what kinds of social interactions a gender-informed study of social stratification does in fact seek to explain' (Lockwood, 1986: 13). In terms of conventional analysis there is and can be no answer. Conventional analyses have manifestly failed to explain the empirically identifiable interactions patterned so that men and women enter them under conditions which are not simply different, but for the most part systematically unequal. Such patterns are observable in all institutional contexts and across historically variable structures. How then are we to explain the persistence and consequences of the sexual division of labour? Brown put the point very clearly in his comments on the research in industrial sociology which saw women in employment from a social problem rather than from a sociological perspective. 'These [sociological] problems can be stated as: in what ways do sexual divisions in society affect the social consciousness of workers who otherwise have in common that they sell their labour power in the market; and how far can comparisons between men and women increase our understanding of the nature and determinants of workers' orientations towards and actions in the work situation?' (1976: 30). Such questions have a direct bearing on class analysis in the 1990s.

Inequalities and the division of labour

The underestimation of the volume of women's economic contribution as employees, paid workers and family supporters is part of the undervaluation of women's economic activity and level of skill more generally and is reflected in lower pay, poorer conditions and lower status (Allen, 1983; Amsden, 1980; Waring, 1988). The evidence from the EOC confirms that, despite legal, demographic and social and economic restructuring, labour market inequalities between men and women persist in the 1990s. Accepting that 'The fact that something should be of concern to the Equal Opportunities Commission does not thereby guarantee its sociological relevance' (Lockwood, 1986: 14) it is nevertheless the case that gender inequalities have real consequences. It is irrelevant whether or not sociologists think these are just or unjust or whether they wish to change them, but highly relevant to seek to investigate and explain them. Theories which take them as natural, or as biologically, genetically or psychologically explicable are plentiful. To arrive at sociologically adequate explanations involves asking a range of questions, some of which challenge class and status orthodoxies.

At present two labour market explanations are put forward for the long-standing inequalities in pay. One is that the gender segregation of labour market work means there is little opportunity for direct comparisons between men's and women's rates and so no legal basis for action on grounds of sex discrimination. This form of gender segregation is more marked in manual and lower-level non-manual jobs. Despite the high profile given to the few women at or near the top of some organisations, and to measures such as Opportunity 2000 which explicitly seek to balance the gender ratio in high-level jobs, there has been little movement in terms of occupational segregation.[14] However, where women do hold higher-status occupations their earnings are also on average lower than their male counterparts, with the gap being wider in the private sector than the public, and the more senior the level the wider it becomes. Full-time women managers in industry and commerce earn two thirds of the weekly earnings of male managers and women in the professions 80 per cent of equivalent males. Neither the provisions of the Equal Pay Act, nor the Equal Pay for Work of Equal Value directive have removed pay inequalities.[15]

The other labour market explanation relates to the ways in which pay is fixed. In the United Kingdom, unlike Europe where the differential is lower, there is no statutory minimum wage (except the minimum rates for agricultural workers set by the last remaining Wages Council).[16] Collective agreements between unions and employers are deemed to be voluntary, so lack statutory status and increasingly, as part of restructuring, nationally negotiated wage settlements are disappearing and being replaced by devolved systems based on market price, performance/merit and appraisal. These forms of pay determination appear to be as susceptible to sex bias as older forms (EOC, 1993a: 11; Bevan and Thompson, 1992). Reporting on qualitative research carried out on both the private and public sectors, the EOC comments that 'Employers' use of flexible and market-based systems of pay during the last few years has tended to widen the gender differential in pay and a degree of ignorance, complacency and prejudice on the part of personnel specialists and trade union officials [was found]' (1993a: 11; see also Randall *et al.*, 1991).

'The pay gap between men and women in Britain, wider than in most EC member states, is a major obstacle to women's economic independence' (EOC, 1993a: 25–6). In view of this the Commission made the narrowing of the pay gap between men and women a priority. A measure of the consciousness of these inequalities among those affected is not available except in complaints about sex discrimination at work, the largest number of which (3,449, almost 40 per cent, in 1992) concerned less favourable terms and conditions. How do sociologists explain this major characteristic of the labour market and its implications?

Casualised working conditions have been discussed in terms of flexibility and 'new' ways of working as constituting one feature of the restructuring of labour markets over the 1980s. The lack of attention to the history of casualised labour and to the extent of gender differentials in it marks much of the discussion. Consequently, it is not only that there is a failure to take into account the routinely casualised conditions of much of the work women do and their role as a flexible workforce in many branches of industry and commerce, long before the present restructuring appeared, but a neglect of the inter- and intra-class differences between men and women in these respects. Most of the employee rights built up over several generations became established only after the Second World War, particularly under the Labour governments in the mid-1960s and mid-1970s. Those in part-time jobs excluded from these rights, as well as from training, promotion and pension schemes were, and are, overwhelmingly women. A pattern of work, seen as particularly appropriate for women by industrial sociologists and by many women, carries extremely high costs, which were given almost no recognition by sociologists (Hurstfield, 1978, 1980, 1987). According to the official count in 1992, some 44 per cent of the workforce was part-time, over

87 per cent of these are women, the vast majority in low-skilled, low-status and low-paid jobs.[17] In the period of full employment for adult males the majority of those remaining outside the provisions which Marshall (1950) argued were essential in conditions of class inequality to embed citizens' rights in social institutions were women (Allen, 1993b). In a period of recession and restructuring this exclusion has been extended to include manual jobs customarily occupied by men and to occupations in the professions and industrial management considered to be secure and protected and the preserve of the middle class. These changes require a radical rethinking of class analyses.

Gender: not just a woman's problem

My concern in this essay to address the gendered inequalities in existing divisions of labour and to suggest more adequate ways to research and explain the persistence in the levels and forms of this type of inequality and to formulate policy to reduce it, has inevitably left untouched many aspects essential to a reworking of the sociology of work and sociology generally. In concentrating on a few issues I have attempted to show that, despite the volume of work undertaken and the many questions raised over the past 25 years, we are still far from integrating these into mainstream ways of thinking.

Research on women workers in the Second World War demonstrates that there was little change in gender segregation or inequality at work. The changes in the work some women did were temporary and only for professional women was there some reduction in inequality (Brown, 1992; Summerfield, 1984). An increase in part-time jobs in the formal labour market marked the post-war period. Though its development varied across industrial sectors and occupational levels, these jobs were almost exclusively done by women. From being seen as appropriate for women in the 1950s and 1960s and as a concession by employers, by the late 1970s the disadvantages of part-time employment were recognised by some sociologists as reinforcing women's subordinate position in the household as well as the labour market. By the beginning of the 1990s the pattern of inequality between men and women showed few signs of diminishing. The relative gap in earnings persisted at all occupational levels and the occupational and industrial distributions were little changed. Changes in the 1980s through deregulation, privatisation and the effects of recession brought high levels of job loss and insecurity, with worsening conditions for those still in employment. The proportion of non-elderly households in poverty increased in the UK from 8.5 per cent in 1979 to 12.5 per cent in 1986 (Smeeding and Rainwater, 1991). Household and labour market changes both played a part, but it is argued that labour market changes were more significant (Buck, 1993). These, together with the reduction of collective welfare provision and eligibility for benefit, intensified the labour burden in households, which falls especially on women.

Sociology has only slowly taken up the gender dimension of social relations and begun to examine the vocabularies, assumptions and measures which produce theories and explanations which obscure or distort the divisions of labour between men and women. Supply-side explanations of female labour still rely heavily on mechanistic models of socialisation and fall back on unimbedded notions of 'choice'. Yet, as Richard Brown pointed out in his discussion of orientations to work, the influence of the labour market where the demands on women and the rewards are not such 'as to increase their involvement in the world of work at the expense of their . . . home and family' and 'because of the reactions of employers to the knowledge that a woman is married or has children [these] have . . . consequences regardless of the woman's own priorities' (1976: 33). Studies of the processes which maintain occupational segregation by gender as a major organisational characteristic in the formal labour market and those which explore the use of women's labour in sex-segregated jobs by multinationals provide the basis for a better understanding of the continued structuring of employment along gender lines (Cockburn, 1991; Elson and Pearson, 1989). The systematic investigation of the interconnection of the division of labour found in employment with that found in other forms of work is central to the understanding of persistent and marked gender inequality and to the formulation of policies for removing it. More than this, however, generalisations about social action, structure and organisation are possible only when they are based on the condition and experience of both genders. Only when this becomes the norm in sociology can we begin to analyse the salience of gender relative to that of other major divisions.

Notes

1 In 1973 when Diana Leonard and I were organising the Sexual Divisions and Society conference for the BSA we wrote to several 'established' male sociologists asking them if they would present a paper reviewing the research field in which they were/had been working for its attention to sexual divisions and suggest some questions which they thought should be addressed in future research. One of the two positive replies we received was from Richard Brown.

2 A range of theories has developed which draw on a variety of standpoints. These provide not one perspective, but many. While they cannot be adequately summarised here, those which engage with the central issues in mainstream social science and its various disciplines, particularly sociology and its sub-disciplines, are the most relevant for this essay. See for instance, Gross, 1992; Harding, 1992; Maynard, 1990; Moore, 1988; Stanley, 1990.

3 In saying this I am not intending to deny the value position which I share with many others, that of wishing to transform gender relations. Rather I

see scholarly enquiry as integral to achieving such a transformation. There is nothing to be gained from characterising this position as political or as one which fails to work with the assumptions made and the knowledge produced by social scientists with other value positions (see Hammersley, 1994).

4 This is no easier nor different from what social theory aims to do in relation to diversities among men. But this very obvious point is frequently overlooked by critics of feminist theories.

5 For discussion and references to relevant work see Allen, 1987; hooks, 1984; Phillips, 1987; Ramazonoglu, 1989.

6 These projects were Homeworking in West Yorkshire, funded by the SSRC, 1979–81; Women in Mining Communities, funded by the ESRC, 1985–8; and Women in Business Enterprise, funded by the Leverhulme Trust, 1988–91.

7 Studies of the family rarely included the paid work done by wives or children. The labour aristocracy may well have adopted the ideology of the domesticated, maternal wife and been in a position to put it into practice as the 'family wage' policies of craft unions indicated. Despite attempts by some employers, philanthropists and the state to impose it, it does not become widely practised in many sections of the working class until well into the twentieth century (Poster, 1978).

8 I do not discuss the underestimation of the economic contribution of unpaid work for reasons of length. Much has been written on who does what in the household and how the division relates to whether the 'wife works', the number and ages of children and the employment status of the husband (Gregson and Lowe, 1994; Morris, 1985; Roberts *et al.*, 1985; Wheelock, 1990). Whatever differences of intepretation exist, the evidence strongly suggests that women carry a major share. Less attention has been given to devising measures to estimate the value of this contribution (Goldschmidt-Clermont, 1982, 1987).

9 Both Martin and Roberts (1984) and Warwick and Littlejohn (1992) provide much interesting and valuable data. However, using a different overall approach which took women as the prime respondents, wording questions to elicit details of all paid work, and probing reasons for not having a job the 1986 study found a lower rate of economic inactivity (32%) compared to 35 per cent (Martin and Roberts, 1984) and 43 per cent in the 1987 West Yorkshire survey (see Allen, 1993a).

10 The 1960s and 1970s brought a considerable change in the analysis of class structuring with a development of varieties of neo-Marxism and attention being given to the issues of imperialism, immigration and of racial ordering.

11 See for instance, Runciman, 1966; Wedderburn, 1974.

12 The context in which he was writing included high-profile debates about and legislation on equal pay and sex discrimination and might have been expected to be part of academic and policy discussions.

13 These debates are not about women only, but have taken on board questions central to the sociological enterprise and in this sense can be regarded as a success for the challenges mounted by feminists on orthodox analyses. It is not possible to consider these debates further here, but see Crompton and Sanderson, 1990; Delphy and Leonard, 1986; Goldthorpe, 1983; Lockwood, 1986; Mann, 1986; Marshall *et al.*, 1988; Pahl, 1989; Scott, 1986; Stacey, 1986; Stanworth, 1984; Walby, 1986). What has not so far developed either

in the theoretical literature or in empirical investigations, is a conceptualisation which systematically explores the interconnectedness of class and gender.

14 Since the Equal Pay Act became fully operational in 1975 the reduction in the pay differential between men and women resulted mainly as a consequence of the abolition of the 'women's rate' for jobs done by both men and women.

15 In 1992 32 per cent of employees in managerial and administrative occupations were women, but they were only 13 per cent of senior staff and less than 1 per cent of chief executives. They were concentrated in particular occupations, forming a majority of office managers, but only 6 per cent of production managers in manufacturing, construction and related industries. In some sectors there has been an increase in the proportion of women employed. For example, women are now 25 per cent of solicitors in private law firms and 14 per cent of police constables. They are only 5 per cent of law partners and less than 3 per cent of Assistant Chief Constables (none is a Chief or Deputy Chief Constable).

16 A statutory minimum wage of £3.60 per hour (excluding those under 18) comes into force in April 1999 and it is estimated that some 3 million workers will benefit. Much will depend on how far the law is enforced.

17 Only 17 per cent of women managers and 27 per cent of women in the professions are employed on a less than a full-time basis. The concentration varies across professions; only 10 per cent of those in legal, business and financial occupations but a third of women in teaching are part-time (EOC, 1993b).

CHAPTER 4

A classless society?

HUW BEYNON

In contemporary analysis British social science has been accused of an obsession with class. In its defence it can – with justice – be claimed that British society has been deeply affected by class-based inequalities, prejudices and understandings. In the 1950s British Rail sold first-class, second-class and third-class tickets; it also provided a further type of seat which was referred to as the 'working man's ticket'. In 1991 a member of the government observed that the railways should be re-quired to provide a first-class executive service; alongside this some-thing would be needed for the secretarial staff of the offices and he described this as a 'cheap and cheerful' service. In recent times man-agers in German, Japanese and US-based trans-national companies have commented upon the ritualised patterns of avoidance in British com-panies with their segregated lavatories, car parks and eating places.

This interpretation of British society has been supported in the 1990s by public opinion polls which indicate the general strength of ideas of class within British culture. Gallup, for example has, since 1961, sys-tematically polled the British public with the question: 'There used to be a lot of talk in politics about the class struggle. Do you think that there is a class struggle in this country?' When first asked, 56 per cent of those questioned answered 'yes'. This level of response was main-tained, with some fluctuations, until the early 1980s. Since then, how-ever, it has increased markedly to reach a peak of 81 per cent in the autumn of 1995. In that poll, the number of 'don't knows' had declined from the 22 per cent recorded in 1961, to just 4 per cent. In interpreting this data, Bob Wynbrow of Gallup related it to the growing pattern of inequality in society. In his view: 'more people believe that there is a class struggle, there are two nations, the haves are gaining and not everybody has a chance'.

In contrast, politicians, social scientists and historians have been com-ing to opposite conclusions. Frequently debates in scholarly journals like *Social History* and *Sociology* have questioned the usefulness of class as an analytic tool. Reddy, for example has argued that 'the whole notion of class as an explanatory principle in history is (currently being) brought into question' (Reddy, 1987: 15). In most formal political discourse, the idea of the 'class struggle' is seen as theoretically weak and empirically unsubstantiated. Generally changes in society are seen to have weakened the efficacy of any analysis of society conducted in such terms. In the 1990s the British Tory party talked of 'the classless society', and New Labour of being the party of the middle class, the country and 'the people'. It is an interesting conundrum.

Classes and boundaries

The use of social class as the basis for a general conceptual framework through which to analyse society and social change has been the subject of detailed debate and discussion for over a century. This debate has taken place both within the Marxist tradition and between it and other schools of thought. Often the lines of disagreement have been more apparent than real; occasionally the opposite has been the case (Skocpol, 1979; Meicksens-Wood, 1986). In reflecting on this it is hard to resist the view that the idea of class is, at one and the same time, the most useful and the most problematic of concepts employed by historians and social scientists. Its attractiveness lies initially in its potential for identifying coherent groups of people via their economic position within society. Furthermore, if these groups are seen as being in conflict or competition with each other, class position can be seen as a significant key to an exploration of people's motives and political action. The problems arise in different ways. To begin with it is not clear how and upon what basis groups can be located in the economic structure of a society. Furthermore whichever scheme is chosen there is likely to be ambiguity and marginality. In Reddy's words 'once the microscope is brought into focus neat class boundaries dissolve' (Reddy, 1987: 9). In addition, and perhaps most importantly, it is arguable that people, however located, will behave and think in ways which are not simply determined by their economic position. Again in Reddy's view, it is difficult 'to speak of socially distinct sets of individuals, united by some identifiable trait or traits, (and) having shared intentions' (Reddy, 1987: 8).

This problem can be understood as having two dimensions: one involving the problem of classification (by some 'objective' set of criteria) and the other interpreting the subjective experiences and understandings of people. A third problem arises in attempting to relate these approaches.

In assessing these issues it is helpful to place them in historical context. Kolakowski has maintained that most of the significant questions relevant to Marxist theory were fully discussed in the nineteenth century, and there is some justice in this view (Kolakowski, 1978). Certainly the writings of Marx show a keen awareness of these problems. In the judgement of recent authors he was 'irrefutably ambiguous' in the ways he resolved them (Marshall *et al.*, 1988). While this may be over-harsh, it is helpful in drawing attention to the variety of different ways in which Marx addressed this central issue.

On questions concerning the social basis of classes and class relationships, for example, Marx's writings occasionally establish the analysis
with great clarity. Here he relates class in capitalist society directly to
property (or propertylessness) and to the operation of the division of
labour, and the labour process which produces a tendency toward
polarisation and class conflict. In a much quoted passage he identified
the 'three big classes in modern society':

> the owners merely of labour power, owners of capital and landowners whose
> respective source of income are wages, profit and ground-rent, in other words
> wage labourers, capitalists and landowners. (Marx, 1971: 885)

However, Marx observed that the social and technical division of labour
operating within these classes had produced an 'infinite fragmentation
of interest and rank'. Here, as all Marxologists inform us, 'the manuscript breaks off', leaving us with what has become known as 'the
boundary problem'. It was this problem which was picked up by Weber
in his detailed distillation of the variety of economic processes at work
upon group formation in a market economy. As a result the possibility
emerged of Marx's 'three big classes' fragmenting into a greater number
based not only upon position within the production process but through
competition over a range of marketable goods. Given this, Reddy's view
that it is 'difficult to be precise about class boundaries and class membership' is undeniable (others would call it a truism). It is also the case
that it is not a new problem.

Certainly, within any broadly defined class of people a great variation
exists – both in terms of economic rewards and interests, and in sets of
ideas and beliefs. Michael Bush, for example, has provided an account
of the European peasantry (Bush, 1992: 136–158) which is particularly
helpful in outlining both the diversity of fates associated with pre-
capitalist social relations, and their multiplicity of causes. Patterns of
land utilisation and landholding, taxation policies as well as kinship
and democratic factors all contributed to the fates of peasants. It was
for these and other reasons that Shanin referred to the peasantry as 'the
awkward class' (Shanin, 1973). They too were the people who severely
taxed Marx's own conceptual scheme and drew from him an assessment
of class in terms of their relationships. In France he wrote of 'small-
holding peasants, forming a vast mass, the members of which live in
similar conditions but without entering into manifold relations with
each other'. From this he concluded generally:

> in so far as millions of families live under economic conditions of existence
> that separate their mode of life, their interests and their culture from those of
> their classes and put them in hostile opposition to the latter, they form a class.
> In so far as there is merely local interconnection among these smallholding
> peasants and the identity of interest begets no community, no national bond and
> no political organisation amongst them, they do not form a class. (Marx, 1963:
> 123–4)

This element of community is, in different ways, seen as critical by both proponents and critics of class analysis and has been taken up forcefully in the variety of writings of Patrick Joyce (see e.g. Joyce, 1996). His account of industrial workers in the nineteenth century reveals the extent to which the working class was made up of fragmented groups, often locally isolated and divided rather than united by their economic position as wage labourers. While aspects of this account can be questioned, it shows clearly that it is particularly difficult to establish evidence for a single coherent 'working class' in Victorian England. This (via discussion of the 'labour aristocracy' and the 'reserve army') has been recognised for some time. Joyce's writings take us a further step along the road of deconstruction, and uncovers another awkward class.

To this problem of the internal variation within a class (and the related question of subjective class identity) can be added a further set of problems relating to class boundaries. Again Bush's account of the peasantry is suggestive. He raises questions about the experiences of free peasants in relation to those of serfs and slaves, and suggests circumstances in which the latter states would be preferable to the former, thereby raising the possibility of a severe disjuncture between analytical categories and everyday experience.

Similar ideas have influenced the discussion of slavery in the Americas. Here attention has been drawn to the variability of slavery as an institutional form (between Africa and the USA and within the Americas), and the similarity and difference between the experience of slaves and free workers in the industrialising USA. The workers in the USA and Europe were well aware of the ways in which their lives were similar to those of slaves. Marx's notion of a 'wage slave' flowed from a popular discourse that was influenced, in part, by the fact that significant numbers of workers were involved in a tied relationship to their employers. Of these, the coal-miners of Scotland and the north of England were the most significant group. These workers were employed as bonded servants until 1872. As the first General Secretary of the Durham Miners Association put it in 1871: 'when you felt the full weight of the burden you longed to be free; you looked around but found no means of escape; you were lashed to the PLACE by English law, and while there, constantly scorched by the employers' scorpion whip' (Beynon and Austrin, 1994: 29). In this way, perhaps Snell's observations on the blurring of distinctions between peasant and agricultural labourers in the English and Welsh countryside could be extended to a group of workers whose centrality to the working class has become almost legendary (Snell, 1992: 158).

The miners in the eighteenth and nineteenth century were employed by landowners, under arrangements similar to those experienced by agricultural labourers. Equally, and in spite of an over-enthusiastic interpretation of industrialisation as an *urban* process, they lived in villages which were most often situated apart from the towns and cities.

As such John Campbell in his biography of Nye Bevan draws close attention to the link between solidarity and 'local chauvinism' amongst mine workers and how in any assessment of Bevan it is important to understand that:

he was in a real sense a country boy. The mining communities are not truly urban but *valleys* with open hillside in between them . . . the mountain – more accurately the bare heather moors – came almost literally to his doorstep. (Campbell, 1987: 7)

These problems, of establishing clear class categories based upon forms of labour and production, are exacerbated when we consider the vexed question of the 'middle class'. The historical dilemma has been to identify a class whose name denotes not a role or activity but 'a space, a between . . . a group that fails or refuses to fit the dominant social division between rich and poor' (Snell, 1992: 158–185). This problem has been compounded by the rise of large-scale organisations and a growing non-capitalist salariat to form 'one of the most intractable issues in contemporary sociology' (Abercrombie and Urry, 1983). Here the problem is partly one of definition (why 'middle' class) and sociologists have suggested new terms to handle modern conditions – the 'service class' being the most common (Goldthorpe, 1980). More significant is the question of class boundaries and the allocative process whereby people are placed in the class categories.

This problem, of course, is a general one and not peculiar to sociology and history. One of the features of modern states has been their concern with classifying and collecting data about their populations. Often this has created considerable conceptual difficulties. In the British case, the 1851 census, for example, located the royal family in the 'professional class'. This classification system became refined in the twentieth century into the widely used Registrar General's scale. While more comprehensive, this outline of categories was not without its idiosyncrasies. Its underlying theoretical assumptions were those of the eugenicists and their views of 'superior' and 'inferior' types. It has frequently been pointed out that the scale is based on a range of intuitive and *a priori* assumptions, and Nichols has observed how, in this scheme of things, capitalists and inmates of mental hospitals are brought together in the same class (Nichols, 1996). Against this background, sociologists and historians have attempted to develop more refined classificatory systems. In his assessment of historical researches into the middle class Seed points to the 'limited value of using occupation as an index of social position' (Seed, 1992). Much contemporary sociological research bears this out. Elaborate and sophisticated attempts at establishing scales which link occupation to class have indicated the problematic nature of this exercise. They have also pointed to the critical role played by the evaluative judgements of the researchers themselves (Marshall, 1983). Even given these problems, however, empirical sociological researchers would argue that while class categories (like all categories) contain internal variation, they remain a powerful explanatory tool accounting for people's attitudes at work, voting preferences, education performance and so on. But this is the beginning and not the end of an analysis. To go beyond this requires an assessment of the ways in which class inequalities relate to other major sources of differentiation in society. Of these, gender and ethnicity are undoubtedly the most significant. Some (see Pahl, 1993) would wish to add others, like car ownership. Above all, an extended analysis requires more detailed, ethnographic evidence and qualitative investigations into people's lives and the processes which relate inequality and identity formation.

Classes in daily life

It is, of course, at this broad level of subjectivity that the argument becomes most complex. Classificatory systems are all inherently difficult to establish and historians and sociologists recognise this as a necessary evil. For Reddy the classificatory problem is a stalking horse for a greater enemy; that is the view that classes themselves become agents in history, being ushered on and off the stage by historians to explain (or explain away) particular events and developments. Here too (as with the 'infinite fragmentation of interest and rank') the problem, the challenge and the crisis is not a new one. Certainly in their own empirical analyses it is possible to discern an awareness of this issue in the minds of Marx and Engels. Marx's reference to the peasantry has already been noted. To this could be added Engels' account of the religious views of the English middle classes in the 1850s. Engels makes clear that the class interest of this particular group had become effectively masked by the depths of their religious beliefs and could not, as such, be used as an explanation of their behaviour. In this he concludes that 'religious views and their further development into systems of dogmas' in many cases predominate in determining the 'form' and the 'course' of historical struggles (Engels, 1892). As Abrams has astutely observed, the problem here (and elsewhere) is *not* that the analysis 'too closely explains all historical events and developments in terms of the relations of production, ownership and class, but that it makes such generous provision for the *mediation* of these influences by political, cultural and ideological factors that the causal connection between economic relationships and historical change becomes extremely difficult to trace' (Abrams, 1982: 49).

These accounts leave us with a paradox. In one reading Marx's observations on the peasantry (reinforced by the reference to 'potatoes in a sack') leads to the sharp dichotomy he draws between 'true' and 'false' consciousness, between reality and illusion. It is this framework which allows the 'interests' of classes to lurk undetected for decades before finally emerging at critical moments in the agency of class action. This is the Marxism of the Third International and it shares many assumptions with more liberal and empiricist researchers. This is the root of much contemporary scepticism with class analysis (Pahl, 1993). However, these same observations can also lead to a theorisation of class which sees economic and political classes (and the arena of 'class struggle') as non-reducible categories, a view which is compatible with radical interpretations of Weber. It was in his pursuit of this solution that E. P. Thompson wrote of the importance of cultural processes for:

If the experience appears as determined, class consciousness does not. We can see a logic . . . but we cannot predict any law. Consciousness of class arises in the same way in different times and places, but never in just the same way. (Thompson, 1968: 13)

Such an approach ushered in an investigation of the subjective worlds of (in Thompson's case) workers as a central and necessary part of any class analysis. This view has greatly influenced social historians and sociologists and ironically (given Thompson's antipathy toward much sociological work) it has been instrumental in generating common approaches and questions between the two disciplines, which have pointed to the need to investigate the vocabulary of class used in popular discourse.

This view draws attention to the fact that, whatever the classification problems, people have used and continue to use a language which identifies other groups and classes in society. Often they have used the idea of class in imaginative and metaphysical ways. Snell, for example, recounts how the term 'burglar class' was used in the fields of England and Wales in the nineteenth century as a means of defining groups who lived off the work of others (Snell, 1992: 176). In contemporary society French car workers have described their managers as 'the grey suits' (Linhart, 1978) and British chemical workers theirs as 'the big books' (Nichols and Beynon, 1977). Both these terms, and the manner of their utterance, were used to convey a sense of the 'otherness' of the senior managers, and the manner of the worker's subordination. This naming process can also be incorporated into patterns of resistance. In the Brazilian steel town of Volta Rodanda, the different grades of workers are identified by the colours of their helmets and overalls. On the Bessemer furnaces the engineers arrive when there is a crisis, and the manual operators observe their arrival from high above them. The engineers wear yellow helmets and white overalls and they are universally referred to as 'margarida' (a daisy-like flower with white petals and a yellow centre) which carries many of the same overtones as 'pansy' in the UK.

Similar kinds of evidence can be found from the everyday language of other, more powerful groups in society. If the language of the Brazilian steel workers is gently mocking, the allusions of their superiors often carries a harsher edge. In the 1930s the populist regime of President Vargas saw a new, socially insignificant, leader replaced the powerfully extended landowning families who had previously dominated the politics of the state. In this period, the social characteristics of the new political groups were identified by the ways their supporters carried their lunch to work in handkerchiefs ('marmiteiros'). This capacity for powerful groupings to identify subordinates through their life-styles, language and eating habits extends into contemporary Brazil. 'Farofeiros' became a general term applied to poorer people who eat farofa. The political campaigns of Lula, the leader of the Workers' Party, were disabled by similar taunts, referring to the 'social inadequacies' of the presidential candidate.

This is not a phenomenon peculiar to Brazil, nor is it simply an aspect of a transitional society *en route* to modern forms of political discourse. In the USA, Calvin Trilling has provided a detailed auto-biographical account of Yale in the 1950s which makes clear that class and status was a central part of social life. He explains how, amongst the privileged undergraduates, 'one of the adjectives in common use was "shoe"'. This, it seems, was derived from 'white shoe'. 'Shoe' referred to the students whose background was 'patrician or old money' and it came to refer to a style of dress and 'also something approaching cool or scarce'. He notes that

a few years before we arrived, the term 'white shoe' was often heard . . . along with 'brown shoe' and 'black shoe'. The white shoe people were, of course, shoe. Apparently, the brown shoe people were the bright student council presidents from white middle class high schools . . . the black shoe people were beyond the pale. (Trilling, 1993)

Trilling describes eloquently how at Yale these undergraduates viewed the future as a 'stairway to heaven' with them all 'moving upwards through the clouds on a blissful escalator'. For not only were these young men privileged socially, they were also 'demographically blessed':

we were white males who were born in a baby boom during the depression and came of age at a time when the privileged position of white males was so deeply embedded in the structure of society that we didn't even think about it. (Trilling, 1993)

By the 1980s the embeddedness of this privilege had been under-mined by feminist movements and changes in the economy. In the UK, however, the diaries of the patrician Tory minister Alan Clark make clear the ways in which much of social life continued to be understood through notions of origins and background. On one occasion he writes of his irritation with his fellow MP Nicholas Soames and how his wife chides him: 'Don't be beastly. So few of the upper classes go into politics nowadays, you've all got to stick together' (Clark, 1993: 78). Clark gave strong support to Mrs Thatcher, who is referred to throughout

the text as 'the lady'. He recounts how 'the upper classes' were so convinced that her personal qualities were at odds with her lowly origins
that rumours were spread linking Thatcher's mother with the aristocracy. While this attempt to appropriate the Tory leader to a historical
class failed, the Tory grandees held true to their convictions. On one
occasion, Clark writes of how, when sitting next to her in the House of
Commons he noticed that:

she has very small feet and attractive – not bony – ankles in the 1940 style.
Julian Amery will nod his head sagely and say in a gruff voice, 'There's blood
there, you know, no doubt about it, there's blood'. And I see what he means.
(Clark, 1993: 69)

This notion of social classes being held together through blood lines is
a powerful one, and Clark's diaries demonstrate the ways in which this
sense of identity and purpose was held together politically through the
practices of daily life: through the institutions of the gentlemen's club,
the house party and the family. It was Clark who sustained the jibe
at the renegade Hesletine: 'he had to buy his own furniture'. The ire he
directs toward the *nouveau riche* contrasts with his views of the workers.
True to his patrician origins this oscillates between an acceptance of
the critical role they play within the social structure ('Salt of the earth'
and all that) and irritation and anger when social life is disrupted. Hence
on one occasion he is driven to Heathrow by his driver, Dave:

I rose early and confident. But Dave *lost the way* in light fog. . . . Like all the
lower classes, he went to pieces quickly and sat rigid at the wheel, slightly
leaning forward, squinting into the fog, being overtaken by vans on either side.
Too flush-faced to admit that he's 'done wrong', he would neither turn round,
nor even stop to get his bearings. . . . Finally, with only seven minutes to spare,
we found ourselves at the familiar Spelthorne entrance. I leapt out and asked
for directions. Naturally, it was a gate some distance along the perimeter which
I had already suggested. (Clark, 1993: 230)

His forbearance is further tested by rail transport:

I am sitting in a first class compartment of the Sandling train, odorous and
untidy, which, for reasons as yet undisclosed, and probably never to *be* dis-
closed, has not yet left Charing Cross. 'Operating Difficulties', I assume, which
is BR-speak for some ASLEF slob, having drunk fourteen pints of beer the
previous evening, now gone 'sick' and failed to turn up. (Clark, 1993: 169)

This idea of a socially distinct grouping of people, almost of different
species, identified by 'blood' and social indicators of style, manners
and so on is a commonly held view within British society. These are
powerful devices for emphasising the 'otherness' of the identified group.
Undoubtedly, Alan Clark expressed them with a particular verve, but
his views should not be seen as exceptional. They are often encountered
amongst professional groups (like teachers and social workers) who
work in deprived areas. They are ever-present in the world of business.

For example, a turkey manufacturer expressed surprise when the food correspondent of the *Guardian* newspaper asked if he could extend his investigations into turkey production by interviewing the workers. He was told to remember that:

these are the sort of people who eat crisps and fish and chips. They are totally different from you and me. Sometimes they don't shower in the morning. (*Guardian*, 24 December 1994)

Occasionally these worlds collide. In cases of social mobility, this collision is contained within individual biographies. For example, Alan Hughes worked as a graphic designer for *New Internationalist* in Oxford. His father had been a factory worker in Birmingham and on one occasion in 1996 he returned to visit his uncle and cousins and to watch Aston Villa play football. At the end of the match they were reluctant to leave the ground quickly. On being implored by a steward to leave Hughes replied: 'It's OK, we're just taking in the *ambience.*'

I couldn't believe it, I just said it. The word came out of my mouth, italicised for emphasis, as though I had no control over it. I groaned inwardly. He looked at me as if I was from another planet. 'Are you taking the piss, mate?' he queried, now more menacingly.

This encounter led to a protracted discussion with his cousins over the nature of class and its various signifiers in language, style, dress and attitude: 'fuckin' clever types who think they'm better than us'. It also led Hughes to some profound reflections on the way things were changing in society and in his own life:

I see the working class; low achieving, lacking confidence, willingly accepting their fate, destructively turning in on themselves; drug abuse, crime and violence. Or turning outwards, looking for scapegoats. . . .

I see an increasingly nervous middle class with their traditional values of hard work and thrift under threat. The spectre of unemployment and insecurity now hangs over them and they are more than willing to pull up the ladder on the masses below. . . .

And for me? I continue to live in my cultural limbo land – feeling guilt at betraying what remains of the struggle for working class emancipation, then thanking God that I'm not there any more. (Hughes, 1996: 25)

The attack on class

The examination of what might be termed the phenomenology of class is revealing, and serves as a corrective to assertions of the 'end of class'. However, it raises questions about the construction of these ideas and how they fit with an analysis of class relations. In considering these issues, Patrick Joyce and others have emphasised the role of political discourse and narrative in the construction of such class understandings in Britain in the nineteenth century. Such an approach can helpfully be related to the United Kingdom in the 1980s. In this decade, the Tory party under the leadership of Margaret Thatcher attempted to arrest the United Kingdom's economic decline through an audacious and radical strategy which operated at a number of different levels. The most important of these involved the linked deregulation of international capital markets and local labour markets. In this strategy, the trade unions and the form of the British working class were together seen as a major obstacle to renewal. Legislation was passed which limited the powers of trade unions, and privatised the state monopolies.

This economic strategy, however, was combined in an intriguing way with a new kind of political rhetoric which involved selective borrowing from radical traditions within the left. It was Thatcher who talked of giving 'power to the people', and who attacked state officials for being bureaucratic and uncaring. In this discourse, however, society was reconstructed around the idea of individual consumers, rather than one of collectively organised producers. It was a dramatic switch, which played ruthlessly upon the structural changes which were under way. Within this new discourse, there was 'no such thing as society'; all forms of relationships became dissolved into the dominant ones of consumption, and 'value for money' became the slogan for the new age. The market model has come to dominate all forms of social exchange. In the 1980s football fans from the south of England who visited the north with their teams would often chant 'Loads of Money . . . Loads of Money' and wave wads of notes in the direction of the opposing (poorer) fans.

This theme of consumption and classlessness was developed through advertisements, often by state bodies, which reassembled elements of the iconography of the left. In this way British Coal used a photograph of a coal-miner in his working clothes to symbolise business, similarly Cardiff Bay used Karl Marx to advertise enterprise opportunities (see Figures 4.1 and 4.2). While the past was being parodied in these images, other physical symbols of the old order were being torn down. Across the coal fields with an almost indecent haste the winding gears of the coal mines were dismantled and the shafts filled. In previous periods this process could take years rather than months. As one man put it: 'I think they are trying to tell us something. This is the end.' The working mines, steel mills and factories were replaced with heritage museums which recreated the past and often employed ex-workers to replay their previous working roles. Such museums were opened, on average, each day of the year in the late 1980s. These museums have tended to create a view of the past which emphasises the simplicity of life and of living arrangements; it is a sanitised past dominated by tradition and the absence of conflict. Many authors have pointed to the ways in which these and other cultural enterprises both reorder the past (obliterating issues of class) and reaffirm a particular kind of *English* heritage which, among other things, excludes ethnic minorities (see Gilroy, 1987; Hall, 1992).

One of Britain's most successful businessmen.

Figure 4.1 **British Coal advertisement (reproduced courtesy of British Coal)**

This attempt to reconstruct society can be understood as an attack upon class. It was developed by Thatcher's successor John Major as he talked repeatedly of the classless society and in a different way by Tony Blair when he talks of 'the people'. Within this meritocratic world, the very idea of class became seen as irrelevant and a further aspect of

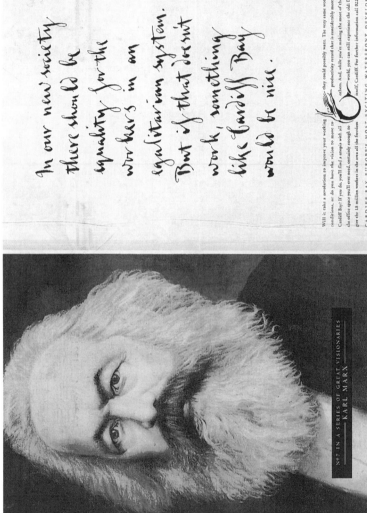

In our new society there should be equality for the workers in an egalitarian system. But if that doesn't work, something like Cardiff Bay would be nice.

Will it take a revolution to improve your working conditions, or do you have the vision to move to Cardiff Bay? If you do, you'll find a utopia with all the office space you'll ever need, certainly enough to give the 18 million workers in the area all the freedom they could possibly want. The very same workers have a productivity record that is considerably more equal than others. And, while you're making the most of the brave new world, you can still experience the olde Das Kapital itself, Cardiff. For further information call 0222 58 58 58.

CARDIFF BAY, EUROPE'S MOST EXCITING WATERFRONT DEVELOPMENT

Nº 7 IN A SERIES OF GREAT VISIONARIES
—— KARL MARX ——

Figure 4.2   *Cardiff Bay advertisement (reproduced courtesy of Cardiff Bay)*

a discredited past. As if to emphasise this, in 1987 the government announced that it intended to alter its methods of data collection. On 30 October *The Times* noted that 'the working class is to be abolished, statisticians in the Office of Population Censuses and Surveys (OPCS) have decided. To ensure social inequality the middle and upper classes are being abolished too'. This decision (later to be revoked) was warmly endorsed by the Secretary of State for Health and Social Security who remarked that he was 'keen on the idea of a classless Britain'.

This, of course, sat well with the supposed ordinariness of John Major. A party political broadcast on 18 March 1992, for example, dwelt on the story of a poor boy from Brixton rising to the highest office in the land. This account emphasised his lowly social origins, his experience of manual labour and unemployment and his modest life-style. While the accuracy of this account is questionable, it is clear that the party through the biography of its leader was attempting to establish a view of society in which hard work and thrift brought its own re-wards. This is, of course, a classic middle-class view; by locating the young Major amongst the poor it represented a further attempt at 'declassing' the Conservative project, a strategy that was exaggerated in the attention it drew to the social origins of the leader of the New Labour party and the education of his children.

The restructuring of class

As a result of these political developments, it might be expected that perceptions and understandings based upon ideas of class would have weakened over the past ten years. Certainly the political project initi-ated by Thatcher had a crucial bearing upon the transformation of the Labour party to New Labour, and informed the change in *its* rhetoric. In this context the Gallup findings on 'class struggle' seem all the more incomprehensible. Further data collected by NOP for the *Sunday Times* add to the puzzle. This was expressed well by the newspaper's leader writer. 'It has become a truism of modern politics that most of the population is middle class', yet oddly:

> the majority of people regard themselves as working class even when they are (according to the people who decide these things) middle class. In an NOP poll in the *Sunday Times* today, more than half said they were working class, 1% upper class, and 17% (some cheer for John Major) said they belonged to no class at all. The middle classes were left with a miserable 28%. Confused? Either they are or we are. (*Sunday Times*, 22 September 1996)

Part of the confusion resides in the analysis offered by 'the people who decide these things' and the problems inherent in moving quickly from occupational structures to class categories. In orthodox class analysis, skilled non-manual occupations are located in the middle class. Yet analyses of occupational flows indicate that these groups are now made up of new kinds of jobs, often done by women many of whom work part-time. These, and other features of the changing occupational hierarchy, have introduced serious ambiguity into traditional lines of class division (see Bradley, 1996; Crompton, 1993) and make it thoroughly understandable that people in 'middle-class jobs' would describe themselves as 'working-class'. That they should do so at a time when both of the major political parties have expunged the phrase from their vocabularies is nevertheless perplexing.

Further clarification can be obtained if we go beyond political rhetoric and examine political strategies. In doing so it should be emphasised that much more was involved in the politics adopted by Margaret Thatcher than a change in the *language* of politics. 'Thatcherism' also involved a determined attempt to check the problem of economic decline in Britain, a problem which Blair has inherited. Principal amongst these policies was an attack upon labour market regulation by the trade unions and other institutions. In a television interview in June 1992 Alan Budd, Professor of Economics at the London Business School and erstwhile advisor to Mrs Thatcher, reflected upon these policies in this way:

raising unemployment was a very desirable way of reducing the strength of the working classes. . . . what was engineered – in Marxist terms – was a crisis in capitalism, which recreated the reserve army of labour, and has allowed the capitalists to make high profits ever since.

So interpreted, the attack on class can be seen as the defence of class and the establishment of different kinds of class relationships.

There is no doubt that in the 1980s, the levels of income inequality in the United Kingdom accelerated. In this period, the proportion of total income received by the bottom 20 per cent of households fell steeply. The official statistical summary in *Economic Trends* explains how:

the distribution of household income has become more unequal. The bottom quintile group's share of disposable income fell (between 1977 and 1988) from 9.7% to 7.6% while the share of the top fifth of households went up from 36% to 42%.

When real incomes are assessed we see that the income of the top decile increased by 38 per cent between 1984 and 1990, while that of the bottom two deciles rose by 0.7 and 1.8 per cent respectively. This bottom group on average has less than £5 in savings. The 10 per cent above them exist below the official poverty line of 40 per cent of median income.

These findings were supported by a survey conducted in 1995 by the market research group Mintel. The survey contrasted the positions of 'the Rich' (the top 20 per cent of earners with average gross household incomes of £42,818) with 'the Poor' (the bottom 40 per cent with gross average incomes of £6,088). It concluded that the rich had increased their share of total expenditure from 35 per cent in 1979 to 49 per cent in 1995. In contrast the share of the bottom 40 per cent halved from 24.5 to 12.5 per cent in the same period.

This survey and Gallup's were conducted around the same time. They coincided with the considerable publicity given to the salary increases of senior executives in the privatised utilities – the so-called 'fat cats' – and the general salary levels of senior businessmen. The pay of the top ten directors in 1995 ranged from the £17.4 million awarded to Peter Wood of Direct Line Insurance to the £935,000 paid to Sir Richard Sykes of Glaxo Wellcome. The publicity which these salaries attracted was linked to a general criticism of 'greed', and undoubtedly influenced many people's views about the salience of class in British society.

That this should be understood as 'class struggle' can perhaps be understood in relation to the changes that were taking place within workplaces and in labour and housing markets in the 1980s and 1990s. The recession of the early 1980s severely reduced employment levels in manufacturing industry and changed the character of the old industrial regions. This decline was linked with notions of post-industrialism and the emergence of a new kind of society. The gloss was taken off this account in the late 1980s and early 1990s when recession hit directly at the new post-industrial service economy and its heartland in the South-East. An investigation by *World in Action* (10 November 1992) into the local economy of Slough (the boom town of the 1980s) documented 'the fear that affects every office and shop-floor in Britain'. In a sample of 1,000 they found that 9 per cent had recently been made redundant, 43 per cent were worried about being made redundant and 60 per cent expected there to be an early redundancy within the family. The leader of the local council remarked:

everyone is depressed on the borough council . . . this country seems to be geared up for one thing – unemployment. You can't plan your future.

A year later, a MORI/IRS survey commissioned by the *Financial Times* found that:

the number of workers who fear they might lose their jobs in the next twelve months rose to more than 50 per cent in December – in spite of last week's sharp fall in unemployment. (*Financial Times*, 20 December 1993)

In this way, economic insecurity became increasingly widespread and in spite of Ian Lang's view that it was 'a state of mind', repeated research reports indicated that fears and anxieties about security were rooted in the changed nature of labour markets and the 'flexibility' being required by employers (see Beynon, 1997). These insecurities compound the stress which is related to the intensification of work itself. In the year to March 1993, the United Kingdom's largest 1,000 companies shed 1.5 million workers (the *Director*, March 1993), cutting costs and restructuring their operations. In the view of Alistair Anderson, managing director of Personal Performance Consultants UK:

downsizing in companies has meant that often people have been left ill-equipped and ill-prepared for the job expected of them. This itself creates great stress.

He added that in his belief: 'the demands on the workforce are greater than they have ever been' (*Financial Times*, 8 December 1993). And there has been little compensation in the housing markets either. As part of the project of denying class and building a property-owning democracy house purchasing by all groups was encouraged by the government and by financial institutions. Council house sales in fact represented the greatest of all the privatisations. However, unlike the 1960s and 1970s, house prices did not continue on an upward spiral and could not continue as an investment ('a nice little earner') to compensate for misfortune in the labour market. In fact house prices exaggerated these recessionary processes. In so doing a new term was created – 'negative equity' – and with it the prospect of the 'dream home' becoming a living nightmare.

These changes affected groups throughout the occupational structure. They meshed with dramatic technological changes to transform the experience of life inside and outside the workplace. One dimension of these changes has served to intensify a sense of insecurity and vulnerability amongst people. It has also served to make clear the locus of power and privilege in society. These processes were readily converted to a language of class.

Conclusions

It is clear that some fundamental changes have taken place in the British social structure. However, it would be difficult to conclude that inequalities have been eroded, or that class-based understandings of society are no longer appropriate. The changes outlined in this chapter have clearly contributed to a disruption of previously established forms of social solidarism which held groups and social classes together. For example, institutions which once supported collective forms of understandings have been severely weakened. The power of trade union organisations, which once enabled groups to regulate their workplaces and create a sense of occupational or workplace solidarity which, at times, informed and developed an understanding of class has been eroded. Equally, professional groups which once ordered their lives through ideas of service, trust and security have also found their worlds turned upside down. As a group during this century, their understanding of class has been built upon their denial of it, and their emphasis upon the individual and upon personal qualities. In the 1980s and 1990s many of these individuals faced the impersonal vagaries of the market: many of them resent what has happened to them. These changes have inevitable complications for social cohesion across generations and for established relationships between men and women.

In attempting to resolve some of these puzzles it is helpful to move from a static to a dynamic framework, and from ideas of *class structure* to those of process and *class formation*. It certainly seems possible to use a language of *remaking* in the present context (see, e.g., Savage and Miles, 1994). However, in discerning the fabric of these new class relations, it is clear that they have remarkably different characteristics from the previous ones, which derive from a rapidly changing and globalising system of production and communication.

In this context it is possible to see British society in terms of that *Long Revolution* which Raymond Williams wrote about so eloquently: a process in which industrial and technological forms change, but through which values and beliefs are maintained and developed through a continuity of adapted cultural practices and institutional forms of life (Williams, 1965). In such a view, the working class in the United Kingdom was not 'made' in 1832 in a way in which a reading of Edward Thompson might imply; rather it has gone and goes through a process of making and remaking – at each turn drawing upon institutions and values previously established. In these ways class relationships can be seen to continue in changing contexts and with changed contents. As they change *class* itself will continue to be contested as a concept in social science. It will be argued about in pubs, restaurants and television studios in ways which will challenge and undermine the very idea of a 'classless society'.

CHAPTER 5

'Race', racism and the politics of identity

PANDELI GLAVANIS

'Within 10 years Britain will have solved its "black problem"': that was the message contained in the British government White Paper issued in September 1975. The instrument of legislation to achieve this was the Race Relations Bill of February 1976. The problem, as defined by the White Paper, was 'the political control of a rebellious second genera-tion' and the solution was 'to divert militancy into national achieve-ment' (Sivanandan, 1976). Twenty years later however, David Mason writing on *Race and Ethnicity in Modern Britain*, argues that 'the evi-dence of inequality, discrimination, and exclusion is so pervasive that it would be a dereliction of duty to the truth not to give it major promin-ence' (Mason, 1995: 3). In fact, most studies published in the first half of the 1990s highlight the dramatic deterioration of 'race relations' both in the United Kingdom and the European Union,[1] and emphasise the danger that derives from 'the growing malignancy of racist violence and the increasing ramifications of what has been termed "ethnic cleans-ing" (or the extermination of populations by ethnic (racial?) violence)' (Anthias, 1995: 299).

It is of some interest, therefore, to consider some of the reasons which may account for the failure of the 1976 legislation to *solve* the 'black problem'. To achieve this it is necessary to understand the back-ground that led to the legislation in 1976, namely immigration and immigration acts and legislation that preceded it. Like most West Euro-pean countries after the Second World War, the United Kingdom was faced with a labour 'shortage' that was only partially alleviated by the half million refugees admitted to the United Kingdom between 1946 and 1951. Thus, the Ministry of Labour found it necessary to systema-tise the recruitment of labour from overseas, and it was no surprise that British government officials turned to British colonies and ex-colonies (Sivanandan, 1976: 348).

This initial recruitment of labour in the 1950s immediately produced two problems for the immigrants: employment in low-status jobs, and living in decaying inner-city slums. Immigrant labour was recruited to do the jobs British white workers were not willing to do, and since most of these jobs were in large metropolitan areas, immigrants settled in the slums of these urban areas while the more affluent white working class started to move to the new housing estates in the suburbs (Sivanandan, 1976: 348–9). Immigrant labour, of course, was very cheap; they were born and socialised in the colonies and ex-colonies and they were imported as 'ready-made workers'.[2] In fact, it was estimated that depending on age and skills, immigrant labour represented a saving of between 8 and 16 thousand pounds per worker, representing the social cost of producing labour and taking into account the fact that immigrant workers came primarily as single men (Gortz, 1970).

Given that immigrant labour was so cheap, it could have been expected that the British state might use some of the savings to improve the social conditions for immigrant workers. This did not happen, as the British state adopted a *laissez-faire* immigration policy, and the social conditions of immigrants deteriorated as the numbers increased. Thus, immigrants were welcome as workers, but socially undesirable, given their social conditions of existence. It is not surprising, therefore, that this generated new racial stereotypes and a new kind of colour racism in the United Kingdom. The immigration policy of the British state, therefore, contributed to the first stage of the 'ideological racialization' of 'black' immigrant labour (Solomos, 1992). In fact, as Sivanandan argues, 'the economic profit from immigration had gone to capital, the social cost had gone to labour, but the resulting conflict between the two had been mediated by a common "ideology" of racism' (Sivanandan, 1976).

The deteriorating social conditions of existence for 'black' immigrant workers led to the race riots of 1958, and the British state recognised the dangers implicit in its *laissez-faire* immigration policy. However, the response from the government was not in the direction of improving the social conditions of 'black' immigrants. Instead, it signalled the start of immigration legislation which had a dual objective: to curb immigration from the colonies and ex-colonies and to deal with racism in the United Kingdom. In the 1950s, however, the majority of immigrants to the United Kingdom were white Europeans. The intervention of the British state through its policies, therefore, contributed to the process by which 'race', and in particular its identification with 'black' and immigration became synonymous in public discourse (Solomos, 1992). This was confirmed by the series of Nationality Laws (definition of patriality) that were introduced in the 1960s. The first of these laws was the Commonwealth Immigrants Act of 1962, which disregarded the fact that many immigrants from the colonies and the ex-colonies held British citizenship and limited the right to settlement in the United Kingdom only to those who had employment vouchers.[3] Thus by the mid-1960s racial discrimination was given the sanction of the state; it was institutionalised. But in so doing the British state placed itself squarely in the middle of the construction of modern racism in the United Kingdom with immigration policies which in fact defined the process of 'ideological racialisation'. In effect, immigrant workers from the colonies and the ex-colonies were transformed into a particular category of 'racialised' labour within the British labour market.[4]

In the meantime history was being transformed in the colonies and the ex-colonies. In 1967, for example, Kenyatta's Africanisation policies in Kenya, placed Kenyan Asians in an impossible situation: they were suddenly 'aliens' in Kenya and, given the devaluation of their British citizenship, they were virtually stateless. The uproar that ensued forced the British state to allow Kenyan Asians to settle in the United Kingdom on 'special' vouchers, but this also led the state to introduce a new piece of legislation, the Commonwealth Immigrants Act of 1968, which restricted even further the rights of British citizens from the colonies and ex-colonies – i.e. those who were 'black'. Finally, by 1971, another Act (which came into force in 1973) classified all immigrants, irrespective of what nationality they had, as 'aliens'; immigrants from the colonies and the ex-colonies would have to register with the police as 'aliens', even if they carried a British passport (Sivanandan, 1976).

The discussion so far has highlighted one of the dimensions of the immigration policy, abolition of the right to enter and settle in the United Kingdom for immigrants from the colonies and ex-colonies, and indicated how it contributed to the institutionalisation of racism in post-war the United Kingdom, i.e. state-sanctioned racism and discrimination. The policy also intended to reduce 'racial' tension within British society; i.e. how to deal with those immigrants who had already settled in Britain. This was to be achieved by the Commonwealth Immigrants Advisory Council, which was created by the Commonwealth Immigrants Act of 1962, and its function was to advise the Home Secretary on the welfare of immigrants. Very quickly, however, this advisory council, whose name was changed to the National Committee for Commonwealth Immigrants (NCCI) in 1965, also contributed to the construction of racial categories and stereotypes rather than reduce them.

The first thing that the NCCI did was to produce the first Race Relations Act of 1965. This act prohibited racial discrimination in 'places of public resort' and by default encouraged discrimination everywhere else, in housing, employment, etc. More important, however, is the underlying objective of NCCI and the manner in which it perceived the immigrant population. The underlying objective was the integration of the immigrant and settler populations into British society, and in this context the Asian and West Indian populations were perceived differentially and thus 'racialised'. The NCCI assumed that West Indians were closer to British culture, spoke the same language, shared the same religion, etc., whereas Asian immigrants were 'different'. So the emphasis for integration was directed at Asians, as they were seen as the 'problem'. This enhanced racial stereotypes within British society. In effect the British state, via the mediation of its own institutions, was actively engaged in the process of constructing and legitimating different forms of social exclusion and 'racialisation'.[5]

This 'ideological racialisation' of the immigrant and settler populations failed to note that the West Indian population, and especially the younger generation, were in effect socially excluded and marginalised. Even more so it failed to consider the effects of developments in another ex-colony (the USA) where the Civil Rights campaigns had already gained significant visibility in the public and political domain. Given the 'common' historical origins of American 'blacks' and British West Indians, the failure to consider the effects of the 'Black Power' movement in the USA only underlined the extent to which 'racial' stereotypes defined state policy in the United Kingdom. Thus, it is not surprising that the British state also failed to note that Martin Luther King's visit to the United Kingdom in 1964, on his way to Sweden to receive the Nobel Prize, had a profound effect on the West Indian community. By the end of the 1960s, therefore, British society and the state were faced with an American-style 'Black Power' movement originating from a community that had been ideologically perceived as 'docile'.[6]

This was also a particularly important turning point in contemporary 'race relations' in the United Kingdom. In adopting 'Black Power' community politics, the West Indian immigrants and settlers were also constructing a new social identity. West Indian children (i.e. second generation) rejected British culture and values and even the English language. The British state quickly realised that it had to do something to prevent 'race relations' deteriorating even further. In effect, the British state was looking for ways to govern and rule a subject population which had already been 'racialised' and whose assimilation into the dominant white culture had failed. It is not surprising, therefore, that the British state, with its colonial history, would turn to its own history and introduce at that moment of crisis colonial practices in Britain. The Race Relations Bill of February 1976 provided the legislation. Thus, by 1976, the United Kingdom had moved from 'institutionalised racism' to 'domestic colonialism' (Sivanandan, 1976). As with earlier legislation, of course, the 1976 Bill failed to deal with the 'problem', even though several academics believed that it had at the time. Sivanandan, for example, argued that government legislation had achieved 'the accommodation of West Indian militant politics within the framework of social democracy [and] the Asians had already settled into the cultural pluralist set-up ordained for them by the state' (Sivanandan, 1976: 365).

In fact, the legislation contributed to the increased militancy from some sections of the Asian community in the 1980s, and especially the emergence of the 'Muslim Voice' as an empowered alternative to the 'Black Power' movement. Once again, the 'Muslim Voice' in the United Kingdom derived from policies introduced by the British state, but gained its dynamism and vitality from events taking place beyond the United Kingdom; the Islamic Revolution in Iran, the Gulf War, and the spread of Political Islam in a number of ex-colonial societies.[7]

The immigration policies of the British state during the two decades of the 1960s and 1970s had a dual objective: to reduce immigration and resolve the problem of 'racial' tension. The state achieved its first objective, but in doing so accentuated the second problem. In fact, by the end of the 1980s British society and the state were confronted by two groups of militant second-generation settler communities: Afro-Caribbeans and Muslims. Thus immigration policies, and especially the socio-political legislation which accompanied them and was intended to define the nature of British nationality (identity) as a means of limiting the entry of British subjects from the commonwealth (i.e. 'blacks'), contributed to the emergence of a new kind of 'race' politics in modern Britain, the politics of identity. The manner in which the state employed 'racialised' categories in defining its policies articulated with global transformations, and especially in the ex-colonies, so that immigrant and settler populations started to define their collectivitiy and identity in juxtaposition to British nationality and identity.

In this respect, however, the growing militancy of the newly empowered immigrant and settler 'voices' did not challenge only the British state and its concern to govern. Such developments since the 1980s also challenged much of conventional social science whose object had been the analysis of 'race relations' in contemporary society. For 'race relations' accounts derived from a social science paradigm which for more than a century had accepted that the assimilation of cultural and religious identities into a national society was a necessary precondition for socio-economic and political development. In fact, diverse and competing ethnic and religious communal identities were seen as a primary factor in dividing post-colonial societies and hindering development. European scholars perceived ethnic and religious identities as inimical to rational social planning and economic development, and instead highlighted the classical European model where, it was assumed, modernity had eroded communal identities in favour of citizenship and loyalty to the state.

Nevertheless, and despite the resistance from conventional and institutionalised social science, the emergence of the politics of identity in social and political formulations of citizenship and nationhood have forced some social scientists to re-think their analytical and conceptual agendas. This is particularly so since the recently empowered voices of the different immigrant and settler communities within the United Kingdom and the European Union are seen to articulate with a global revival of ethnicity, race and religion as modes of organising socio-political order. Furthermore, these newly empowered voices, within Europe and outside, also constitute an important challenge to prevailing Eurocentric conceptualisations of modernity. In fact, it can be suggested that it was as a response to the increasingly militant ethnic/racial/religious voices within Europe that some social scientists started to recognise the importance of 're-introducing' in their studies of modernity one of the prime divisions in the social ontology of collectivity, namely 'race'.

The urgency of the task cannot be emphasised enough as most European Union citizens and governments (including the European Union political and administrative hierarchy) are presently in a state of alarm and surprise caused by the growing immigrant and settler populations in their midst, and especially as they face an impressive roster of newly empowered 'voices' asking for their narratives to be heard. Such alarm and ignorance can, of course, and does lead to the emergence of 'racist' legislation, policies and practices which only contribute to an increase in the militancy of the newly empowered 'voices'. This is well documented in some recent studies, such as Glyn Ford's book, *Fascist Europe: The Rise of Racism and Xenophobia* (1992), and Paul Gordon and Francesca Klug's study, *New Right, New Racism* (1986). Nevertheless, important as these and other similar studies may be, they only document the consequences of the failure to understand the reasons why so many ethnic and immigrant communities have responded wholeheartedly to the call of the newly empowered 'voices'. What they fail to do is to present an analytical account which can explain the manner in which immigrant and settler communities have abandoned assimilation and multiculturalism in favour of the politics of identity (Anthias and Yuval-Davis, 1992). It is of some interest, therefore, to highlight some of the central issues in the contemporary academic debate around the terms 'race' and racism.

Rethinking 'race' and racism

In her review of contributions to the debate on 'race' and racism, Floya Anthias notes that 'writing on "race" and racism in the last few years is indicative of the ways in which the "race" paradigm is changing [and] the idea of a new racism embodies a shift in the central organising elements of racist discourse away from explicit biological notions to culturalist or nationalist ones' (Anthias, 1995: 279). This is supported by David Mason when he argues that 'there are no races, in the biological sense of distinct divisions of the human species. Rather there are social interactions which are constituted by their participants as a particular kind of social relationship: race' (Mason, 1995: 1). It seems that a significant number of writers are abandoning the term 'race' in favour of such concepts as ethnicity and nationalism and in this respect the new discourse is gradually replacing the conventional one, with its deterministic and unitary forms (Anthias, 1995). This is clearly reflected in a study by Harry Goulbourne (1993: 177) which argues that 'in Britain too, where militant nationalism has never received a serious hearing, the question of national identity is now high on the general public agenda'. In spite of these changes Miles has noted how much of the public agenda retains the idea of 'race':

Newspaper headlines report that 'Race riots hit Los Angeles', that there is a 'Race bias in employment' and that an 'MP plays the race card'. In Britain, the Commission for Racial Equality comments annually on the state of 'race relations'. (Miles, 1993: 1)

Thus, Miles goes on to suggest that 'if "race relations" are a feature of contemporary society, it seems obvious that academics should study them' (Miles, 1993: 1), particularly as incidents of racism, racist attacks and racist practice have dramatically increased during the last decade. Richard Skellington has documented these developments and noted their significance for the 'experiences of young black people . . . across the breadth of institutional contexts negotiated in daily life' (Skellington, 1992: 11–12).

All this illustrates both the complex meanings associated with the term 'race' and its persistence as the predominant paradigm through which the exclusion, oppression and subordination of immigrant and settler populations in contemporary British society is organised. As with categories such as class and gender, the term 'race' will be the subject of extensive and often polemic academic debate, which will not necessarily influence its use in public discourse. This is made clear by Miles who, while arguing forcefully against the use of the terms 'race' and racism, also acknowledges their extensive use in public discourse. In fact, he argues that the 'strongest case made in favour of the retention of the notion of "race" as an analytical category arises from the fact that it has been used by the victims of racism to fashion a strategy and practice of resistance to their subordination' (Miles, 1993: 3). Even here, however, the situation is far from simple; the use of 'race' as a focus for political organisation and action, by the victims of racism, reflects a similar variety of meanings and practices.

For many sections of the immigrant and settler populations in the United Kingdom during the decade of the 1980s, 'race' became associated with the idea of 'black'. Notions of 'race struggle' and 'black struggle' became synonymous and both terms were employed as a means of political mobilisation by the various victims of racism. In this way both terms also lost their specific biological meanings, and the term 'black' was no longer associated solely with the subordination and oppression of peoples from exclusively African origin. Both terms were assumed to embody and reflect a universal notion of resistance against racism that could be used for all immigrant and settler populations irrespective of their origins (Anthias and Yuval-Davis, 1992).

By the end of the decade of the 1980s, however, the assumed universalism of 'race' as a unitary mode for the political mobilisation of the victims of racism was seriously challenged, most clearly with the events surrounding the publication of Salman Rushdie's book *The Satanic Verses.* These events marked a turning point in the form of political organisation and practice against racism and the socio-political exclusion of immigrant and settler populations. They also highlighted the fact that for British Muslims, in their mobilisation especially against the publication of the book, the terms 'race' and 'black' had practically no significance. Even in daily life, 'race' reflected a variety of meanings and its assumed universalism and association with 'black' could no longer be sustained.

This truth was reflected in the reaction of British 'black' activists who distanced themselves from what were seen as 'Muslim Fundamentalists' and beyond the scope of the 'race struggle'. In some respects they were right. What outraged British Muslims was the blasphemy contained in the book and as such their demonstration can be seen as a religious one. Certainly this was the view of prominent anti-racist activists, including 'black' Labour members of Parliament. One prominent MP of Caribbean origin argued that

these demonstrators were out on the streets not as blacks, but as outraged Muslim fundamentalists. Not all Muslims are black, and not all Muslims take the fundamentalist position. Why then should black socialists give support to hardline religious leaders? (Miles, 1993: 4)

However, it is helpful to deconstruct the assumptions which guided this response and locate the behaviour of British Muslims in their social and political context. In 1989 the British state refused to ban *The Satanic Verses*. Furthermore, it 'warned Muslims not to isolate themselves from their host society' (Asad, 1993: 239). The Home Secretary, Douglas Hurd, and his deputy, John Patten, made statements which emphasised

the importance of proper integration for ethnic minorities, the need to learn about British culture without abandoning one's own faith, and the necessity of refraining from violence . . . were widely applauded by the liberal middle classes, whose pronouncements both before and after the government's intervention repeatedly denounced 'Muslim violence'. (Asad, 1993: 239)

Newspapers and television unanimously condemned the 'Muslim Fundamentalists', and quoted at length from a document produced by John Patten entitled *On Being British* (Patten, 1989). This document was widely circulated to the media and the United Kingdom appeared to be experiencing a serious political and apparently violent crisis. However, there was little evidence of any sustained threat to law and order and very few arrests or injuries occurred during the demonstrations by British Muslims. In explaining the severity of the government's response we need to recall the innumerable angry demonstrations through the streets of London during the 1980s. These had involved anti-racists and fascists, feminists and gays, abortion rights activists, trade unionists, students. As Asad notes:

Scuffles had broken out between demonstrators and police – involving accusations and counter accusations of violence, including death threats – in which injuries were sustained and arrests made. More significantly, Britain had witnessed a number of major urban riots (in Nottingham, Notting Hill Gate, Brixton,

Bristol, Birmingham, Liverpool, etc.) in which pitched battles were fought between police and non-white immigrants, cars and buildings burned, blood spilt – though, incidentally, South Asians [the majority of British Muslims] were rarely if ever involved in any of these violent confrontations. (Asad, 1993: 240)

Furthermore, a steady stream of racist murders of non-white immigrants and settlers and an even longer list of physical assault, spitting and verbal abuse had been taking place for some time (Gordon, 1989). Nevertheless, the white majority had never been previously warned against the violence, nor had the government felt it necessary to lecture British citizens on 'Being British'. Thus, it is important to reiterate Talal Asad's question, 'What exactly was the danger sensed by the Tory government and "liberal opinion" in Britain?' (Asad, 1993: 241); what were the underlying factors and socio-political forces that turned an otherwise legitimate expression of religious sentiment by a section of the British population into such a serious crisis.

Clearly the external intervention from Iran and in particular the issuing of a *fatwa* (religious proscription) by Ayatollah Khomeini legitimating the assassination of Salman Rushdie by any Muslim was of great significance. The life of a British citizen was being threatened by a foreign government and a section of the British population were seen to collude with this power. Nevertheless, in itself this is not sufficient to account for the scale of the response. It is of some interest, therefore, to quote Talal Asad's answer:

It was a perceived threat to a particular ideological structure, to a cultural hierarchy organised around an essential Englishness, which defines British identity. . . . Thus, the Rushdie affair in Britain should be seen primarily as yet another symptom of postimperial British identity crisis, not – as most commentators have represented it – as an unhappy instance of some immigrants with difficulties in adjusting to a new and more civilized world. (Asad, 1993: 241)

Thus, Asad challenges the prevailing account that sees the British Muslim response as primarily religious. Asad's argument, however, goes further to suggest that the British state itself, the media and liberal public opinion perceived these religious demonstrations in political terms – the politics of identity and of a developing struggle over the meaning of being British and civilised. He suggests that by the end of the 1980s 'the politics of identity' had entered the public arena as an important element in structuring the socio-political relations between different sections of the British population as well as between sections of the immigrant and settler population and the British state. Furthermore, the term 'race', which in the academic debate had already acquired cultural and nationalist dimensions, was now being attributed with an additional religious dimension.

This brief account lends support to Robert Miles' view that the term 'race' is a contested one and thus generates problems when used as an analytical concept (Miles, 1993: 5). In fact, the above example has highlighted the fact that even in its political use, the term 'race', as defined in the current struggle against racism, conceptually excludes certain sections of the immigrant and settler populations, given that 'race' cannot be assumed to reflect any form of universalism or for that matter representation of *all* such populations. It is not surprising that Miles rejects it as a useful concept and instead proposes an analytical paradigm founded solely on the political economy of labour migration to Western European capitalist societies (Miles, 1993: 3). This solution is attractive analytically. However, such a paradigm fails to address the critical issue of the politics of identity. This is a particularly serious limitation, not only because it cannot properly account for the Rushdie affair, but also because it fails to engage with and consider a variety of other recent contributions which have already abandoned a unitary system of representations and practices in favour of a notion of the plurality of racisms (Cohen and Baines, 1988; Anthias 1990, 1992, 1995).

To raise this criticism is not to imply an acceptance of the current preoccupation with group identification and culture and the postmodernist tendency to talk about the proliferation of identities and the growth of new ethnicities (e.g. Hall, 1988; Goldberg, 1993). This approach has unfortunately shifted the debate away from racial disadvantage and the persistence of various forms of social inequality within contemporary British society (Anthias 1995: 280). It has also contributed to the undermining of a new political agenda creating unity across ethnic, religious, gender, class and other forms of 'difference' and diversity. What is needed is an analytical paradigm that avoids the current polarisation between 'political economy' and the 'postmodernist' approaches. The politics of identity should be incorporated as a central component of any analytical paradigm that accounts for the oppression, subordination and socio-political exclusion of immigrant and settler populations. This, of course, implies the urgent need for a political economy of modernity. The more so as the polarisation of the academic and political debate has serious implications for the formulation of a coherent strategy to confront and combat racism, and to develop new policy initiatives:

the legal framework has not been up to the task of tackling racist violence and the institutional structures of the race relations industry have been largely paralysed by lack of resources, co-optation and confused interventionism. The multiculturalist and anti-racist practices in schools have been seen as less than effective, working with fairly simplistic notions of prejudice formation and a belief that racist responses, which are seen as irrational, should be tackled by rational means. In addition, there is an absence of radical perspectives from the left on racism in Britain. (Anthias, 1995: 280)

Of course, this crisis does not derive from the failure of academics to formulate a coherent concept of 'race'. The demise of socialism and the right-wing backlash with regard to policy and government initiatives is certainly more important. Furthermore, the fragmentation of social forces and social movements and their inability to challenge the 'conservatism' of the state has not helped the immigrant and settler populations confront their increased marginalisation. Nevertheless, analytical reasoning and theoretical debate does have an impact upon policy agendas and the forming of political responses to change. Social scientists are obliged to occupy a space between their 'scientific' categories. Therefore, Miles' rejection of the term 'race' is unsustainable in a world where it is central to the way in which society, socio-political movements and political activists formulate strategies against oppression and struggle for the development of a substantive and participatory democracy. Thus, it is necessary to pursue the debate that will enable a clearer understanding of the factors that contribute to the persistence of both 'race' and racism in contemporary society.

Globalisation: the contruction of 'racial' categories

The polarisation of the current debate with regard to the use of 'race' and racism as analytical categories derives in part from a wider theoretical and methodological debate within sociology. The dualist theory of sociological knowledge which separates historical and structural analysis and assigns to each a discreet sector of reality, and so distinguishes methodologically between the logic of a social system – which is subordinate and needs to be 'realised' – and its origins and historical evolution – which is dominant and explicit. Thus, the political economists are concerned with change (history) and the postmodernists with structures of meaning (logic), and this because changes, or processes, are conceived not as analytical objects but as the particular way in which a temporality is *experienced* by a *subject*. It is not surprising, therefore, that Miles is primarily concerned with the political economy of Western capitalism and labour migration while Hall and Goldberg are preoccupied with the diverse forms by which the subjects experience their social reality.

It is the unique commitment of capitalism to maximise production and profit, however, that constitutes the rationale of modernity and hence the mode in which the histories and identities of all immigrant and settler populations in Britain have been subordinated (conceptually or in practice) to the history and identity of the hegemonic (ruling) British middle classes. The politics of identity, therefore, has to be examined as part of the process of capitalist expansion which in turn conditions the parameters within which modernity is apprehended. Thus, it is the political economy of modernity, incorporating both the politics of identity and the political economy of labour migration, that constitutes the analytical paradigm within which we can account for both the characteristics of immigrant and settler populations and the various forms of struggle against their oppression, subordination and social exclusion. Let me elaborate.

Conventional and mainstream sociology accounts for modernity by reference to the concept of 'society' – as a self-defined system. This limited conceptualisation of modernity has been challenged, and Anthony Giddens (1990), among others, has produced a particularly interesting account by arguing that 'modernity is inherently globalising', and sociologists need to account for social phenomenon as they are ordered and transformed across time *and* space. Thus, globalisation, conceptualised as a process, intensifies the interaction of world-wide social relations 'in such a way that local happenings are shaped by events occurring many miles away and vice versa' (Giddens, 1990). Such an approach, of course, does direct our attention (and focus) to the complex relationships between local/regional structures and social transformations and interactions across regional and national boundaries. This was already highlighted in the previous section with reference to emergence of both 'Black Power' and the 'Muslim voice'. The globalisation of modernity, however, has a history that parallels that of industrial capitalism.

Lancashire textiles mills and cotton textiles, for example, played a pioneering role in British industrialisation, and contributed to the formation of the first fully developed industrial organisations in the British economy. The problem confronting sociologists, and in this particular example industrial sociologists, is how to determine the unit of analysis within which to account for this significant development – modernity. In other words, how do industrial sociologists construct an analytical framework which in addition to taking into account the conventional concerns of the discipline can also consider the analytical importance of such issues as: the role of the slave plantations in the 'Deep South' that produced the cotton for the textile mills; the role of Egyptian long-fibre cotton for the labour process and technological innovations; and the role of the British Empire that guaranteed both markets and cheap raw materials. Furthermore, how does industrial sociology theorise the relationship between 'free' and 'unfree' labour, where the latter reflects the process by which certain sections of the global labour force were coerced into producing for the requirements of industrial capitalism. In other words, how can industrial sociology account conceptually and theoretically for the process which at one and the same time generated a 'free' (that is from feudalism) industrial working class in Lancashire and enslaved and coerced millions of non-Europeans to work on cotton plantations in the 'Deep South', Egypt, Sudan and India.

Robin Cohen, in his pioneering contribution, *The New Helots*, is one of those social scientists who has theorised the relationship between 'free' and 'unfree' labour within modernity when he argues 'that capitalism has historically coexisted with a combination of labour regimes' (Cohen, 1987: 3), in which non-European labour has always played a central role. Thus, Cohen provides a formidable critique of conventional industrial sociologists who focus solely on immigrant labour within Europe by noting that 'the phenomenon they identify is part of a much older game: one that has always had profound implications for the survival of the system [industrial capitalism] itself' (Cohen, 1987: 253). The thrust of Cohen's argument is that:

historically, the international division of labour wrought by the capitalist mode of production has not been characterised by the exclusive use of free labour but by a combination of free and unfree labour regimes. This has applied throughout the history as much as the 'pre-history' of capital and has taken a variety of forms in different areas. (Cohen, 1987: 25)

Cohen then proceeds to examine the role of immigrant labour in West European economies in order to challenge the assumption that it constituted a 'structural necessity' for the development of European capital. He argues that as immigrant labour became established in West European societies the fundamental relationship between capital and labour was transformed. By the early 1970s, immigrant labour started to become unionised, the cost of reproducing immigrant families started to constitute a financial burden on the West European states, and many European trade unions started to adopt anti-racist policies. Cohen concludes, therefore, that West European capital realised that it was no longer profitable to 'import' workers and, thus, decided to 'export' capital to the Third World. In contrast to the structural necessity argument, Cohen notes that

the mix between free and unfree labour is spatially redistributed in a complex and continuously changing way in response to the mix of market opportunities, comparative labour-power costs, the course of struggles between capital and labour and the historically specific flows and supplies of immigrant and other forms of unfree labour. (Cohen, 1987: 144)

The discussion of immigrant labour in the West European economies permits Cohen to elaborate in some detail on three of the themes related to the changing relationship between capital and labour. First, he notes that 'while capital has an expanding global horizon, workers have been corralled into narrower pens, their physical and psychological frontiers being policed by the national state' (Cohen, 1987: 147). Cohen examines the policies adopted by the states in the USA, South Africa and Western Europe and concludes that these discriminatory and often racist policies play a central role in subduing immigrant labour which in turn 'permits a maximum level of exploitation' (Cohen, 1987: 178). Second, because it is the nation states which play a central role in subjugating immigrant labour, they also constitute the central focus for resistance. Cohen, highlights the manner in which immigrant labour in South Africa has mobilised against the apartheid state, and thus transformed a capital–labour conflict into a nationalist and anti-apartheid struggle.[8] Third, as the immigrant labour–state struggle develops, capital finds it necessary to relocate itself in order to secure further new supplies of cheap labour; thus creating a 'problem' for those immigrants and settlers who are resident within the European Union and are no longer needed. Thus, Cohen is able to conclude that what appears to be a new situation generated by the new Europe is in fact another dimension or form of the development of capitalist production. In other words, the parameters of the capital–labour relationship are constantly changing, and trade union federations or for that matter social scientists, who remain within the confines of conventional perceptions, are threatened with irrelevance.

The process of globalisation, as elaborated by Giddens (1990) or Wallerstein (1979), differs fundamentally from the conceptual structures employed by conventional sociology which has 'society' as its focus. Thus, what is required is a framework which can account for the fact that 'capitalism was from the beginning an affair of the world economy and not of nation-states' (Wallerstein, 1979). It is in such an analytical framework, therefore, that Berger and Mohr's *A Seventh Man* (1975) is at one and the same time an account of underdevelopment in Turkey (generating a reserve of cheap labour) and the 'miracle' of industrial development in post-war Germany, which relied extensively on 'racialised' (Turkish) labour. Similarly, an examination of the working conditions of overseas female domestic workers in the United Kingdom, in Bridget Anderson's *Britain's Secret Slaves* (1993), is both an account of underdevelopment in the Philippines and a critique of contemporary British labour relations which exclude ('racialise) Philipina maids working for Middle Eastern families in London because they are non-citizens. Labour, however, as a productive category, as with capital, has no nationality, sex, religion or colour. Such identities are socially constructed in the process of 'globalisation' and the power relationship between labour and capital; this is how 'racialised' labour categories are constructed.

Sociologists, therefore, need to adopt alternative analytical and conceptual frameworks which give priority to the process of globalisation and especially the manner in which capital has made and continues to make use of social, political/national, religious, gender and racial differences in order to maximise the production of surplus value and profit. What is needed, therefore, is a 'sociology of work and working practice' which accepts the process of 'globalisation', as its analytical parameters, but goes further and deconstructs the social construct 'society' as a self-defined socio-political system.[9] In other words, social scientists need to acknowledge that the process by which labour has been and is 'racialised' is mediated by the political project of the nation state, the construction of national and 'racialised' boundaries and the policies of social and political exclusion. Capital, of course, makes the most of such situations and initiates new working practices which can benefit from the availability of marginalised and 'racialised' labour. In effect, therefore, it is the development of the nation state, the political project of modernity, which constructs the 'racialised' boundaries for the benefit of indigenous and multinational capital. Thus, it is a political economy of modernity within an analytical framework which acknowledges globalisation, which will enable social scientists to account in a dynamic manner for the persistence of 'race' and racism.

The persistence of 'race' and racism

Labour and immigrant and settler populations respond to the process by which they are 'racialised'. Most political economy accounts of immigrant and settler populations, however, fail to account for such responses since they present a single-sided account of the development of capitalism and tend to focus solely on the diachronic (time) relationship between capital, nation-state and labour, for example Robert Miles (1993). As indicated above, however, what is needed is an account for modernity by reference to both time *and* space. It is the synchronic account, the politics of identity, which is neglected by such social scientists and thus suggests that they accept 'racial' categories as static ideal types which are solely defined by state legislation or political projects (e.g. Turks, Germans, Albanians, Greeks, etc.). In other words, such contributions are marred by the use of 'racial' categories solely at a substantive level and ignoring the analytical dimension, the political project of modernity.

This is a particularly important point because such studies tend to portray labour as passive and accepting the 'racialised' categories produced by the nation state political project. Labour, however, is not absent from the process. Labour does respond, and it is the synchronic and subjective struggle between labour and the nation state project which needs to be highlighted in these studies. In other words, it is necessary to grasp 'the dynamic of capital vs labour via a deconstruction and account of the relationship between collectivity and belongingness ('race') and economic placement (class)' (Anthias, 1991: 30). In some respects European political leaders have played a role in the recognition of the challenge posed by the politics of identity.

During the last few years, and especially since the publication of the *White Paper on Growth, Competitiveness and Employment* in 1993, the European Council of Ministers and other political leaders and personalities have started to show signs of coming to terms with the fact that their various macro-economic policies and measures are unable to stem increasing unemployment, social marginalisation and poverty in the European Union. In fact, it can be argued that they are starting to accept that such economic measures, and especially those aimed at increasing European economic competitiveness in the global economy, carry with them 'societal effects' (Brown and Crompton, 1994: 1). Given that these same European leaders are also keen to follow the introduction of the Single Market, with more radical forms of socio-political integration, it is not surprising that these 'societal effects' are starting to achieve a degree of visibility and seen to constitute critical problems for the new Europe.

Thus, European political leaders have come to accept what has already been argued by some social scientists, namely that 'a major consequence of economic restructuring throughout Europe has been an intensification of competitive pressure, and this is likely to reinforce divisions between rich and poor nations and people' (Brown and Crompton, 1994: 5). Of course, some European social scientists have been arguing for some time that the European political agenda to create a Single Market and to enhance European economic competitiveness in the global economy is in effect leading to the development of a 'two-tier' Europe. Brown and Crompton, among others, have argued that this 'two-tier' Europe is likely to be characterised by different forms of social exclusion of which two can be highlighted:

'fortress Europe' that imposes barriers on east Europeans and Africans seeking entry to EC member states . . . [and] . . . those forms of exclusion that typically affect the life chances and material circumstances of those who have EC citizenship rights. (Brown and Crompton, 1994: 5)

An important dimension of the restructuring of the European economies is the manner in which the informal sector of employment has increased in significance. This has been highlighted in a report which accompanied the above-mentioned White Paper. The report to the European Commission's Employment Task Force noted that a primary concern of the European Union is how to 'enable the re-entry into the formal labour market of many citizens who have to work at the margins' (Mingione and Magatti, 1994: 1). Mingione and Magatti also argue the fact that most of those caught in the informal employment sector are immigrants and settlers and this raises the question of how to conceptualise the relationship between the expansion of the informal forms of employment and the marginalisation of immigrant and settler populations. In other words, it raises the issue of whether there is a relationship between the persistence of 'race' and racism and the changing patterns of employment within Europe.

The answer is provided by Annie Phizacklea who notes that the pursuit of flexibility in the European Union encourages casualised employment practices and that although their contribution remains unquantified and therefore unacknowledged, they constitute the most exploited and vulnerable workers in the EU. Phizacklea goes on to argue that this is most clearly the case for immigrant workers who are not full citizens of member states, since 'the Treaty of Rome established sex equality as a fundamental right to be pursued, but there is no similar provision for the pursuit of ethnic or racial equality'. Thus, in the context of 'the increase in casualised employment and the much greater control and surveillance of migrant populations within the EU . . . it is important to recognise the socially and culturally embedded gendered and racialised hierarchies in employment' (Phizacklea, 1995: 1–2).

Gendered hierarchies have already been recognised to some extent by industrial sociologists, but most studies of the changing labour markets have failed up to now to develop the analytical tools which would allow them to consider 'racialised' hierarchies. Phizacklea, therefore, is right to highlight the fact that the significance of 'racialised' hierarchies as a central issue in the structuring of 'new' employment patterns within the European Union has yet to be recognised. In other words, globalisation and the political economy of modernity have yet to be accepted as necessary analytical paradigms for the study of immigrant and settler populations. Neverthless, the significance and visibility of the response of some immigrant and settler populations to their increased marginalisation and 'racialisation' has been noted. Philip Brown and Rosemary Crompton, for example, note that

as the 20th century draws to a close, the economic and political changes in contemporary Europe seem to be as profound as those that dominated the concerns of Sociology's founders in the 19th and early 20th centuries. (Brown and Crompton, 1994: 1)

This theme is starting to gain acceptance among some social scientists who note that the global economy itself is in a time of acute and unprecedented flux and transformation with profound effects on social, cultural and political realities. This is emphasised by Appelbaum and Henderson, who argue that as we approach the end of the twentieth century we are at a critical point around which history is turning – a hinge of history. Change, of course, opens up new possibilities and closes others but until the new ones are consolidated the situation is inherently unstable. Thus, we are in a situation which simultaneously presents opportunities and danger. Furthermore, Appelbaum and Henderson also note that the necessity to develop new analytical paradigms that can account for the fact that the globalisation of economic, social and cultural processes has profound effects for the concept and practice of the long-standing Western model of the nation state (Appelbaum and Henderson, 1995; Glavanis, 1996a).

What has yet to be incorporated into the academic debate, however, is the fact that globalisation raises questions of national and supra-national interests and in particular how these are expressed and managed. Furthermore, the speed with which globalisation is taking place also raises issues of people's changing values, identities and their attitudes towards the traditional nation state, and especially the mechanisms and state structures by which individuals, social groups and communities are integrated into the national project. This rapid social change, the disruption of traditional political, cultural and societal allegiances and the changing form of governance and political participation is a central concern to those responsible for constructing and maintaining political communities. This is particularly the case as the changes have profound implications for such issues as the future of democracy and civil liberties, citizenship, civil society and nationalism. Changes in technology and employment patterns (flexibility) have also accentuated social divisions and created social categories with neither access or understanding of the new developments. This in turn has given rise to new supra-national, national and regional social and political identities that reflect increasing marginalisation and social exclusion of particular social groups and communities; in particular certain sections of the immigrant and settler populations.

Thus, it is not surprising, for example, that the ability to account for Political Islam and the newly empowered 'Muslim Voices' within the European Union has failed up to now, and instead we are confronted with an account which concerns itself with the spectre that haunts Europe – after communism it is Political Islam (Glavanis, 1996). The 'Islamic Threat', therefore, has become the subject of many studies which fail to account for this socio-political phenomenon in a broader analytical framework. In particular these studies fail to account for the reasons why some European Muslims no longer give their loyalty solely to their respective European nation states, or for that matter why they challenge the notion that the nation state should continue to incarnate popular sovereignty. For European Muslims appear to reject the idea of popular sovereignty and instead place their faith above loyalty to the nation state. Thus, it is not surprising that European Muslims, where the nation state is deeply embedded, are seen as causing disruption since they seek to re-negotiate what has been considered part of the political common sense. But these European social scientists try to read Political Islam with an 'obsolete' European template, hence the accounts that Political Islam is backward, traditional, conservative and against modernity (Glavanis, 1996; Sayyid, 1994).

What such European social scientists fail to consider is that globalisation and the post-colonial era have dramatically transformed the socio-political, cultural and economic research agenda. Eurocentrism and the European narrative is being challenged and deconstructed, and this has opened up the possibility of articulating projects which make a virtue of their antagonistic relationship to the West. The passing of 'The Age of Europe' and the creeping recognition that the West is only one civilisation among others has to become a central analytical focus of contemporary theorising and accounts of immigrant and settler communities within the European Union (Glavanis, 1995, 1996b; Sayyid, 1994).

It is for the above reasons that this essay has argued that the construction of a dynamic and analytical framework necessitates that we account for contemporary forms and processes of social exclusion as part of a theoretical and conceptual model which engages with the process of globalisation in a synchronic and diachronic analysis. For although social exclusion, 'two-tier' Europe and marginalisation constitute critical problems in contemporary Europe, finally recognised by European political leaders and some social scientists, the process does not originate solely with the formation of the New Europe. On the contrary, this essay has argued that it is a process which has deep historical roots, and that its recent visibility derives primarily from the fact that some of these socio-cultural groups of immigrants and settlers have recently started to challenge the European project from within – the 'Stranger Within'. In fact, it is this internal challenge – from some European citizens such as the British Muslims in the Rushdie affair – which has alarmed both political leaders and social scientists to the extent that they have recognised the necessity to develop theoretical and methodological tools to enable them to understand what they perceive as the threat from within.

This is a particularly important issue, as these populations and 'voices', of course, have been resident in Europe for some time, thanks to the globalisation process set in motion by capitalism, slavery in the 'new world' and colonialism. What is new, however, is that during the past few years we have witnessed the terminal decline of the assimilationist model of ethnic relations in favour of a politics of identity. No longer do immigrant populations submerge themselves into the dominant host culture, rather many groups argue that they want to maintain a distinct identity. Thus, for example, some populations are likely to identify themselves as British Hindus or British Indians or British Muslims rather than as South Asians.[10]

Religious affiliation, and in particular an Islamic or Muslim identity, constitutes one of these newly empowered voices in a number of states within the European Community. Muslim populations from different ethnic origins have existed within Europe for several decades: Turks in Germany, Pakistanis and Bangladeshis in the United Kingdom, North Africans in France, Turks in Greece, etc. What is of particular interest is the manner in which some of these populations are making new choices with regard to their identity, and specifically how they are constructing new identities which attribute to the Islamic religious affiliation a privileged status. Thus, an analysis and understanding of this particular process of constructing identity and difference (the politics of identity), must constitute one of the primary objectives of an alternative paradigm which can account for the persistence of 'race' and racism; this is the political economy of modernity.

Notes

1 See among others: Anthias and Yuval-Davis, 1992; Braham, Rattansi and Skellington, 1992; Donald and Rattansi, 1992; Modood, 1992; Skellington, 1992; and Solomos, 1993.

2 For an elaboration of this argument see John Berger's account in Berger and Mohr, 1975.

3 In order to highlight that this was the reaction of the British state, and not of a particular political party, it is important to note that when the Labour party renewed the Act in a White Paper (August 1965), they set a numerical ceiling for the first time (8,500 per year), and declared that no unskilled worker would get a voucher. This had immediate implications for 'family re-unification'; most immigrants in the 1950s had arrived as single males (Sivanandan, 1976: 354).

4 The 'racialisation' of labour was not new, it had already taken place in the slave plantations of the 'Deep South' in the new world and in the colonial labour markets as part of the process of the globalisation of capitalism: i.e. modernity. This will be discussed in more detail below. It was the first time, however, that it was happening in the United Kingdom.

5 This was the origin of the Cultural Diversity thesis (multiculturalism), introduced by the then Home Secretary, Roy Jenkins (August 1965), which in effect was aimed at integrating and assimilating what was perceived as the outsider – 'other'.

6 This perception derived to a large extent from the mythology about 'black' slaves in the plantations of the 'Deep South' that prevailed at that time among whites in British society.

7 This particular development will be discussed in greater detail in the next section.

8 This is similar to the argument developed in this essay with regard to the emergence of empowered 'voices' within the immigrant and settler populations which challenge the state.

9 Richard Brown has made a significant contribution in this direction with his exemplary study, *Understanding Industrial Organisations: Theoretical Perspectives in Industrial Sociology* (1992).

10 See the confusion caused by the 1991 census which attempted to classify the ethnic populations by reference to state defined categories. For a detailed discussion of this issue see Ballard and Kalra, 1994.

CHAPTER 6

Patterns of inequality in education

ROBERT G. BURGESS

A persistent theme in the sociology of education for the last 50 years has been the analysis of patterns of social and educational inequality (Halsey *et al.*, 1997). It has been examined by sociologists focusing on patterns and processes associated with educational systems and was a theme that I was commissioned to write on by Richard Brown in the early 1980s when I examined patterns and processes of education in the United Kingdom by focusing on evidence from the different educational systems in England and Wales, Scotland and Northern Ireland (Burgess, 1984). Here I combined statistical and ethnographic evidence, much in the style of Richard Brown's work. In contributing to this volume it therefore seems appropriate to return to this theme so as to update the evidence available on patterns and processes of inequality in education by drawing on some of the original evidence and updating it in relation to the English educational system.

Education is still big business in the United Kingdom. Expenditure on education in the public sector in 1995/96 represented 5 per cent of the gross national product and the total public expenditure in the United Kingdom was 11.5 per cent. In 1995/96 there were just over 33,000 maintained and non-maintained schools in which $9^{1}/_{2}$ million pupils were taught by 535,000 teachers (see Table 6.1). In post-compulsory education 87 per cent of sixteen-year-olds and 53 per cent of eighteen-year-olds engaged in education and training (the latter being among the lowest participation in OECD countries). At a later stage 24 per cent of eighteen- to twenty-one-year-olds were engaged in full-time and part-time study in higher education (see Table 6.2). New entrants to degree courses in 1994 constituted 44 per cent of the relevant year group. This was a considerable increase and represented a higher rate of participation than in most OECD countries. Similarly, the United Kingdom had the highest graduation rate at first degree level (27 per hundred of the relevant year group) in the European Union (Statistics of Education, 1998).

Education is, therefore, a familiar experience for residents of the United Kingdom. Many of them are actively engaged in the educational system in some capacity as pupil, student, trainee, parent and so on. In turn, it is the current Labour government's objective to place education at the top of the political agenda – an objective that is to be achieved

Table 6.1 **Numbers of schools, pupils and teachers and pupil–teacher ratios by school type in the United Kingdom 1995/96**

	Schools	Pupils (000s)	Teachers (000s)	Pupil/ teacher ratios
Public sector schools				
Nursery	1 486	61.8	2.9	21.4
Primary	23 426	5 142.5	227.3	22.6
Secondary	4 462	3 676.2	228.2	16.1
Non-maintained schools	2 436	589.6	58.3	10.1
Special schools – maintained	1 458	106.2	16.8	6.3
Special schools – non-maintained	109	6.7	1.5	4.4
All schools	33 377	9 583.0	535.1	17.9

Notes:
1 Excludes sixth-form colleges that became further education colleges from 1 April 1993.
2 Includes 1994/95 data for Wales.

Source: *Statistics of Education 1996* (London, Stationery Office, 1997).

Table 6.2 **Participation in post-compulsory education and graduation ratios for 1994**

Age[1]	%[2]
16	87
17	74
18	53
Higher education[3] Participation of 18–21[4] Year olds in HE	
Full-time and part-time	24
Sub degree	31
First degree	16
Graduation rates[5]	
Sub degree	25
First degree	27

Notes:
1 Excludes students in private FE and HE, adult education centres and YT with employers.
2 Based on full-time and part-time headcount.
3 Excludes private HE.
4 Number of full-time and part-time students aged 18–21 as a percentage of the population aged 18–21.
5 Based on students qualifying divided by the average population of the age group.

Source: *Statistics of Education, 1996* (London: Stationery Office, 1997, pp. 10 and 11).

through a policy of lifelong learning (Stationery Office, 1997). It is the sociologist's task to probe behind these basic patterns, and explore the nature of this educational experience.

Sociologists who studied education have looked at the school system, the school curriculum, assessment, testing and so on in order to analyse the educational experience as it occurs in schools, colleges and class-rooms. In turn, they have also focused on structures and the ways in which they operate to affect the perennial problem of equality of educational opportunity (Silver, 1973). The impact of social class on edu-cational achievement remains a concern. Several studies have examined social mobility and the relationship between education, employment and unemployment (see Halsey, Floud and Anderson, 1961; Karabel and Halsey, 1977 and Halsey *et al.*, 1997). They have been comple-mented by others which have questioned the 'black box' approach to education and suggested that studies of schools and classrooms are also needed if we are to understand more about social and educational pro-cesses, and the assumptions made about teaching and learning.

Given the salience of education in our society, it is not surprising that its study has not only been concerned with a series of substantive contributions but has also been the site of theoretical and methodolo-gical advance (Deem, 1996). It is in this arena that feminist scholarship (which has focused on the importance of gender relations in shaping areas of social life), has made one of its greatest contributions. This has emphasised the patterning of gender inequality in the educational system through differential treatment in the school, choices in the school cur-riculum and performance in examinations. Ethnicity has been examined in similar ways (Gilborn, 1990). As a result, class, gender and ethnicity have been key concepts that have been used in understanding patterns of inequality within the educational system. This chapter utilises some of the sociological evidence derived from these perspectives to exam-ine patterns of inequality within education. Here both quantitative and qualitative data will be used to examine educational practice, but before turning to the key phases of education, the educational systems in the United Kingdom need to be placed in context.

The context of education in the United Kingdom

There is a tendency to oversimplify the educational system within the United Kingdom, with the result that many writers still discuss it as if there was one single system. In reality three spatially separate educa-tional systems co-exist within the United Kingdom: those of England and Wales, Scotland and Northern Ireland. The structures are broadly similar and much of the sociological evidence within this chapter will focus on the English school system. Children who enter the educational system pass through a number of phases – from nursery school to university – and the main phases of the English education system are

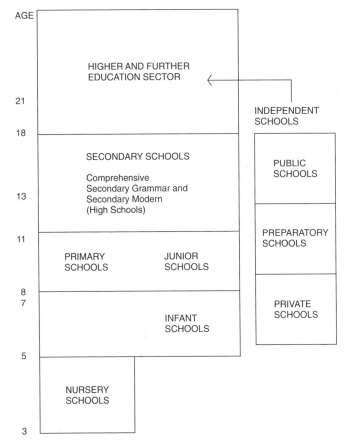

Figure 6.1   **The educational system of England and Wales**

Source: Adapted from R. Bell and N. Grant (1977) *Patterns of Education in the British Isles*, p. 212.

summarised in Figure 6.1. Within the United Kingdom, state schools are maintained by local education authorities but schools also have had the opportunity to become self-governing or grant-maintained whereby their funding is provided by a central government agency.

Since the mid-1940s English education has been characterised by change, involving a partnership between central government, local authorities and schools. This was well summarised by a government report on local authority arrangements for the school curriculum (1979) which stated:

The Secretaries of State do not intend to alter the existing statutory relationship between these various partners . . . with responsibilities for school education: central and local government, school governing bodies and teachers. . . . Indeed,

Table 6.3   **The curriculum: the 1980s and after: landmarks**

1980	A Framework for the School Curriculum (DES): A View of the Curriculum (HMI)
1981	The School Curriculum (DES): The Practical Curriculum (Schools Council)
1982	Technical and Vocational Education Initiative (TVEI)
1983	DES Circular No 8/83: Enquiry into Curriculum Arrangements
1985	Better Schools – White Paper (DES): The Curriculum from 5–16 (HMI)
1986	Secretary of State announces the intention to introduce a national curriculum
1987	The National Curriculum 5–16: A Consultation Document
1987	Task Group on Assessment and Testing (TGAT)
1987	Education Reform Bill presented to Parliament
1988	The Education Reform Act
1989	DES Circular No 5/89: The Education Reform Act, The School Curriculum and Assessment
1989	National Curriculum Council (NCC): School Examinations and Assessment Council (SEAC).

Source: Tomlinson (1993), p. 93.

they believe that the effective development and implementation of curricula policies must be based upon a clear understanding of, and must pay proper regard to, the responsibilities and interests of each of the partners and the contribution which each can make. (DES, 1979: 2)

The local education authorities were therefore perceived as the lynchpin of the English educational system and some commentators, such as Tomlinson (1986) argued that they had been principally responsible for innovation and development in areas like school-based curriculum development, records of achievement, education–industry liaison and so on. However, since the early 1980s a series of government decisions saw the relationship between central government, local authorities and schools change (see Table 6.3). Central government now has a much greater influence on the overall structure of the educational system, the provision of schools, the content of the curriculum and the subjects taught. To many, it seems that we are witnessing a slow demise in the educational role of local authorities, and this has been associated with changes in the emphasis of the educational debate. Increasingly these have been concerned with the relationship between education, economic perform-ance and work.

This has had a strong impact upon teaching matters, the content of the curriculum and the role of teachers. While these issues are most commonly associated with the 'Thatcherite' agenda, James Callaghan first raised them in his speech at Ruskin College in 1976. Many of them were addressed in the 1988 Education Act, which raised the question of a National Curriculum, and a linked system of assessment and testing. It also developed the powers of school governing bodies and established city technology colleges and grant-maintained schools. These changes were subsequently built in under the Conservative governments. The end product has been a radically changed educational system, with greatly increased power for central government. These developments have been of great interest to sociologists and to policy groups concerned with education and work (see National Commission on Education, 1993).

These changes have not been limited to the school system. Further education colleges have been removed from the control of local education authorities, and the polytechnics have been upgraded to universities. Major educational reviews have taken place examining the role of schools, colleges and higher education by Sir Ron (now Lord) Dearing, which have paralleled investigations by social scientists. In the 1990s we have returned to some of the perennial questions concerned with educational opportunity and educational inequality.

The pre-school phase

For children aged five and under, educational provision comes from attendance at nursery schools, playgroups and day nurseries, although only nursery schools are under the direct control of the Department for Education and Employment. Nursery education has traditionally been perceived as a means of promoting equality of educational opportunity. It was with the publication of the Plowden Report (1967) that a new impetus was given to the provision of nursery schooling, as it was argued that this was desirable for education, health and welfare among those below the age of five. Indeed, the committee argued that 90 per cent of four-year-olds and 50 per cent of three-year-olds should be provided with nursery schooling. In the early 1970s the White Paper, *Education: A Framework for Expansion* (1972), supported Plowden's view that nursery education should be provided to assist the social and educational circumstances of all young children and expressed a desire to see the development, not only of nursery schools but playgroups. As a result a modest development took place in nursery schooling during the 1970s, so that 53 per cent of four-year-olds and 15 per cent of three-year-olds were being educated in maintained schools. However, this was far short of the Plowden recommendations. During the 1970s, the proportion of children attending nursery or primary schools, playgroups or day nurseries rose from 17 per cent to 40 per cent. Over the last 20 years there has been a steady increase in the proportion of children under five attending nursery schools. While in 1970–1, 50,000 pupils were attending nursery, this had risen to 83,000 in 1996–7 (58 per cent of the age group). Indeed, it is now government policy for local authorities to enter into partnership with private, voluntary and independent schools to provide three terms of pre-school education for all four-year-olds. Nevertheless, the provision of nursery education is un-even throughout the country. In 1996, 71 per cent of children under five attended local authority nursery schools and classes in Wales, while only 59 per cent did so in England.

Throughout the period social scientists have provided evidence to suggest the importance of nursery education for children under five (Burgess, Hughes and Moxon, 1989, David, 1990; Sylva and Moss, 1993). Much of their data, together with evidence from government reports, has been reviewed by the National Commission on Education, which reasserts the importance of nursery school provision. Clark (1988) pointed to the range of services provided: nursery education; recep-tion classes in infant and junior schools; day nurseries; playgroups and child minders. However, great disparities still existed both nationally and between local authorities. For example, Walsall was found by the Select Committee (Select Committee Report, 1989) to have the highest rate of provision, with places for 93 per cent of children under five, whilst West Sussex had places for only 9 per cent of children in that age group. Where a child lived in England and Wales clearly influenced participation and life chances. While there has been an increase in places available, there has also been an increase in the number of places that depend on private funding and the ability of certain social class groups to get access to nursery education. It is this provision that con-tributes to the social, educational and compensatory objectives which prepares children for schooling (Select Committee Report, 1989).

This emphasis upon pre-school provision should not mask the impor-tance of parental participation in education for the under-fives. Hughes, Burgess and Moxon (1991) indicate that this can take many forms. In their study of nursery schooling in Salford (where unemployment was 9.6 per cent), they found that the Council made provision for 83 per cent of children under five. Interviews with headteachers of nursery schools and headteachers and matrons of combined nursery centres examined the ways in which parental participation was defined. They revealed that despite the ways in which 'parent' is portrayed as a gender-neutral term 'parent' really means 'mother', as fathers were frequently absent from any involvement in early years education. One headteacher remarked:

We are just in the process of putting together a reading meeting to show parents what they can do, perhaps at home or whatever with their children's reading. While we were talking about reading, it suddenly struck me that when we were doing the harvest festival and were showing them things that the children had brought and there was a tin of beans, but not one bean on the label whatsoever and one child said Heinz Baked Beans, they are reading it and you can call it reading, so I want to explain to mums what it means at this level, reading.

In this context, the word parent becomes transposed as mums who are the dominant figures involved in helping children read at home and in the nursery setting. Indeed, the study found that mothers were often involved as helpers. As one head commented:

We have a parent-helper scheme, where parents are encouraged to come in and help to work with children in small groups. They do cooking, they do baking, they help at PE times, they help with reading groups when they play reading games, they come out on visits and outings, and when we are going out to do environmental education on walks and visits to parks and the shops, etc.

From this evidence it would seem that mothers were taking on a major responsibility for settling children into school. And it seems that class also played a role. As one head remarked:

The parents who are very committed to their child's education are usually parents who are working, who are very intelligent women who have a career and a job and perhaps some crisis where her husband has walked out and we've helped them over that crisis so the children are in the centre and they want to get involved but they haven't got the time to actually come in and work in the nursery. The parent who's got the time to come in . . . is the parent who wants to leave the child and go home and have some peace.

In this context, some parents are in a no-win situation as they are blamed for their lack of participation – a situation that Finch (1984) also found concerning the devaluation of the working-class parent's provision for the under-fives. This is at odds with the links between parent and professional that are often dominated by those in the higher social class groups (a trend that has also been noted in the General Household Survey over the years).

The primary school phase

While there has been much work from sociologists on primary schooling, concerned with the proportion of teachers in the school system, the curriculum that is transmitted, and so on, it is around the topic of educational attainment that issues concerned with class, gender and race re-emerge. In the past sociologists have looked at educational attainment in relation to the eleven-plus examination and the use of IQ tests. Today new evidence is available. With the passing of the 1988 Education Act, there is a requirement that a comprehensive system of testing is in place in all schools. Formal tests are now established at age seven (key stage one) and at age eleven (key stage two) in the primary years. Pupils are tested in English, Mathematics and Science, and the results of the national tests in 1996 are summarised in Table 6.4.

The evidence demonstrates that in 1996 three in five eleven-year-olds reached level four at key stage two of the national curriculum within English and Mathematics and that a slightly higher proportion achieved level four in Science. Once again, residence is important.

Table 6.4 **Pupils reaching or exceeding level four at key stage two: 1996**

England and Wales	Inner London	Outer London	Metropolitan districts	Shire counties	England	Wales	England & Wales (Percentages)
Boys							
English							
Teacher assessment	50	55	50	55	53	53	53
Test	41	50	47	52	50	48	50
Maths							
Teacher assessment	55	61	55	60	59	60	59
Test	48	55	51	57	55	56	55
Science							
Teacher assessment	58	64	60	66	64	66	64
Test	52	59	58	64	62	64	62
Girls							
English							
Teacher assessment	63	69	64	70	68	68	68
Test	55	66	62	68	65	65	65
Maths							
Teacher assessment	57	64	59	64	62	64	62
Test	46	54	50	56	54	56	54
Science							
Teacher assessment	62	67	63	69	67	70	67
Test	54	62	59	65	63	66	63

Source: Social Trends (1998), p. 64.

Children who attended schools in Shire Counties, in outer London and Wales, performed better than their counterparts in inner-London and metropolitan districts. More significant, however, were the gender differences. A much higher proportion of girls than boys attained a higher level in English, but there was little difference in Science and Mathematics. This kind of evidence began to raise questions about curriculum choice and especially boys' underachievement in schools.

Sociologists have also been interested in the introduction of the national curriculum in schools and the ways in which assessment influences the transmission of the curriculum. A key study by Andrew Pollard and his colleagues was based upon interviews with 88 teachers who were asked about their role and how it had changed as a result of the national curriculum and assessment procedures. Many of them felt negative about the introduction of the national curriculum and assessment in primary schools. As one teacher reports:

I'm just more stressed now. I feel pulled in different directions and I feel the need to fulfil attainment targets and to cover the core subjects as a constant unspoken pressure. The relaxed atmosphere I used to have in my class has gone. I can't spend so much time with individual children and I don't feel able to respond in a spontaneous way to some initiative introduced by the children. I no longer have the luxury of being responsive and creative. (Pollard *et al.*, 1994: 85)

These feelings were also echoed by other teachers:

It's just a different place. There's a pressure and a feeling that you're never doing enough . . . You look at the documents and you think 'how can I possibly fulfil all these demands? How can I fit all this in?' It's just overwhelming sometimes. You feel you're just going through a wheel. You're desperately covering stuff because you must give an assessment for it and you think, 'this is just not what it's about. Learning is not about this and this is not what it should be like'. (Teacher quoted in Pollard *et al.*, 1994: 85)

These views influenced not only the way in which teachers perceived the national curriculum, but also influenced their own sense of professionalism. Many felt there was a loss of autonomy in pedagogic decision-making. Many also *accepted* the imposed changes and with this came a professional ideology. For these teachers, greater control began to be perceived as acceptable or even desirable. Most commonly, however, teachers went along with changes by *incorporating* them into existing modes of working. In this way, methods were *adapted* rather than changed, and the effect of change was considerably different from that intended. Others took *active control* of the changes and responded to them in a creative but selective way; while others *submitted* without any change from professional ideology, leading to resentment, demoralisation, alienation and resistance, hoping that the sanctions available would not be sufficiently powerful. Of all these changes, *incorporation* was the most common. As one headteacher remarked:

I think I feel less uncomfortable than I did. Just about this time last year I wrote a letter to my senior adviser telling him that I was very seriously thinking of resigning because I was not prepared to have a dictated curriculum. I was not prepared for somebody to change the job I loved into one I didn't even recognise. He was very good about that and we had a long talk about acting subversively – sounds awful – but if you were really convinced that while what you were saying was right, then you looked at the national curriculum and you used it as a tool really, rather than letting it drive you. . . . I feel happier about it than I did a year ago. (Pollard *et al.*, 1994: 100)

In these circumstances, teachers take ownership and control of innovation in the process of developing new forms of pedagogy and assessment, while others engaged in other actions. But how did this influence assessment? Many teachers felt constrained by the national curriculum and the way in which it influenced their individual decision-making. As one teacher remarked:

It's changed dramatically; there's no longer the great freedom to do what you would like to do with the children. This is controlled by the policy that the school has adopted in whole school planning and internally forecasts where topics are determined two years in advance. I think we have to guard not picking up on opportunities when they present themselves, because you have to get through your topic or your theme for that term. Teachers must be allowed that spontaneity because often those are the moments that children will remember and learn from. (Teacher quoted in Pollard *et al.*, 1994: 121)

In turn, pupils also perceived differences in terms of the way in which the national curriculum was introduced. Indeed, Pollard *et al.* indicate that the national curriculum had made little difference to the pupils and their perceptions of the curriculum, so much so that they were much the same as had been reported before its introduction. However, Pollard also asked teachers about their views on assessment. Many stressed the need for assessment and highlighted how it could be used to encourage pupils. As one teacher remarked:

Every time a child brings a piece of work up I do make sure that I read it, read it with them or they read it to me and then if there's anything there that is to do with language, to do with spelling, to do with organisation, I draw it out of them, then and there. I mean, spelling hits me immediately. I notice them straight away and if I can use something that's a howling mistake with all the children, for instance the spelling of OU sounds we were doing this week. If so many were putting the spelling of OW or whatever, then I'd draw that out for the whole class. But I suppose time – I'm not sure – I don't often accept the piece of work as it is. I'll always try and make some constructive comment about that piece of work. Either 'yes, that's lovely handwriting, that's very neat, you've really worked hard on that' or 'can you see what mistake you've made with this?', so there is an assessment going on with every piece of work. (Pollard *et al.*, 1994: 191)

In this respect, teachers were involved centrally in debates, not only about the curriculum, but also about the shape of assessment and how far standard assessment tasks can be incorporated into teaching and the curriculum.

A major primary school project that focused on teaching, curriculum and assessment in the primary years was the Observational Research and Classroom Learning Evaluation study (ORACLE) that was conducted in 60 primary schools in the mid-1970s (Galton, Simon and Croll, 1980). This study has now been repeated in 1996–7 in 38 primary schools (several of which had been included in the earlier study). Among the key findings reported by Galton (1998) is that teachers spend less time with individual pupils (43 per cent down from 56 per cent in the 1970s' study) and less time hearing pupils read, marking in class and monitoring pupils. However, much pupil to pupil interaction has increased from 18.6 per cent to 26.9 per cent.

Richmond tests were given to children in years 4, 5 and 6 in September 1976 while in 1996 the tests were taken in June. Galton reports that adjustments were made so as to compare the 1976 and 1996 test scores with the result that only in year 6 were differences positive for mathematical concepts. However, he found that mathematical problem-solving had declined in years 4 and 5. As far as reading was concerned, improvements were found in year 5 but language and spelling had worsened in all years except in year 5. Only in year 6 could the researchers point to an overall improvement in language usage. In accounting for these changes, Galton highlights the shift from individual teaching to whole-class teaching, an emphasis on subject specialism and reduction in topic work as a consequence of the national curriculum (Galton, 1998).

Evidence from all these studies acts as a backdrop to the patterns of assessment that continue through the schooling process and emerge within the secondary school phase. Many of the trends that have been noted throughout the nursery and primary school phases come together in secondary schools through the formal assessment systems. Indeed, many of the debates in the last ten years have centred around different forms of assessment, including the introduction of records of achievement into schools and the development of the examination technology in the form of GCSE coursework. It is research on these topics that will be drawn on in the next section, together with a commentary on the statistical trends in examination performance, by social class, gender and race, to highlight some of the patterns that have emerged within the English school system.

The secondary school phase

Since the passing of the 1944 Education Act, secondary schooling in England and Wales has undergone considerable change. Central to it all has been a debate about the pattern of schooling. First, there were questions about the division of secondary schools into grammar, technical and modern. Subsequently, this was overtaken by the debate on the concept of comprehensive education and in turn the introduction of comprehensive schooling. While many commentators would argue that the comprehensive school has been dominant since the mid-1960s, the evidence is somewhat different. Indeed, the percentage of pupils attending comprehensive schools in England in 1965–6 was only 9.9 per cent. This rose to 34.4 per cent in 1970–1, doubling to 68.8 per cent in 1975–6, after which it climbed steadily into the 1980s. However, other patterns of schooling have also emerged: city technology colleges, grant-maintained schools and more recently the development of specialist sports and technology colleges. The pattern of schooling in England at secondary school level has therefore undergone considerable change. Alongside the debate about structure, there has also been a debate about the curriculum and the kinds of provision made for pupils of different ability levels, but it is perhaps not the type of school or the curriculum on which one should focus, but rather the pattern of assessment and examination that occurs within the English school system.

Alongside the development of the tripartite system, England also witnessed the introduction of the General Certificate of Education in 1951, an examination that was principally designed for those pupils attending a grammar school and a small number of pupils who were in other types of schooling. Indeed, Broadfoot (1996) is able to report that by 1960 only one in eight pupils were sitting for examinations in the General Certificate of Education. This was the context for establishing the Beloe Committee in 1958 which came out in favour of a new examination: the Certificate of Secondary Education (CSE) that was introduced into English schools in the mid-1960s for approximately 60 per cent of the pupils in the school system. However, in the following 20 years Broadfoot (1996) identifies four significant developments in patterns of assessment. They are: the pursuit of a common system of examining at 16+; the rise of teacher assessment; the development of post-16 qualifications; and the rise of the profiling (records of achievement) movement. For our purposes, we will focus briefly on the development of the common examination at 16+ and also on records of achievement, as they have had a considerable impact on schooling through the curriculum and assessment systems in place.

While the debate about a common examination at sixteen plus has a long history in English education, it culminated in the publication of a set of national and subject criteria in March 1985 with the first group of students sitting the national examinations in June 1988. The purpose of

GCSE was placed in the rhetoric of raising standards. However, one of its most important features was that teacher-assessed coursework became a feature rather than students just having to sit formal examination papers. Coursework was assessed by those who taught the students and was based upon a range of skills, which included those which were experimental, research based and interactive, as well as including co-operative learning and work based on fieldwork and original research. In a case study on coursework and coursework assessment in six schools, David Scott (1990) examined the content and timing of coursework, teacher input, pupil input, and parental influence. It is interesting to note the way in which Scott identifies parental influence in two forms. First, the provision of important resources, such as books and equipment, and second, assistance provided by parents with specific pieces of work. In these circumstances, the influence of parents relate to social class in the form of different kinds of capital, especially cultural capital. As a consequence, a debate has occurred about whether some pupils are more advantaged than others. Indeed, a teacher in Scott's study remarked:

And it does certainly favour the pupils from the more advantaged homes quite definitely. More so I mean, before they used to go into the exam and you know they'd go on with the exam: now with all this work that they are doing at home, quite a few of them have brothers and sisters who have gone through, you know, who might have done the course last year, they're doing the same books. Some parents are far more helpful. They have far more resources to provide at home, so in the coursework, certainly quite a proportion of children are at a disadvantage.

Certainly, Scott found that the input took a variety of different forms, whereby parents provided resources that included writing and re-writing assignments, providing detailed answers, the provision of practice sessions at home, re-visiting fieldwork sites for geography coursework, and the purchase of appropriate books for some subject areas, as well as the access to computer equipment and software packages.

Nevertheless, Scott did not find it a widespread practice within his six schools. Indeed, most parents were providing very little direct assistance with specific pieces of work. Rather they were concerned whether they had the necessary technical knowledge, and whether it was fair to give their children an unfair advantage over others. The role of parents, while being seen as significant in the English educational system, can also be seen as potentially divisive in these circumstances, perpetuating the social divisions that have been identified in other ways.

Alongside the debate about the introduction of a common examination at 16 and the use of coursework, has been a debate about developing other means of recording and reporting achievement and learning of a formal and informal kind. This has been developed through records of achievement or profiles that are designed to make pupils partners in assessment and to provide a basis for future decisions about careers, career options and learning targets. The record has often been seen as a means of making links between school and work, as the DES/ Welsh Office commented:

The benefits to employers go wider than the availability of better information through records of achievement. The development of self-appraisal and self-management skills can help pupils, not only to take increasing responsibility for their own learning whilst at school, but also later on to be better equipped to present themselves for selection and interview for jobs and later still to manage their work in employment and evaluate their careers performance. (DES/Welsh Office, 1989)

While these are the purposes of records of achievement, we need to look at the practice, as revealed in a study by Christopher Pole (1993) that challenges the rhetoric of records of achievement through target-setting, dialogue and the promotion of learning. As Pole indicates, records of achievement are not the innovative development that some would claim.

In his case study school, Pole reports that records of achievement had an influence on teacher–pupil relations. For example, the Head of Benton School saw records of achievement as a means of promoting relationships between teachers and pupils. As he commented:

I don't think there are any children too bright to benefit. Because you are academically able doesn't make you socially competent or give you personal skills . . . (high academic ability) doesn't stop us trying to identify areas of strength and weakness . . . I would have thought to continue to talk to children like that on a one-to-one basis is the key to get them to think about what they are doing (and) can only be a positive help. (Pole, 1993: 39)

However, as Pole indicates, the one-to-one discussion often concerned considerable negotiation where the power and experience of teachers and pupils came to the fore. He documents several ways in which teachers took control of the records of achievement discussion and negotiation, as indicated by the following comments:

CP: When you are in the negotiation room, who does most of the talking, you or the teacher?
SIMON: Well, if you agree on everything, it's the teacher because he is just going through (the descriptor sheets) saying yeah right, that's agreed, and he just keeps going until you don't agree. (Pole, 1993: 51)

This is a situation where the teacher is in control, but we might ask what occurs when disagreements arise and negotiation is involved. As Pole indicates:

CP: Have either of you been in a situation where you couldn't agree?
SALLY: Yes I have.
CP: What happens then?
SALLY: Well Mr Shaw just batters you down.
CP: Batters you down?

SALLY: Yes, say you've got like six against one i.e. the opinion of six teachers to one pupil like I put two (descriptor number two) and they put four Mr Shaw just talks you round. (Pole, 1993: 52)

The pupils in this study also indicated how they argued against the evidence which had been collected from teachers, as Sally and another pupil, Paul, indicate:

CP: Is it difficult to argue with six against one?
PAUL: Yes it is a bit.
SALLY: It's annoying because they are all teachers and if they don't agree you can't say a lot about it because . . .
PAUL: Because there are six of them and just you.
SALLY: Yes (about) schoolwork you can't really talk them down because they are teachers. (Pole, 1993: 52)

As well as teachers being involved in negotiations with pupils, there are also compromises as recorded in the following conversation:

CP: Right so if you come to a negotiation session with some ideas about yourself and the teacher has other ideas what happens then?
DAVID: Well, you discuss it for a while and finally you come to some agreement.
CP: Have you ever had a disagreement with a teacher over a descriptor?
DAVID: Yes I did once but we eventually resolved it. I think it was about library skills. I thought I was pretty good at that.
CP: Library skills?
DAVID: Yes, it was finding books in the library, using the codes and that, and the teachers commented, and they put me lower down than I thought I was. And so eventually we middled it out.
CP: Middled it out?
DAVID: Well sort of. I went down and he came up. We compromised. (Pole, 1993: 54)

Within these illustrations, Chris Pole indicates that teachers are in control of the negotiation process. Such a situation suggests that rather than records of achievement being a panacea for developing new modes of assessment and challenging traditional teacher–pupil relationships, they reinforce some of these elements and highlight negotiation, compromise and control. Indeed, in this respect the traditional patterns of secondary school assessment were reinforced at this level.

While much of the research on examinations, especially at secondary level, has focused on the relationship between social class and educational achievement, there has also been much interest in the relationship between gender and success. The evidence from statistics in education concerning GCSE and advanced level examinations demonstrates that there is a differential pattern of achievement between girls and boys at both levels (see Tables 6.5 and 6.6). Indeed, the tables suggest that particular subjects become predominantly associated with either boys or girls with scientific subjects (apart from Biology at advanced level) being more associated with boys and humanities and social science

Table 6.5   **GCSE selected achievements 1995/96**

Subject	Male passes	Female passes
Biology	21 778	17 761
Chemistry	21 203	13 583
Physics	21 727	12 145
Mathematics	150 076	151 300
Geography	76 467	68 562
History	55 648	65 446
Social Studies	6 185	17 950
English	148 079	194 696
French	63 241	94 771
Music	10 029	16 412

Source: *Statistics of Education: Public Examinations GCSE and GCE in England*. Table 11 (adapted).

Table 6.6   **GCE Advanced Level selected achievements 1995/96**

Subject	Male passes	Female passes
Biology	15 784	23 596
Chemistry	17 365	13 801
Physics	19 862	5 374
Mathematics	35 044	18 973
Geography	17 014	14 190
History	14 818	17 800
Social Studies	16 566	35 121
English	21 856	50 568
French	6 606	14 526
Music	2 072	3 251

Source: *Statistics of Education: Public Examinations GCSE and GCE in England*. Table 26 (adapted).

subjects being more associated with girls. It is these patterns that are reinforced when candidates make their way through to higher education.

The training system

Not all children move through the educational system to university. The majority continue their learning through the workplace and through the formalised provision of training. However, as the commentary in training statistics for 1995 indicates, there is very little agreement as to what constitutes training, other than to view it as:

Intentional intervention to help the individual (or the organisation) to become competent or more competent at work. (HMSO, 1995: 9)

United Kingdom

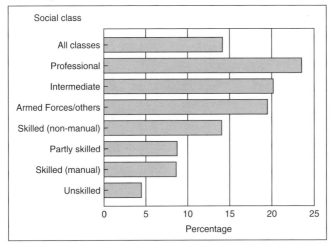

Figure 6.2   Employees[1] of working age[2] receiving job related training[3] during the last four weeks[4,5] by social class

Notes:
1 Employees are those in employment excluding the self-employed, unpaid family workers and those on government employment and training programmes.
2 Working age is defined as Men aged 16–64 and Women aged 16–59.
3 Job related training includes both on-the-job and off-the-job training.
4 Figures from spring 1992 onwards have been calculated using 1991 Census of Population figures and are not consistent with earlier figures.
5 Due to a change in the LFS questionnaire data from summer 1994 onwards are not comparable with earlier figures.

Source: Labour Force Survey, spring 1995.

The patterns associated with who gets training reinforce the earlier interlinked relationships between social class and education. Those in the professional and intermediate classes were much more likely to have received job-related training during the last four weeks (25 per cent) than those in the skilled non-manual and skilled manual classes (10 per cent – see Figure 6.2) and for those drawn from other ethnic groups. Training for men and women showed similarities in pattern, with 15 per cent of women and 13.7 per cent of men receiving training in the four-week period under study (see Table 6.7). There has been a tendency for white employees (especially white males) to have a greater chance of training than non-whites. In these ways it would seem that the world beyond school reinforces trends that have been found within the schooling process. But what happens when individuals move into higher education?

Table 6.7   Employees[1] of working age[2] receiving job related training[3] during the last four weeks[4,5] by ethnic origin and sex

United Kingdom thousands and percentages[6]

Ethnic origin	Total			Men			Women		
	Base	No.	%	Base	No.	%	Base	No.	%
Total	21 132	3 026	14.3	11 195	1 529	13.7	9 937	1 497	15.1
White	20 158	2 896	14.3	10 690	1 464	13.7	9 508	1 432	15.1
All non-white—Other	929	179	13.9	503	64	12.8	426	55	15.2
Black	292	51	17.5	134	19	14.3	158	22	20.2
Indian, Pakistani	423	45	10.6	253	27	10.8	170	18	10.4
& Bangladeshi	214	33	15.5	116	18	16.5	98	15	15.4

Notes:
1   Employees are those in employment excluding the self-employed, unpaid family workers and those on government employment and training programmes.
2   Working age is defined as men aged 16–64 and women aged 16–59.
3   Job-related training includes both on and off-the-job training.
4   Figures from 1992 have been calculated using the 1991 Census of Population figures and are not consistent with earlier figures.
5   Due to changes in the LFS questionnaire data from summer 1994 onwards are not comparable with earlier figures.
6   Expressed as a percentage of the total numbers of people in each cell.
    Less than 10,000 in calls estimate not shown.

Source: Labour Force Survey, spring 1995.

The higher education phase

The pattern of higher education in the United Kingdom has undergone a transformation in recent years, with a movement from an elite to a mass system. This has been accompanied by the removal of the 'binary line' which divided polytechnics from universities. In these circumstances there have been greater opportunities for individuals to participate in the higher education system, both at first and higher degree level. Indeed, there have been increased registrations in the system at both levels, with expansion at undergraduate level occurring in the 1980s and at post-graduate level in the 1990s. By 1995, 11.5 per cent of the population held a degree or equivalent compared with 6.8 per cent ten years earlier (see Table 6.8). Men (13.7 per cent) were still more likely to hold a degree than women (9 per cent), but the difference was diminishing. The increased participation of women in higher education was reflected in an increase from 9 per cent obtaining a degree or equivalent to 13.7 per cent over a ten-year period. However, there has been little change in the 'gender bias' of subject (and thereby career) choice. Many of the subject patterns in the school system are reinforced in higher education (see Table 6.9). More women than men are studying biological sciences and far more men than women are in the physical sciences, mathematics and engineering. In the social sciences and humanities, more women than men study languages and in the social sciences these trends are reinforced through study at postgraduate level for taught courses and research degrees, where women are still under-represented (Coffield and Vignoles, 1997). Such patterns hold implications for the gendering of occupational groups within the professions. In medicine, it has been argued that the numbers of women becoming doctors has resulted in career breaks and shortages, provoking considerable debate about the numbers of students who should be accepted and trained for the medical profession. Similarly, in school teaching, which has predominantly attracted women, there has been debate about the absence of male role models in schools; especially primary schools (Pascall and Cox, 1993).

Discrepant patterns of subject choice have continued, therefore, and this has been the source of considerable debate. More pressing has been the question of inequalities of access to universities. Here, social class differences remain of concern. This is a subject that is high on the political agenda in the late 1990s and was the subject of some concern to members of the Dearing Committee in their analysis of participation in higher education (National Committee of Inquiry into Higher Education, 1997). The age participation index for socio-economic group 1 is now 79 per cent, while in socio-economic group 5 it is only 12 per cent. (see Table 6.10). While this is slightly less of a bias than ten years earlier, it still points to a massively uneven process adversely affecting the life chances of students from lower socio-economic groups

Table 6.8   Trends in highest qualifications held by sex for people of working age[1]

United Kingdom thousands and percentages

Highest qualification	1984	1985	1986	1987	1988	1989	1990	1991	1992	1993	1994	1995
All people (thousands)	33 125	33 301	33 424	33 620	33 750	33 851	33 922	33 947	34 245	34 293	34 351	34 445
Degree or equivalent	5.8	7.2	7.8	7.7	7.6	7.9	8.4	8.5	9.9	10.9	10.8	11.5
Higher education below degree level	5.4	5.7	5.4	5.5	5.6	5.6	5.8	5.9	6.9	7.6	8.2	8.2
GCE A level or equivalent	21.8	22.2	21.9	22.2	22.1	24.0	25.0	25.8	26.6	25.5	26.2	25.1
GCE O level or equivalent	15.5	16.0	16.4	17.0	17.5	17.7	18.4	18.6	18.3	16.8	17.4	18.4
Other qualifications	8.7	9.1	10.3	10.6	12.0	12.0	11.2	10.1	10.3	11.9	14.6	15.5
No qualification	40.0	38.4	37.2	35.7	34.1	32.0	30.0	30.3	27.8	27.3	22.4	21.0
Don't know/no reply	1.8	1.5	1.0	1.3	0.9	0.9	1.0	0.8	0.2	0.0	0.3	0.3
Men (thousands)	17 361	17 427	17 476	17 549	17 606	17 657	17 694	17 705	17 901	17 929	17 964	18 017
Degree or equivalent	9.0	9.5	10.3	10.1	9.8	9.8	10.4	10.5	12.1	13.3	13.0	13.7
Higher education below degree level	3.9	4.2	3.7	4.0	4.3	4.3	4.6	4.9	5.8	6.3	7.1	7.2
GCE A level or equivalent	30.9	31.2	30.7	31.2	30.7	32.8	33.7	34.3	35.2	32.6	33.2	32.4
GCE O level or equivalent	11.4	11.6	12.3	12.5	12.6	13.0	13.5	13.8	13.5	12.9	13.5	14.0
Other qualifications	6.9	7.2	8.4	9.2	10.9	10.7	10.0	8.6	8.8	11.2	14.0	14.6
No qualification	35.9	34.6	33.3	31.4	30.4	26.4	26.5	26.8	24.4	23.7	19.0	17.7
Don't know/no reply	2.1	1.6	1.2	1.5	1.2	1.0	1.2	0.9	0.2	0.0	0.3	0.4
Women (thousands)	15 764	15 874	15 947	16 070	16 143	16 194	16 228	16 242	16 344	16 365	16 367	16 428
Degree or equivalent	4.5	4.8	5.0	5.1	5.2	5.7	6.2	6.4	7.4	8.3	8.5	9.0
Higher education below degree level	7.0	7.3	7.3	7.2	7.1	7.0	7.5	7.0	8.2	8.9	9.5	9.2
GCE A level or equivalent	11.8	12.4	12.3	12.4	12.8	14.5	15.6	16.5	17.2	17.8	18.5	17.2
GCE O level or equivalent	20.0	20.6	20.9	21.9	22.9	22.7	23.7	23.8	23.6	21.1	21.8	23.2
Other qualifications	10.7	11.1	12.3	12.0	13.3	13.4	10.6	11.6	11.9	12.6	15.3	16.6
No qualification	44.6	42.7	41.5	40.3	38.2	35.9	33.8	34.1	31.6	31.3	26.1	24.5
Don't know/no reply	1.5	1.3	0.8	1.1	0.7	0.7	0.9	0.6	0.1	0.0	0.3	0.3

Note:
1 Working age is defined as men aged 16–64 and women aged 16–59.

Table 6.9 **Subjects studied by UK undergraduates in 1995–6**

Subjects	Undergraduate		
	Male	*Female*	*Total*
Medicine and dentistry	13 200	13 453	26 653
Subjects allied to medicine	9 774	28 923	38 697
Biological sciences	20 320	31 104	51 424
Veterinary science	911	1 482	2 393
Agricultural & related subjects	3 765	3 554	7 319
Physical sciences	31 695	17 671	49 366
Mathematical sciences	9 024	5 593	14 617
Computer science	30 718	7 298	38 016
Engineering & technology	71 712	12 436	84 148
Architecture, building & planning	19 580	5 683	25 263
Social, economic & political studies	31 113	39 501	70 614
Law	14 458	17 248	31 706
Business & administrative studies	47 676	46 618	34 294
Librarianship & information science	4 466	6 740	11 206
Languages	17 421	41 836	59 257
Humanities	15 244	17 417	32 661
Creative arts & design	26 469	35 600	62 069
Education	12 919	41 711	54 630
Combined	46 416	58 640	105 056

Source: Students in Higher Education Institutions 1995–96 (HESA 1996).
Table 1a adapted, p. 29.

Table 6.10 **Percentage age participation index by academic year and socio-economic groups in the United Kingdom**

SEG	*1991–2*	*1992–3*	*1993–4*	*1994–5*	*1995–6*
I	55	71	73	78	79
II	36	39	42	45	45
IIIn	22	27	29	31	31
IIIm	11	15	17	18	18
IV	12	14	16	17	17
V	6	9	11	11	12
Total	23	28	30	32	32

Source: DfEE, 1996.

(Robertson and Hillman, 1997). While there have been many initiatives to attract working-class students, through the availability of access courses and the like (see Wakeford, 1993), there is still a considerable challenge for higher education to improve on patterns of recruitment from these groups.

The pattern of inequalities associated with ethnic minorities is complex. Perhaps surprisingly, members of certain ethnic groups are more strongly represented in higher education than their white counterparts. This is even stronger when we compare groups chosen from the same social class background. In part, this may relate to the ways in which the members of these groups value education. Interestingly, the participation of Bangladeshi women and Afro-Caribbean men are significantly lower than their white counterparts (UCAS, 1996). However it should not be assumed that the influence of the educational system is a benign one. A closer analysis also reveals than many of the ethnic minority students are concentrated in the less prestigious post-1992 universities and still face discrimination and isolation (Coffield and Vignoles, 1997).

Conclusion

In concluding my essay on patterns and processes of education in the United Kingdom in 1984, I pointed to the changes that had occurred in the educational system since the Second World War and posed the question: to what extent have different social groups benefitted from these changes? At that stage I was able to conclude:

The overall pattern is based on distinct social divisions by gender, race and social class. Indeed, it could be ·argued that the divisiveness in education is cumulative with the result that the patterns established in pre-school and in the early years of schooling result in a series of selection processes which have a marked effect on the educational routes that can be taken in secondary, further and higher education. (Burgess, 1984: 119)

But how, might we ask, has this changed? At the close of this account, I can point to some improvements while still highlighting the continuity of these same basic social divisions and patterns of inequality in education. They represent an acute challenge to researchers, policy-makers and practitioners at the start of the new millennium.

CHAPTER 7

Culture at work

JOHN ELDRIDGE

In the present post-colonial world, the notion of an authentic culture as an autonomous internally coherent universe no longer seems tenable, except perhaps as a 'useful fiction' or a revealing distortion. In retrospect, it appears that only a concerted disciplinary effort could maintain the tenuous fiction of a self-contained cultural whole. Rapidly increasing global interdependence has made it more and more clear that neither 'we' nor 'they' are as neatly bounded and homogeneous as once seemed the case. The stock market crash of October 1987, for example, was global not local. News from Tokyo and Hong Kong mattered as much as a word from New York or London. Similarly, Latin American and African fiction influence and are influenced by French and North American literary production. All of us inhabit a late-twentieth-century world marked by borrowing and lending across porous national and cultural boundaries that are saturated with inequality, power and domination (Rosaldo, 1993: 217).

The meanings attached to the word culture are so diverse, the topics covered so numerous, the connotations so extensive, that we are at once fascinated and confused by it. There is a stretching of the concept that can take us from the work group culture to global culture. In between, as we vary the focus, we can, for example, identify references to class, gender, community, ethnicity, organisation, corporation, bureaucracy, nation. We notice that what are sometimes treated as distinct categories such as economics, politics, technology, science, religion and culture, can be elided, as when we speak of a political culture, a scientific culture, and so on. We can think of culture in descriptive terms, a way of life, identifiable practices expressed in symbols to which meanings are given and collectively understood. We can think of it in evaluative terms, as in judgements of 'high' and 'low' culture, or as a basis for a critique of society, whether by people actively involved in some kind of struggle – cultural resistance – or by theorists who write about hegemony and anti-hegemony, dominant and emergent cultures and such like. Questions of value come into play both in describing the conflicts that may be identified between different groups and in the theorist making value judgements and offering interpretations. Cultural analysis can thus become cultural critique and such critiques may be informed by political, moral and philosophical considerations. I want now to take some examples that impinge upon the world of work and reflect upon them.

We will begin with Raymond Williams who, for most of his academic life, was preoccupied with the the concept of culture and knew well the variability of its meanings. We can see in *Culture and Society*, first published in 1958, how he selects five key words – democracy, art, class, industry and culture – and then proceeds to show how the idea of culture had been used as a critique of capitalism in the work of people as various as Blake, Cobbett, Ruskin, Morris and Lawrence. This recovery of a tradition, mainly literary at this point, was not only a way of re-appropriating it from those who saw culture and cultural ideals in elitist terms set against the 'masses' in a profoundly inegalitarian framework, but as a way of working towards a critique of contemporary capitalism and seeking to make connections between socialism and democracy. He is both a critic and an advocate. Thus in the follow-up to *Culture and Society, The Long Revolution*, he applies his thinking to Britain in the 1960s and argues for an educated participative democracy. This, we may say, was the cultural ideal for a new way of life, to be set against the existing one. As he reviews the nature of the consumer society with its emphasis on the individual rather than social needs, generated by the ideology of the market, he points out:

It is easy, to get a sense of plenty from the shop windows of contemporary Britain, but if we look at the schools, the hospitals, the roads, the libraries, we find chronic shortages far too often. Even when things are factually connected, in direct daily experience, as in the spectacular example of the flood of new cars and the ludicrous inadequacy of our road system, the spell of this kind of thinking seems too powerful to break. Crises of this sort seem certain to dominate our economy in the years to come. (Williams, 1961: 324)

This was not a yearning for a pre-industrial organic society, as he made abundantly clear. Industrial production keeps us from starving. Large-scale organisation enables us to extend communications which make for new participative possibilities. But what was lacking was an adequate sense of society: 'For my own part,' he wrote, 'I am certain, as I review the evidence, that it is capitalism – a particular and temporary system of organising the industrial process – which is in fact confusing us. Capitalism's version of society can only be the market, for its purpose is profit in particular activities rather than any general conception of social use, and its concentration of ownership in sections of the community makes most common decisions, beyond those of the market, limited or impossible' (Williams, 1961: 327). Within industry itself, Williams suggest that the democratic impulse was only weakly evident; decision-making is grounded in hierarchies from which most of us are excluded. Depending on circumstances the excluded may respond with apathy, petitions or revolts.

Is a socialist culture the answer? As he points out, there are both liberals and socialists who are worried about the state-controlled, centralised version, and with reason. Against the speculators who operate in the market economy are the bureaucrats and officials of the state:

This difficulty has a representative significance. It is not only in cultural questions but in the whole area of thinking about change in in our society, that this knot is tied. Here is the deepest difficulty in the whole development of our democracy: that we seem reduced to a choice between speculator and bureaucrat, and while we do not like the speculator, the bureaucrat is not exactly inviting either. In such a situation, energy is sapped, hope weakens, and of course the present compromise between the speculators and the bureaucrats remains unchallenged. (Williams, 1961: 367)

The long revolution he was advocating was one which envisaged the steady extension of democracy, as people broke out of the restrictions and blockages of the existing society, creating and discovering new institutions. Trade unions and the mutuality that could be found in some communities and co-operative associations indicate some of the possibilities, despite their own limitations and, in the case of trade unions, sectionalism and exclusiveness. There was no inevitability about this but there were still grounds for hope: 'If we look back over recent centuries, the successes are truly spectacular, and we ought to keep reminding ourselves of them, and of the incomprehension, the confusion and the distaste with which the proposals for things now the most ordinary parts of reality were received' (Williams, 1961: 375). The question of democracy was related to the extension of education, to ownership and control of the means of production and communication. This was seen as a political and a cultural struggle against existing forms of class inequality: 'With that basic inequality isolated we could stop the irrelevant discussion of class, of which most of us are truly sick and tired and let through the more interesting discussion of human differences, between real people and real communities living in their valuably various ways' (Williams, 1961: 363).

To put the matter starkly: the culture of democracy was set against the culture of capitalism. This, indeed, is one of the ways in to the concept of a 'mass society'. Both Williams and Richard Hoggart (notably in *The Uses of Literacy* (1958)) see the developments that had taken place in the wider society, especially with reference to the system of communications as a form of cultural robbery. It is commercialism that has put real power into the hands of the few owners of the means of communication. The democratic project had, as it were, been hijacked. This was not to deny the real democratic gains over a long period but to suggest that clamps were placed on it by capitalism as an economic formation. There is a mirror image of this kind of argument to be found in Martin Wiener's *English Culture and the Decline of the Industrial Spirit: 1850–1980* (Wiener, 1985) where the central argument is that the enterprise culture was eroded by the critics of industrialism, and this has to be taken into account when considering the secular decline of the economy. But to speak of a culture of capitalism is to speak of a set of values and a way of life, as Weber made very clear in writing of the *spirit* of capitalism. This spirit was about making money, with acquisition as the ultimate purpose of life. Economic activity no longer becomes a means to satisfy material needs, but an end albeit with no fixed destination. In his aptly named *The Culture of Capitalism*, Alan MacFarlane has pointed to the double meaning of 'culture' in this respect. There is the anthropological sense of 'the way of life' – the mentality, morality and emotional structure (which is broadly equivalent to what Williams had termed the structure of feeling) and the products and activities that typify it. There is also a connotation relating to what is cultivated and, in consequence, develops and flourishes. It has developed to become a world-wide phenomenon. As MacFarlane comments:

It flourished and sprouted and many of its seeds were to spread all over the world so that it is now part of the air we breathe. So wide has been its influence that formal distinctions between 'capitalist' and 'socialist' countries have broken down. Much of the 'culture of capitalism' is now to be found in Moscow, Havana or Beijing, as well as in Los Angeles, Paris or London. . . . The phenomenon is worth our understanding, prisoners as we are in this world culture, yet partly liberated by knowing something of the roots and growth of the tree high up in whose branches we nervously rest. (MacFarlane, 1987: xvi)

We should not be too surprised, therefore, when shop-floor studies of management–worker relations at the point of production reveal similarities. It is instructive, for example, to compare the American shop-floor studies of Donald Roy (e.g. Roy 1952, 1954, 1960) with Harastzi's Hungarian plant-based study *A Worker in a Worker's State* (1977). The pressure to obtain enough output under the application of piece-rate incentive schemes could lead to the development of tactics and coping strategies on the shop-floor, sometimes, but not always, with the collusion of management or supervision. What was important in each situation was to get through the week and 'make out' on the take-home pay. Or, in the case of the much-studied car industry, the pressures of the mass assembly production line are experienced in similar ways to the USA (Walker, 1952), the UK (Beynon, 1975), France (Linhart, 1981) and Japan (Kamata, 1983). We are dealing not only with similar technologies in these cases, but also with a competitive system which, in turn, provides the context within which managerial strategies are developed.

When, therefore, we speak of such entities as working class culture – whether in the work situation or more generally – it is within this sense of wider capitalist processes. There are both conflicts and struggles against as well as co-operation with these ever-extending developments. The specific example of the making of the English working class was worked through most famously by E. P. Thompson. In the book of that title he tells us that the working class was present at its own making and that the experience of productive relations into which they were born or entered involuntarily, when it was embodied in traditions, value systems and institutions, constituted a culture, which could be distinctive enough to be identified in terms of class consciousness. Thompson was aware of the long historical journey that had brought English society to the industrial revolution, and that working people had brought into this new situation ideas of liberty, for which they struggled. Against the slower processes were also the sharper struggles between contending groups, of which Peterloo stood as a dramatic example. It is worth recalling how Thompson concludes in his description of what this culture was like, what it was made of, recognising, too, that in his view by the mid 1830s it was defeated:

This was, perhaps, the most distinguished popular culture England has ever known. It contained the massive diversity of skills, of the workers in metal, wood, textiles and ceramics, without whose inherited 'mysteries' and superb ingenuity with primitive tools the inventions of the Industrial Revolution could scarcely have got further than the drawing board. From this culture of the craftsmen and the self-taught there came scores of inventors, organisers, journalists and political theorists of impressive quality. It is easy enough to say that this culture was backward-looking or conservative. True enough. One direction of the great agitations of the artisans and outworkers continued over fifty years, was to *resist* being turned into a proletariat. When they knew that this cause was lost, yet they reached out again, in the Thirties and Forties, and sought to achieve new and only imagined forms of social control. During all this time they were, as a class, repressed and segregated in their own communities. . . . Segregated in this way, their institutions acquired a peculiar toughness and resilience. (Thompson, 1965: 831)

What was being fought was not the machine but the oppressive and exploitative forces of industrial capitalism, based on the premise that production was not for profit but for use. The triumph of the new political economy of the market was the defeat of what Thompson chose to call a heroic culture. His work on the moral economy of the crowd is a further buttress to that, along with his celebrated discussion of time-discipline (Thompson, 1991). In the first he is showing how the economy of provision was broken down by the new commercialism. As he points out, it is difficult to imagine other social configurations to those to which we have become accustomed, to conceive that it could be held to be unnatural for some to profit out of the necessities of others. The food riots in eighteenth-century England were, he argued, expressions of outrage in times of dearth, that individual dealers, millers, farmers, should think to behave in such a way. The effects of these incipient market dealings on local communities were real, to the point of death and starvation, not just inconveniences. As Thompson pointed out: 'Dearth always comes to such communities as a profound psychic shock.'When it is accompanied by the knowledge of inequalities, and the suspicion of manipulated scarcity, shock passes into fury' (Thompson, 1991: 257).

And he concludes that one sign of the triumph of the market economy was in the subsequent thinking about the food riots, that they were irrational responses to hunger rather than a protest that human reciprocities were being damaged and broken in the name of profit. Such reciprocities had themselves been diminished and re-defined in terms of the cash nexus.

It is worth reminding ourselves at this point that Thompson, while seriously engaged with the concept of culture, did not accept the label that he was a representative figure of 'culturalism'. The term culture, he shrewdly observed, is a 'clumpish term, which by gathering up so many activities and attributes into one common bundle may actually confuse or disguise discriminations that should be made between them. We need to take this bundle apart and examine the components with more care: rites, symbolic modes, the cultural attributes of hegemony, the intergenerational transmission of custom and custom's evolution within historically specific forms of working and social relations' (Thompson, 1991: 13). Behind this is the point that it is necessary to distinguish between culture and non-culture and that, moreover, we need to think carefully about the category of 'experience'. As I see it this involves an appreciation of the historical specificities of societies, how they form and change, alongside a sense of how they interact with nature, such that raw life experience is transmuted into particular kinds of understandings among people in those societies and comes to be structured in definite ways. Thus Thompson writes: 'Experience walks in without knocking at the door, and announces deaths, crises of subsistence, trench warfare, unemployment, inflation, genocide. People starve: their survivors think in new ways about the market. People are imprisoned: in prison they meditate in new ways about the law' (Thompson, 1978: 201). This is one way of saying that people make history but not in circumstances of their choosing. Moreover, along with the making there is the breaking. There are victories as well as defeats for contending groups and their consequences can be decisive for generations to come. This, we scarcely should need reminding, pre-dates capitalism. At the time of the Peloponnesian War, for example, Thucydides tells us how the political and economic stability of ancient Athens was destroyed. Not only were lands laid to waste and populations slaughtered or taken into slavery but the plague was estimated to have accounted for more than a quarter of the population (Mosse, 1969). So much for culturalism.

The cash nexus brings us to the question of time and work discipline. Within the emerging factory system of the industrial revolution time was money. This was, as Weber had famously shown, the legacy of Puritanism, where in religious terms we had to give a strict account of our time before God. How did we use our time was a question, the answer to which could determine our eternal destiny. It was a question the entrepreneur could ask himself but also an obligation he felt justified in laying upon his employees. The legacy was transmuted into secular, economic activity, with the calculus of utilitarianism infusing it. Part of Thompson's concern was to show how this concept of time differed from pre-industrial societies and in this respect is culturally variable. From the rhythms of agricultural work and peasant activity, where time is passed, to the situation where time is spent and is, therefore, a cost, we can see that employer–employee relations can be seen as a struggle for time control. It was not only a matter of taking over the time of the worker but also seeking to control the effort. That struggle can be observed as one recalls the array of sanctions used by employers, including deduction of wages, sacking and blacklisting, as well as rewards for effort, as in piecework and various incentive schemes. At the same time there were forms of resistance from workers against speed-ups, tight piece-rates, unsatisfactory working hours and conditions and, indeed, fixing the clocks (which some employers used to lengthen the working day and shorten the breaks), which also led to the formation of the early trade unions. Thompson sums up the learning experience and the changes that took place in employer–employee relations in a cogent way:

The first generation were taught by their masters the importance of time; the second generation formed their short-time committees in the ten-hour movement; the third generation struck for overtime or time-and-a-half. They accepted the categories of their employers and learned to fight back within them. They had learned their lesson, that time is money, only too well. (Thompson, 1991: 390)

The economic growth to which these changes gave rise was also a cultural change. Thompson's case was not that 'tradition' stood for all that was good but that 'the historical record is not a simple one of neutral and inevitable technological change, but is also one of exploitation and resistance to stand to be lost as well as gained' (Thompson, 1991: 399).

Thompson, as we have seen, draws attention to the growth of segregated working-class communities in the later nineteenth century. In a sympathetic critique of Thompson, Eric Hobsbawm has argued that what we have come to understand as a 'traditional' working class in Britain did not emerge until the 1880s (Hobsbawm, 1984). The residential segregation led to working-class areas of the industrial cities – labour for the shipyards, textiles, engineering, iron and steel. The mining communities had a different history, with rural continuities (see, for example, Beynon and Austrin, 1994). Between them and other classes a gulf was fixed, in life chances and life-styles. In her book *Working-Class Cultures in Britain. 1890–1960*, Joanne Bourke has written of working-class communities as a 'retrospective construction'. She reasonably points out that if as many as 94 ways of defining a community have been unearthed this suggests that the term is problematic. She draws attention to the studies of working-class areas and neighbourhoods, with their divisions, internal forms of stratification, treatment of strangers and foreigners. The concept, she suggests, has been used by socialists as a rhetorical device and modern socialist historians have not wanted to give up the concept:

As with their predecessors, 'community' represented resistance to capitalism. It was conducive to class consciousness. The 'community' was the neighbourhood which was, in turn, the class. Thus Jeremy Seabrook believes in the working-class 'idea of neighbourhood' with its 'values' which the best of the working class forged in opposition to the poverty and insecurity of capitalism, the mutuality and the sharing, the imaginative understanding of other people's sufferings. For him the alleged 'retreat from community' in recent years was lamentable. (Bourke, 1994: 138)

Bourke does well to counsel against nostalgic views of solidarity or assumed value consensus. Yet perhaps she deconstructs too much. Writers like Richard Hoggart (1958) or Robert Roberts (1971) did not write about Hunslet or Salford in sentimental ways. They knew from direct experience the fractures and fissions of these streets and places, but they also knew about the centrality of the big dichotomy between 'them' and 'us'. The way this infused work and leisure is well summarised by Hobsbawm:

A vast amount of working-class life until 1914, and even until 1945, was lived in a network of mutual aid and trust largely independent of the law. In workshops men knew that even the infirm and elderly had a right to earn a living, and their 'mates' saw to it that they could. Neighbours helped each other. Complex systems of mutual trust operated smoothly without sanctions, as in the system of cash betting on horses outside race courses, which stretched into every factory or working-class street. . . . Like the more organised and political forms of working class action, it symbolised a certain sense of class independence, but above all the creation of a social space outside the control of the powerful and the rich. Its ambitions were small but it knew how to set limits to 'their' power through a mixture of formal struggle and informal non-cooperation. British workers may not have aimed to overthrow the wages system but no other class has achieved the degree of *de facto* 'workers control' on the factory floor which became characteristic of so many large British factories. (Hobsbawm, 1984: 191–2)

The theme of the breakdown of community has, of course, been with us for a long time, and not only in the United Kingdom, and is usually connected with issues of urbanisation, bureaucratisation and rapid industrialisation (e.g. Stein, 1960; Bell and Newby, 1971; Eldridge, 1971). It is worth recalling the famous landmark in industrial sociology *Management and the Worker* (Roethlisberger and Dickson, 1939). These studies of work group behaviour, observed in meticulous detail at the Hawthorne Works of the Western Electric Company at Chicago, were attempts to tap human resources in the service of management's purposes. Questions of worker resistance to management objectives were typically defined as workers' sentiments versus managements' rationality. The hope was that through new forms of management style and a therapeutic approach to workers' needs, efficiency could be improved and the business flourish. Thus the researchers concluded that collaboration was not only a matter of logical organisation. 'It presupposes social codes, conventions, traditions, and routine or customary ways of responding to situations. Without such basic codes or conventions, effective work relations were not possible' (Roethlisberger and Dickson, 1939: 568). But it was Chicago, a 'melting pot' city of immigrants, with all the displacements that entailed for the lives of many of the employees in Western Electric. The sociologists of what became known as the Chicago school were already producing work on the slums and ghettoes of the city even before the researchers started at Hawthorne (e.g. Wirth, 1928, Zorbaugh, 1929). Zorbaugh, for example, writes of the bleakness of the slums, with its extreme poverty, high rates of infant mortality, with migrant workers and ramshackle buildings and rooming houses. It is interesting, therefore, that in his Preface to the study, Elton Mayo, generalises about the importance of these kinds of work-based systems of group collaboration between workers and managers, in the context of more general societal, even world considerations. He is writing on the eve of the Second World War:

The spectacle of Europe, erstwhile mother of cultures (sic), torn from end to end by strife that she can by no means resolve, should give pause to the 'practically-minded', should make such persons ask what type of research is likely to be most practically useful at the moment. The art of collaboration seems to have disappeared during two centuries of quite remarkable human progress. The various nations seem to have lost all capacity for international collaboration in the necessary tasks of civilisation. The internal conditions of each nation is not greatly better: it seems that only a threat from without, an unmistakeable emergency, can momentarily quieten the struggle of rival groups. In this general situation it would seem that inquiries such as those undertaken by the officers of the Western Electric Company have an urgent practical importance that is second to no other human undertaking. How can humanity's capacity for spontaneous cooperation be restored? . . . How to substitute human responsibility for futile strife and hatreds – this is one of the most important researches of our time. (Roethlisberger and Dickson, 1939: xiv)

This is an astonishing claim. But it is to the enterprise rather than the community that Mayo looks for the exemplary case of collaboration. At the same time we can see that the work does not address the realities of power relations between employer and employee and it was clear that as the Depression hit Western Electric, workers felt a sense of job insecurity, with good reason. This is an early example of treating the organisation as a culture and the work of Durkheim, Radcliffe-Brown and Malinowski is explicitly referred to in the text. The collaborative form of life that could emerge in the enterprise, with its codes and values was both a social order and a moral order. It could pride itself on not defining the worker solely in economic terms. This new human relations could, moreover, be seen as an alternative to Taylorism and scientific management, although we would have to add that wherever the rate fixer and the time and motion office existed the spirit of Taylor could not be far away. The manifold versions since then represent managerial-led definitions of culture. A good deal of managerial linguistic labour takes place, involving rhetoric and powers of persuasion, as (often with the aid of management consultants) new cultures are constructed. It is the manipulative culture of control. Upon such foundations do we see the managerial concerns with corporate cultures. So, for example, as Binns has argued, Total Quality Management (TQM) is inseparable from the concept of corporate culture. It is precisely upon the basis of this shared culture that the expectation is built in that employees will share the managerial strategy of TQM with its quality criteria and procedures (Binns, 1993). Corporate culture may even project a benevolent face that says, not that unions should be banned, but simply that they are not necessary. Yet the difficulty was, and always has been, how do you deliver the bad news. If you lose your job you are, after all, excluded from, say, the Quality Circle. Industrial sociologists in France, one observes, have long been preoccupied with a critique of Taylorism and Fordism. They find themselves challenged by developments that take enterprises beyond this to other forms of social organisation. The special issue of *Sociologie du Travail*, 'Retour sur l'entreprise' (XXVIII) reveals the liveliness of the debate (Borzeix, 1986).

If the impression is given that the enterprise culture can provide the meaning and security and stability that is lacking elsewhere for employees, then observation and research suggests that this is a fiction. Businesses themselves exist in uncertain environments and it is a matter of record that enterprise cultures based on the 'sweet stuff' of consultation, participation and the like can change their character and dispense the 'fear stuff' when senior management decide it is necessary to do so. The language of restructuring and 'downsizing', the re-writing of contracts, with longer hours, fewer benefits, lower wages and greater insecurity no doubt contribute to the low rating on what the politicians and pollsters are pleased to call the 'feel-good factor'. These kinds of things can occur in companies and sectors where a different culture once existed, as in the examples of banking, broadcasting and teaching. What was once known as casual labour, against which trade unions fought long and hard, and with success, has reappeared in the guise of 'flexibility'.

In the 1980s my colleagues and I worked on the topic of industrial democracy and participation in the Scottish-based private sector (Cressey, Eldridge and MacInnes, 1985). Overwhelmingly we found that management were the initiators of participation schemes. Consequently it was typical and not surprising that management defined the forum within which the theatre of participation was presented. It is sometimes suggested that in difficult economic times managers and workers will pull together to ensure survival. The evidence from our case studies did not support this view. In one case a company was keen to promote a system of joint consultation at plant level on a non-union basis. However, as the market situation became problematical, it was senior management from the multinational's headquarters in the USA who intervened directly to say that the workers must either take a pay cut of the order of 16 per cent or the factory would be closed. They were given 48 hours to decide and agreed through a hastily arranged ballot to accept the wage cut. But the system of consultation, which local management had carefully fostered, lost all credibility From the sweet stuff of consultation the company had moved overnight to the fear stuff of the ultimatum. And another of the company's plants in Holland did close as a result of this outcome. Delegated control was seized back by the corporate headquarters. Not only were the local UK management unaware of the package that had been prepared for restructuring but the manager of the Netherlands plant first read of the closure of his plant in *The Times*. In the Scottish plant, as the plans were implemented from above, the workforce and their delegates withdrew from the participation and consultation system. Agreements previously made were broken and local management, in receipt of directives from corporation headquarters, pushed them through without recourse to normal methods. Viewed from this perspective, when it comes to culture at work it is a matter of now you see it now you don't.

The quotation at the beginning of this essay was taken from Renalto Rosaldo's insightful book *Culture and Power* (1993). As he fairly points out, the idea of culture as an autonomous, coherent way of life is problematical and even more so now where cultures intermingle, overlap and clash with one another in terms of values and interests. All of us, he argues, 'inhabit a late-twentieth-century world marked by borrowing and lending across porous national and cultural boundaries that are saturated with inequality, power and domination' (*ibid.*: 217). This is not a settled world. It is disturbed and disturbing. It is a world of highly mobile finance and nomadic capitalism. Occupational communities of miners, shipyard workers, steel workers and the like rise and fall. Industrial deserts can be created in cities where work once flourished.

The reasons for, and significance of, this has been variously discussed. Galbraith's essay *The Culture of Contentment* (1992) seeks to explain why advanced industrial societies like the USA have been able to tolerate such manifest inequalities and can live with their consequences, and explicitly warns against capitalist triumphalism in a post-1989 world. In the UK context Will Hutton's *The State We're In* (1995) is a *tour de force*. At the outset he refers to the mounting and proper sense of crisis that is spreading across all classes about the character and availability of work and its implications for society at large. What is required he argues, 'is creative institution-building and a democratic opening – and confidence that men and women can shape their world' (Hutton, 1995: xiii). Against what he sees as ungoverned capitalism in the United Kingdom, and against its amorality, he advocates a new moral economy, with the rebuilding of institutions based upon a new conception of citizenship in its economic, social and political dimensions. Like Galbraith, he warns against capitalist triumphalism:

Unless Western capitalism in general and British capitalism in particular can accept that they have responsibilities to the social and political world in which they are embedded, they are headed for perdition. The demand for a moral economy is not simply the assertion of a different value system. It is a call to arms in a world which is running short of time. (*ibid.*: 26)

Such a state will not be achieved without a struggle, as Hutton surely knows. But to engage in such a struggle might enable us to witness and participate in (*pace* Thompson) a heroic culture at work.

CHAPTER 8

Industrial sociology and the labour process

THEO NICHOLS

Industrial sociology before the labour process debate

In 1966, in what must once have been one of the most widely read unpublished papers in modern sociology, Goldthorpe sketched the main theoretical approaches which had been followed up to that time by human and social scientists in their attempts to provide explanations for the attitudes and behaviour of industrial workers generally (Goldthorpe, 1966). He set forth a sequence of four movements – early scientific management, the human factor approach, the human relations approach, the technological implications approach – and then went on to advocate the so-called action approach, or as Goldthorpe then put it 'the action frame of reference which industrial sociology has for so long been lacking' (1966: 11).

It is perhaps worth noting here that scientific management was presented by Goldthorpe as one approach among others (a position which was to be anathema to Braverman), and also as an approach which, in one respect at least, was not without virtue (since the key explanatory variable was held by Goldthorpe to be the orientation of workers towards their work and conditions of employment).[1] Above all, though, it should be noted that with this paper and the subsequent Affluent Worker studies a large claim had been made for the part to be assigned to subjectivity in industrial sociology.[2] It is in fact against this backcloth of, in a particular sense, subjectivism, that the arrival of Braverman's work on these shores has to be understood, a further part of the context being the earlier up-skilling thesis of Blauner (1964) and his particular theory of alienation. In fact, given the coming to prominence of the orientation to work approach in the 1970s and the importance in British industrial sociology of Blauner's book prior to this, there is perhaps reason to conclude that British sociology was as ripe as any for the arrival of Braverman – and that whatever its virtue, the widespread criticism of his work for neglecting the subjectivity of workers was predictable (although hindsight is of course a wonderful thing).[3]

A piece published in 1975 by a British sociologist who was at the time 'completing research on the orientations and strategies of engineering workers' perhaps suffices to indicate how the action approach was sometimes interpreted as a break from both systems theory and from a managerial problematic (Elger, 1975: 91). The topics he chose to discuss from 'the array of discrete research which constitutes the bulk of the literature of industrial sociology' are no less interesting. Such topics included: managerialism (which relied quite heavily on my own work (Nichols, 1969), but also took in white-collar crime, Carson, 1970); administrative design and management career concerns, where reference was made *inter alia* to Burns and Stalker, 1961; Dalton, 1959; Flanders, 1964; Gouldner, 1954, 1955; Chandler, 1962; management–worker conflict and accommodation, which was split into two parts:

(a) conflict and accommodation on the shop-floor
(b) shop-floor administration and occupational bargaining strategies.

The discussion of (a) 'conflict and accommodation on the shop-floor', contained many references which were probably then more or less standard for industrial sociology courses (Gouldner, 1954; Roy, 1953; Carey, 1967; Lupton, 1963; Brown, 1962; Cunnison, 1966; Whyte, 1955; Woodward, 1970; Turner, 1962; Hobsbawm, 1964; Trist *et al.*, 1963; Trist and Bamforth, 1951; Walker and Guest, 1952; Chinoy, 1955; Scott *et al.*, 1956, 1963; Sayles, 1958; Silverman, 1970; Crozier, 1964; also Baldamus 1961, and the then more recent Beynon 1973).

The discussion on (b) 'shop-floor administration and occupational bargaining strategies' was less well supported by citations but included references on the theme of technology, technical change and automation (Brown, 1967a; Mann and Hoffman, 1960; Touraine *et al.*, 1965; as well as Goldthorpe *et al.*, 1968). Overall, the weight of empirically based publications, which Elger was able to survey in the mid-1970s, and which were par for industrial sociology courses in the United Kingdom (though far from all references were by British writers) is impressive. Yet, only shortly after, in 1980, Hyman was writing that 'the edifice of industrial sociology is fragmented, its practitioners demoralised' (Hyman, 1982).[4]

One answer to the question of how this demoralisation had come about would be that the 1974 Braverman-prompted development of a problematic of 'the labour process' had triumphed intellectually over that of (traditional) 'industrial sociology'. This answer is not convincing. Not least is this so because industrial sociology itself was always a movable feast and because those who invoked 'the labour process' often evidenced an eclecticism to rival that of industrial sociology. An important boost to interest in the labour process had come from the Conference of Socialist Economists and from the works published by Marglin, 1974; Gorz, 1976; Friedman, 1977 and Burawoy, 1979. But in so far as the institutionalisation of the study of the labour process is concerned, there are two things that are worth noting. The first is that the Nuffield 'de-skilling conference' (reported in Wood, ed., 1982) did not take place until the end of 1978, and was in any case far from a proselytising vehicle for Braverman's ideas. The second is that the first 'Labour Process Conference', which was run jointly (and perhaps significantly) out of the Management Departments of Aston and UMIST – and which is the institutional focus for most of my remarks about the labour process debate below[5] – did not take place until 1983.

After the Second World War the development of industrial sociology in the United Kingdom had taken several twists and turns, guided both by some underlying constraints and opportunities generated by the wider political economy, and perhaps also by some more immediate considerations. A periodicisation provided by Cox (1978) is of interest here, even though, derived as it is from certain supposed movements in sociology as a whole, it is necessarily somewhat rough and ready for our more particular purpose.

Cox distinguished three phases of development of industrial sociology in the United Kingdom up till *circa* 1978. The phases are:

1945 to the late 1950s;
the late 1950s to the late 1960s;
the late 1960s to the late 1970s.

In the first phase, 1945 to the late 1950s, which is part of post-war reconstruction, research grants were provided through Marshall Aid, and to some extent directly influenced by the human relations approach (Sear, 1962).[6] Thus the Committee of Industrial Productivity set up a Human Factors panel in 1947 which funded research into foremanship by the National Institute of Industrial Psychology, into joint consultation at Liverpool and into organisational change by Jaques (1951) at Glacier Metal.

Reconstruction-focused state funding was an important stimulus to the development of industrial sociology at Liverpool University, where the case study approach was practised and training was to be provided for a number of British sociologists – the Banks, Lupton, Halsey, Woodward – and later on, of course, another generation of Blackburn and Roberts and Beynon and Lane (Cox, 1978: 3; Brown, 1965).

A concern with problems of management and technology is clearly evident in the work of both Woodward (1958) and Burns and Stalker (1961). Jaques' work and that of the Tavistock Institute were more closely aligned with company managements through their combined research-consultancy approach (Brown, 1967b). But in addition to their socio-technical systems theory, for which today they are perhaps best known, it must be remarked that they provided, in the longer term, both Friedman (1977) with his concept of 'responsible autonomy' and an illustrative case for Marglin (1974) (Trist and Bamforth, 1951).[7]

One strand that does not readily fit this general picture is the work of Baldamus (1961). Cox comments fairly that this 'had an unwelcome message for management science and yet did not arouse the interest and enthusiasm of industrial sociologists at the time' in the way that Blauner's was to do (1978: 5). (Anyone thinking that the incompleteness of the labour contract was re-discovered by Braverman in 1974 would do well to read Baldamus.)

In the second phase of the development of industrial sociology, the late 1950s to the late 1960s, there is greater concern with academic and professional ambitions and a purer sociology begins to emerge, with less immediate ties to consultancy or policy. The works of Lupton (1963) and then Cunnison (1966) figure here. These predominantly ethnographic works from Manchester seem to have resulted from a social anthropological input by Gluckman, influenced directly by Homans and the Hawthorne studies but shorn of their major defects, though Lupton later travelled a more managerial route (Emmett and Morgan, 1982).

The existence of the BSA Teachers' Section, to which Goldthorpe read his 1966 'Orientations' paper is symptomatic of this emerging tendency – and Cox argues, rightly I think, that the agenda of industrial sociology later became above all set by the Affluent Worker studies, whatever else continued to be published at this time, and despite the fact that for the most part these studies had a much wider remit. Goldthorpe *et al.*, then, opened the door to a more professional approach and, not least, they provided an impetus for industrial sociologists to engage in theory.

From the late 1960s, amidst turbulent political events, a third phase was under way. It was fuelled, Cox argues, by the increased number of students and their teachers, who through the 1960s, as a consequence of the neo-Weberian critique of Parsons and functionalism, had come to think of sociology as a form of critique. About one quarter of sociology graduates in 1966 had gone into academic jobs (Banks and Webb, 1977: 30–1). The teachers needed something to teach. Especially outside the universities, they had little time to do anything else. According to Cox, one effect of this in sociology generally was a proliferation of secondary works and an emphasis on the critical discussion of theory (especially structural Marxism and phenomenology) rather than empirical work.

Another change, according to Cox, was the coming of a new 'freedom of presentation from formal academic norms' which derived from the liberation of sociological reporting 'from the demands of policy relevance and from tight collegiate control'. It is in this context that he focused his attention specifically upon *Living With Capitalism*, the publication of which (1977) had in fact been the cue for him to conduct an exploration of the continuities and discontinuities in industrial sociology over the past three decades. Two remarks he makes about that book are (1) that despite a difference in methodology 'the ChemCo researchers are drawn onto the same conceptual terrain and share similar empirical concerns' to the Cambridge school – that is, the book actually shares the Goldthorpe assumption about the importance of subjective meanings – and (2) that 'what is new for British industrial sociology, however, is the setting of discussion of conflict and workers' reaction in the context of an analysis of exploitation and capital accumulation as the driving forces of industrial life' (1978: 1, 15, 16). My own views on these comments are that the first must be largely true and that I would hope that the second was. But these comments raise an interesting, wider question of whether the linkage to capital accumulation has been more in evidence in industrial sociology in the years since Cox wrote than has a stress on the importance of subjective meanings. Given the coming of a 'Labour Process Debate', which was probably more prominent in British sociology than elsewhere, the answer might seem a foregone conclusion. It isn't.

Enter the labour process debate

A decade and a half has passed since Cox made his comments on the development of British industrial sociology. Labour has been weakened in relation to capital, the manufacturing base, so often the unproblematic site of the 'industry' studied by the 'industrial sociologist', has shrunk. Within sociology, there has been a cramping process which has entailed increased imagined or real demands for policy relevance for research grants; reductions in the number of central government financed re-search students; the tighter structuring of what sort of research is possible; more consultancy and tied research; and the rise of the teachers of methods rather than doers of research. There was also, especially in the 1980s, when sociology was under particular attack from Thatcherite elements, a shift of sociologists into business and management teaching and other related vocational and professional fields (perhaps again with hard-pressed lecturers looking for something to teach). Blend into all this increased pressure on publication deriving from tighter state control over 'performance' and it is proper to consider that the possible consequences are more conferences, more journal papers, more text-books. Enter, then, debate – secondary debate, tertiary debate, and more debate. I guess that none of this is very contentious. Like it or not, it is the way that things have become. But this is also part of the production, and reproduction, the wholesaling and retailing of the 'labour process debate', and with this, its institutional vehicle, the Labour Process Conference.

The Labour Process Conference provides a forum for a whole number of the issues that industrial sociology had embraced hitherto. So, in the 1980s and into the 90s, in addition to discussions about 'flexibility', themselves provoked by a state agenda, we find, once again, the examination of attitudes to technical change. Also to be found are discussions of human resource management, which do not, in many respects, pose issues all that different from the 'human relations' of old (though it must be said that nowadays the bite of writers like Baritz (1960) is often lacking). Even some of the issues raised by the talk of 'flexibility' and yet more so about the inevitability or not of 'deskilling', which concern the potential variability of the ways in which labour can be organised, are reminiscent of the discovery by an earlier generation that there is 'no one best way' (Woodward, 1958). We find also, and this is different, more discussion of gender and work, usually meaning discussion of women and work, other forms of work becoming increasingly recognised and wage labour itself becoming increasingly female. But what we also find is that, at least over the 1980s – aside from the quintessential paper 'The Labour Process, Gender and Chips' (which I feel should exist, but must admit can no more be found than the earlier title 'Orientation to Work of Giro Employees') – there has been much debate of a theoretical kind.

Three features that have been accorded particular prominence in Labour Conference theoretical output are particularly interesting:

1 the continued interest in subjectivity;
2 the relative neglect of capital accumulation;
3 related to the latter, the oddity whereby a managerial purpose is sometimes implicit or even explicit.

The 1990 volume of Labour Process Conference papers edited by Knights and Willmott, *Labour Process Theory*, is worth consulting here. The editors' view of how the book 'explores the theoretical foundations of labour process analysis and suggests new directions for its development', speaks eloquently to the first and second features. Consult the index and 'valorisation' rates only one single page reference. 'Profit' gets no entry at all. Nor does 'wages'. By contrast, 'subjectivity' rates 13 lines.[8]

Things have come to such a pass that Salaman, in finding the ambit of the labour process debate too cramped for his liking because of its concentration on work design and control strategy, should be led to plead: 'It is also interesting, for example, to ask: why are some business organisations much more efficient than others?' (1986: 26). Putting aside Salaman's reference to 'business organisations' (should the primary focus be on 'organisations'?), it really is extraordinary that those who apparently study the labour process from the standpoint of capitalist accumulation (and why use the term labour process if this is not the standpoint?) should pay little attention to accumulation itself. There still is a good case to be made for the view that what comes out of the labour process matters as well as what goes into it; as does the relation between the two (Nichols, 1986b: xv).

With respect to the third point, about a managerial slant, not only has the very first Labour Process Conference recently been described unblushingly as 'an academic forum for management and business researchers working with critical perspectives' (Jermier, 1991: 691), but only a year after it took place one of the organisers was calling for a move 'to advance or renovate bourgeois management theory' (Willmott,

1984: 364). Suffice to say that before the talk about 'the labour process' took hold, people who wanted to do that kind of thing went right ahead and did it. To entertain such a project whilst also issuing Marxist-sounding noises is, to say the least, odd.

In so far as 'the labour process' has been colonised from the shores of subjects like organisational behaviour and management studies it is not much of a puzzle that it should have been exploited (if I may) selectively. As is well known, colonialists often do develop peculiar views of the countries that they invade. A token of this is perhaps that references to 'the capitalist labour process' threaten to become nothing other than an intellectually pretentious way of saying 'work'. A lesson not to be forgotten, however, is that it is most certainly possible for industrial sociologists to survive and flourish by adapting fragments of Marxism, phenomenology, psychoanalysis or whatever. The prising out of 'the labour process' from the political economy of which it was a part may therefore be considered just one case in point. Certainly, this is something that would in no way surprise Richard Brown. As he has put it: 'No subject develops in a neat and entirely systematic way: among other things, personal interests (intellectual and material), external influences, and chance see to that' (Brown, 1992: 33).

To the middle ground

Compared to studies 'industrial', 'organisational' and 'managerial', it would seem reasonable to hold to the view that a labour process approach arises out of a 'primary concern with capital accumulation and class struggle' (Nichols, 1980: 17). This being so, and looking to the future, it would be a welcome step forward were it to be accepted that 'labour process' is not a sexy phrase for 'work organisation', and that the study of the labour process should be related to that of a valorisation process (or what we might simply term a surplus producing process).[9] Whatever specific terms are used, questions to be asked about the labour process concern *inter alia*: how, and under what conditions, surplus is produced out of labour-power and how labour-power is consumed by capital, and with what consequences for capital and for those who labour, not least their health and collective strength. On this view, in short, the study of the labour process should be broadly conceived. Included should be the conditions for the production of surplus out of labour power, theoretically, and also historically and in particular societies, these conditions including the organisation and the consciousness of the people who labour.

In the 1980s debates arose – for example, about skill, about whether managerial strategies exist – which became unduly narrow, not least as compared to the breadth, and historical perspective, of the early post-Braverman works in Britain (consider for example Friedman, 1977).

Indeed, to go back to 1961 is to find that even the early structural-functionalist conception of a sociology of industry extended further than the more or less standard industrial sociology in work to which, as judged by 'the labour process debate', the political economy of the labour process has been in danger of being reduced (Smith, 1961: 72; Hyman, 1982). As a consequence, there remains a region that has been largely neglected from the standpoint of a labour process approach. It has also been largely neglected from what might be loosely termed a 'work, employment and society approach' – this being another approach to have emerged since Goldthorpe's review back in the 1960s, which is more 'work' than 'labour' oriented (Nichols, 1992).

The neglected region occupies the middle ground between the high theory of political economy on the one side and a narrowly defined labour process on the other.[10] Such middle ground includes those conditions which pertain to the production of surplus and which affect the condition of labour but which are not necessarily located within enterprises. Indeed, there is much here to investigate which has major relevance to the lives of millions and millions of people and which does not need any justification whatsoever in terms of theories of the high ground, for example, of theorems about supposed tendencies of the rate of profit to fall (as opposed to variability in the rate of profit).

The gravedigger thesis once constituted a set of middle-range mechanisms supposedly predisposed to the emergence of a more homogenised, massified and objectively interdependent working class out of capitalist relations of production (Murray, 1985). The fact that these middle range sociological processes have not worked out in the manner anticipated well over a century ago has led some to speak of an 'impossible burden'. But this non-occurrence need not spell the dead weight of unwanted intellectual baggage. Rather it can be seen to invite the further exploration of a middle realm of analysis between high theory assumptions about accumulation, on the one hand, and what happens in the labour process, on the other. At the least we have here a series of relations and processes that should command attention in their own right and which should not be displaced by a narrow labour process focus.[11]

It is now commonplace to observe that those who work carry with them identities defined in terms of ethnicity, gender, nationality, etc. But such observations should not be allowed to substitute for the recognition also that those who sell their labour power do not do so free from the specific means of earning a livelihood available to them or free from the specific relation that they have to the state. An analysis of the labour process is far too restrictive if it fails to take into account these other mechanisms which impact (positively or negatively) on the condition of labour. The institutions built by labour outside the 'business organisation' provide highly particular examples of these (union hiring halls for example, but also other extensive infrastructures of diverse types) as do the institutions built by capital (blacklists in construction and NRB systems in off-shore oil for example).[12] But an analysis of the labour process is also too restrictive if, over and beyond such practices, it fails to take into account the enfranchisement of workers, their right to vote and hold office in union as well as other elections; then again the relative possibility of them entering into wage labour; their ability to subsist without entering into paid employment or training, the possibility of them avoiding wage labour entirely; also their right to protection against dismissal, and much else. Such constraints and opportunities as these matter both for the condition of those who labour and for the accumulation of capital. They can have significance also for the geographical location of labour processes and – a rarely investigated question – their longevity (but see Coombs, 1985).

The Labour Process Debate has been much concerned with control. A feature of many of the constraints and opportunities indicated above is, however, that their source often lies outwith the 'control' of the individual employer. It is because this is so that Littler sets down an important plank for the construction of further analysis when he states that 'the labour-market context, together with state regulation, helps to shape the control dynamic and to create, in Burawoy's terms, factory regimes' (1990: 68).

On the view taken here, there is a good case – whether armed with the theorems of high Marxist political economy or not – for viewing the labour process with a wide-angle lens. For, in the context of capital accumulation, the greater the stress on the two-handed nature of Littler's shaping process, the more it appeals – the labour-market context together with state regulation. In some respects Littler's approach directs attention to what would also come to light from an examination of the fine grain of what constitutes free wage labour or, alternatively, from an analysis of variations from a perfectly free wage labour form. Walder's 1986 account, from an essentially Weberian view, of social and economic dependence on Chinese enterprise is also an important source of encouragement to explore further just such issues.

In this context, it is to be regretted, and it is also interesting, that the study of the labour process has lacked stronger linkage with the new international division of labour studies, which do presently occupy some of the neglected middle ground (Cohen, 1987; Potts, 1990; Munck, 1988). It is also to be regretted that the exemplary approach to the labour process adopted by van Olsenen 1976 has been followed so little. That these studies, which do speak to the middle ground, are often located outside the advanced capitalist societies – or deal with linkages between other societies and advanced capitalist ones – makes them potentially more rewarding, not less. In view of the importance of what such studies can tell us about the conditions under which surplus is produced, and under which people labour, they most certainly merit inclusion in a wide angle 'labour process approach'. If such a broader approach be deemed to be more properly called a political economy or an economic sociology, or perhaps more accurately, a political economy of the labour process, then so be it. But bearing in mind the guiding assumption of Braverman's *Labor and Monopoly Capitalism*, to neglect such an approach on the grounds that there has to be a detailed (academic) division of labour would be ironic indeed. On reflection, however, the quite substantial absorption of 'the labour process' into the space previously occupied by British industrial sociology was not without irony either. To invoke Richard Brown again: among other things, personal interests (intellectual and material), external influences (including the political climate), and chance saw to that.

Notes

1 Goldthorpe's point about scientific management was a technical one which bore on its form of explanation. Others had previously written in a less guarded or critical manner. Thus Pugh *et al.* (1964: 46): 'In fairness to Taylor, it must be said that his principles were often inadequately understood. For example, few managements have been willing to put into practice one of his basic tenets – that there should be no limit to the earnings of a high-producing worker. . . . This may inhibit the "mental revolution" Taylor sought, which requires that "both sides take their eyes off the division of the surplus as the all important matter and together turn their attention towards increasing the size of the surplus".' A very similar point was made about the same time by Lupton (1966: 25).

2 Further prompting in the same direction came from Silverman 1970 and Turner 1971.

3 In surveying industrial studies in the United Kingdom after the Second World War and up till the mid-1970s, for reasons of space it is industrial sociology that is predominantly considered here. This means not only that a certain amount of not very inspiring industrial relations material is excluded but also writings such as Turner 1962 and, more off the beaten track, Melman 1956, 1958 and Goodrich 1920.

4 My reference is to a draft paper later published in 1982.

5 A more wide-ranging version of this paper was in fact presented to the 10th Labour Process Conference at Aston in April 1992.

6 The contribution of Marshall Aid to the diagnosis of the presumed British worker problem is noted in Nichols (1986b); its relation to the development of management thought is dealt with by Carew (1987) and taken up by Binns (1991).

7 I look forward with some interest to the day when those contemporary writers who are so much beset with subjective insecurity take up another aspect of the Tavistock work, which invokes the psychoanalysis of Melanie Klein. But it is to be doubted if even they could out-rival Hill and Trist's accounts of industrial accidents (Hill and Trist, 1953 and especially 1955; Nichols, 1994 and Nichols, 1997, Chapter 2).

8 This is a bit misleading. There are after all two lines for 'exploitation'. True to form however, the second is a sub-head for, again, 'subjectivity'.

9 Unproductive labour does not pose insuperable difficulties for such a formulation, as other writers would appear to accept: for example, Brown, 1992: 189; Scase, 1992: 21–23.

10 This view is not the product of some recent conversion on my part. Some of the ground to be covered can be seen from the range of readings in Nichols (1980).

11 They have of course recently received attention – albeit in an often unrecognised Marx-stood-on-his-head formulation – as an often unrecognised ingredient in Piore and Sabel's model of 'flexible specialisation' (Piore and Sabel, 1984).

12 On the former see Austrin 1978; on the presence of the latter in the North Sea see Lavalette 1991.

CHAPTER 9

Manufacturing myths and miracles: work reorganisation in British manufacturing since 1979

TONY ELGER

Introduction

British industrial sociology and industrial relations outgrew their somewhat narrow preoccupation with manufacturing employment comparatively recently, as researchers responded to the sharp decline in manufacturing, the growth then restructuring of public and private service work and the persistence of mass unemployment. Alongside this widening research agenda, the changing character of manufacturing employment has, nevertheless, remained an appropriate topic of vigorous debate. One reason is that work and employment relations within manufacturing have themselves been undergoing significant changes. The growing application of micro-electronics has been paralleled by a whole portfolio of organisational innovations, ranging from briefing groups, through teamworking and 'just-in-time' scheduling to 'continuous improvement'. Furthermore, some commentators have linked the *quantitative* decline in manufacturing employment with a 'productivity miracle' based upon the *qualitative* recasting of the labour process and industrial relations. Finally developments within manufacturing continue to be treated as symptomatic of much wider transformations in the character of work. Thus they are seen, in one particularly influential terminology, to mark a watershed between Fordist and post-Fordist eras. The objective of this chapter is to review aspects of this continuing debate about the changing character of work in British manufacturing, and particularly to assess claims about a transition from Fordism to post-Fordism (as discussed in Brown, 1995).

The changing experience of work in manufacturing over the last 20 years must be seen in the context of the United Kingdom's wider political economy. In this regard the 1979 Thatcher administration marked a major shift in state policies, both towards manufacturing and towards trades unionism. In the early 1980s the pursuit of monetarist policies gave a savage twist to the decline in manufacturing investment and employment, whilst legislative reforms and political exhortation promoted an offensive against organised labour. The significance of 1979 should nevertheless be treated with some caution. Firstly, important aspects of a monetarist regime were already in place before the Conservatives gained power, whilst there were major shifts in policy – involving the dilution of monetarism, growing emphasis on 'supply-side reforms' and the engineering of electoral booms – through the following years. Secondly, such corporate policies as the decentralisation of bargaining and the pursuit of employee 'flexibility', though central in the 1980s and 1990s, were already being pursued by key employers before 1979. Furthermore, the effects of mass unemployment and legislative reforms on industrial relations were less direct and immediate than had been anticipated, resulting in a substantial but incremental and uneven weakening of workplace trade unionism by the mid-1990s (Edwards *et al.*, 1992; Smith and Morton, 1993). Thus our assessment of developments within the manufacturing workplace must bear in mind not only the Thatcherite pursuit of a neo-liberal project, but also evolving and cyclical features of the British political economy over this period.

Models of transformation

A series of overlapping interpretations of changes in manufacturing work and employment have been developed in recent years, identifying the emergence of flexible specialisation, lean production, Japanisation or 'new production concepts' (Wood, 1989; Hyman, 1991; Tomaney, 1994; Elger and Smith, 1994; Brown, 1995). Despite real differences, they all draw a sharp contrast between the currently emerging manufacturing paradigm and a past characterised by the predominance of Fordist mass production. In this sense it is appropriate to group them together as accounts of a transition from Fordism to post-Fordism. From this vantage point they share two key features. The first is a vision of the decline of thoroughly fragmented and tightly paced manual labour with a shift towards more skilled, collaborative and responsible forms of work. The second is the expectation that this will underpin more co-operative and less combative forms of industrial relations. I shall focus on two of these interpretations, namely flexible specialisation and lean production, because they are particularly influential and embody contrasting political projects.

The flexible specialisation analysis was developed in the early 1980s by Piore, Sabel and their collaborators (Piore and Sabel, 1984; Hirst and Zeitlin, 1989b). They argued that a combination of technical innovations (such as CNC machine tools) and the fragmentation of markets during the 1970s reopened the viability of extensive craft-based manufacturing. Initially they emphasised the emergence of mutually supportive clusters of small producers, whose skilled and flexible workers could competitively deliver customised products, though later they suggested that large firms which decentralised, delayered and networked revealed similar capabilities. This perspective promoted a politics of regional industrial regeneration, gave a pivotal role to political and administrative supports in sustaining constructive competition among networks of producers, and envisaged that local political alliances – between manufacturers and municipalities, across different sectors and enterprises and among owners and employees – could thereby be reinforced. As such it offered a focus for a non-statist reformist politics, to nurture the shared interests of communities of producers in revitalised industrial districts.

Critics of the flexible specialisation diagnosis (Williams *et al.*, 1987; Hyman, 1988; Nolan and O'Donnell, 1991; Smith, 1991) have in turn contested their key claims about the break-up of mass markets, the general obsolescence of mass production, and the supposed harmoniousness of the employment relations of small-scale flexible teamworking. They also suggest that both the initial emphasis on agglomerations of small-scale enterprises and the later discussion of decentralised corporations, gloss over the continuing importance of central financial controls in big firms and the extent of small-firm subordination within the supplier networks of such firms.

The notion of lean production was developed in the USA almost ten years later by Womack *et al.* (1990), in a highly influential study of the motor industry which offered an organisational and political agenda with more appeal to corporate managers and neo-liberal politicians. They argued that Japanese corporations, at home and abroad, had pioneered new forms of work organisation which allowed the production of cheaper, more diverse, quality consumer goods. This has been achieved through minimising the amounts of time, labour and materials required in the production process, and enhancing its flexibility, by placing a greater emphasis on the expertise and co-operation of employees. For shop-floor workers lean work organisation has meant team-working (to maximise the utilisation of labour), minimised stocks (to cut costs and increase flexibility), and the responsibility of direct workers for both quality and 'continuous improvement'. The alleged superiority of this approach is such that lean production becomes essential for corporate survival, not only in motors but in other sectors too. Furthermore, proponents of lean production argue that workers will find increased meaning and purpose as they co-operate in meeting the pressures and challenges of the new regime. In this sense the analysis legitimates radical restructuring by senior management, and appeals to those politicians who portray global competition as a relentless engine of progress.

Critics of this approach (Berggren, 1993; Williams *et al.*, 1992, 1994; Lyddon, 1996) have argued that the contrast between mass and lean production does violence to a more complex spectrum of production operations among the motor companies, glosses over the central importance of product and labour market conditions as influences on productivity and profitability, and provides an idealised account of the bases of employee commitment in such workplaces. In analysing the performance of the Japanese motor companies, such critics have insisted on the importance of tightly defined work routines, long working hours and intense work rates in the final assembly factories, and harsh conditions and low wages in the small firms down their components supply chains. They also underline the dilemmas and constraints which now beset such organisational innovations – even Toyota, with its exceptional domination of a local labour market, supplier hinterland and domestic product market (Williams *et al.*, 1994), faces cross-pressures and limitations arising especially from problems of labour recruitment and urban congestion (Nomura, 1993; Berggren, 1995).

Despite their obvious differences, both flexible specialisation and lean production approaches gain much of their appeal from sharp contrasts between an old and outdated Fordist or Taylorist paradigm of mass production and a new and progressive paradigm. Yet the ideal-type constructs of Fordism or Taylorism which underpin such contrasts represent highly problematical templates for interpreting contemporary change, for they provide static and over-coherent characterisations of the relations between such features as standardised production, fragmented tasks, assembly-line processes, unskilled labour and high wages. In practice each of these approaches represented an historically evolving but problematical portfolio of management practices. Taylor, operating as both innovator and publicist within a wider milieu of management experimentation, advanced an evolving battery of techniques for the tighter regulation and control of labour, and his followers added further variants and refinements (Kelly, 1982: 3–29; Whitston, 1996). Meanwhile Ford and his managers developed and pursued mechanised pacing, refined standardisation, harsh supervision and high wages in an uneven and shifting fashion even within the Ford plants (Williams *et al.*, 1993), while his US and European competitors, operating in different product market, employment and political conditions, developed their own modifications (Tolliday and Zeitlin, 1986; Lyddon, 1996).

Such features suggest that management techniques and initiatives are wrestling with a refractory and contradictory set of social relations, and will thus generally be partial in their objectives, contradictory in their effects and incomplete in their achievements. This theme is nicely summarised in Hyman's (1987: 30) aphorism that management strategies inevitably represent varied routes to partial failure. It follows that strands of management doctrine and policy will represent evolving and incomplete portfolios of principles and practices. Thus Wood (1993) emphasises that both Taylorist forms of work measurement and work fragmentation and Fordist forms of standardised and machine-paced assembly were always beset by 'nagging and recurring problems' indicative of limitations, dilemmas and (often low-key) contestation. This implies that our conceptualisation of such management approaches should explicitly address internal tensions (say between work reorganisation and effort intensification, or incremental systematisation and achieving a 'mental revolution') and shifts of emphasis in changing circumstances, rather than seek to define clear boundaries around more or less narrowly defined ideal-types of Taylorism, Fordism or whatever.

This has three critical implications for our understanding of contemporary developments. The first is that sharply drawn contrasts between ideal types of work organisation and employment relations will conceal more than they reveal, so a better starting-point is attention to the evolving mix of continuities and innovations characteristic of management theory and practice. The second is that tensions, variants, shifts and contestation should be at the centre of our attention, for these features are rooted in the contradictory and class character of employment relations. Finally, we need to locate our understanding of the recasting of work and employment relations in the context of the wider political economy, but without reading one directly into the other as a tightly configured functional totality.

Work reorganisation in British manufacturing

With these arguments in mind we must now consider the pattern of work reorganisation in British manufacturing over the last 20 years, starting with a brief commentary on general trends before considering developments in some key sectors. A review of evidence and debate at the end of the 1980s (Elger, 1990, 1991) concluded that workplace restructuring in British manufacturing had primarily involved management efforts to boost worker productivity through the reduction of manning levels and increases in the flexibility of task allocation, though such changes were often incremental and had varied implications for different occupations. This had often meant a significant shift towards the widening and overlapping of job descriptions and activities, but upskilling and upgrading was generally modest and was rarely accompanied by extensive training, so that the resulting job enlargement was primarily oriented towards more continuous and intense work rather than to multi-skilling. These developments were generally driven by increased competitive pressures on firms and workforces, often underlined by an extended internationalisation of production and sometimes coupled with sharpened rivalry with greenfield sites, and they were also facilitated by the debilitating impact of mass unemployment, factory closures, and anti-union legislation. This did not preclude the survival of workplace trade unionism – most changes were negotiated while many involved wage gains for those still employed – but it often involved a process of union and worker concession-making under pressure over issues of work allocation and work effort.

In many respects Geary's (1995) more recent overview of patterns of work reorganisation and shop-floor administration reports similar findings. He emphasises that increased competitive pressures, coupled with labour market conditions and state policies which augmented management power, have stimulated change at the workplace. However, while British managements have debated and experimented with a wide range of changes, most work reorganisation in manufacturing has remained limited in scope, and reduction of staffing levels remains a management priority, rather than more radical experiments of the sort which ostensibly empower workers. Overall, managements have been more concerned with 'the removal of traditional skill boundaries than with making an investment in new skill structures', while the pursuit of employee involvement and flexibility has largely been 'confined to the margins of existing work practices', though more radical innovations have occurred at a few greenfield sites (Geary, 1995: 374).

In this context unions face major problems, but collective bargaining has not been superseded and worker commitment to their employers remains equivocal. Managements have narrowed bargaining agendas while union reps have been forced to accommodate to a management rhetoric of plant survival. However, managers continue to be drawn into formal and informal bargaining as they seek to juggle an advantageous mix of specified work routines and worker initiative, while most workers retain an 'instrumental' rather than a 'committed' orientation to work.

In addition Geary notes that, rather than marking a clear move from a workforce concentrated around semi-skilled tasks to one concentrated around skilled labour, work reorganisation recasts horizontal divisions and vertical hierarchies among manual workers and occupations. He nevertheless emphasises that skilled workers have most often gained skills and responsibilities (though at the expense of tighter discipline), whilst semi-skilled workers have more often faced intensified supervision or new forms of monitoring. In reflecting on the consequences of these developments, he also suggests that changes in stress and work effort should not simply be equated with generalised work intensification. Not only are increased workloads more often a side-effect than the central concern of management policies, but more importantly they can be experienced in a variety of ways. Some workers may view a sustained work pace as less irksome than unpredictable or disorganised work patterns, while others may perceive more intense working as a necessary or a legitimate quid pro quo for improved working conditions or job security. This is a valuable qualification to any account of uniform work intensification, but should not be pushed too far in the light of considerable evidence of increased work pressures and tightened manning levels.

Such general assessments of patterns of change in British manufacturing give little support to the idea that work organisation has been transformed, either in the direction of flexible specialisation or to approximate lean production. The analysts of flexible specialisation appear to accept this but regard it as evidence of a peculiarly British backwardness, especially in the restructuring of sectors traditionally dominated by mass production methods. The protagonists of lean production, however, emphasise that a minority of firms in such sectors have adopted lean methods, though the overall pattern of restructuring remains very uneven (Hanson *et al.*, 1995). In particular, they highlight the apparently innovative role of Japanese firms in the motor and consumer electronics industries, and the dissemination of lean production methods within these sectors.

This suggests that claims that British manufacturing is being transformed from Fordist to post-Fordist forms of work organisation are best assessed through more specific discussion of developments in key sectors of mass production. The remainder of this chapter therefore focuses on three specific sectors which share a history of labour-intensive assembly-line production and a recent record of substantial work reorganisation, namely vehicles, electrical engineering and food and drink. Of course, the car industry has, from its beginnings, been a major arena of innovations in work reorganisation and has provided the type-cases for both Fordism and lean production. Furthermore, research on the motor industry has gained centrality because of the importance of the automobile as an internationally traded commodity and because of its history of union organisation and worker militancy. At the same time the motor industry possesses distinctive features which mean that it cannot simply stand as *the* exemplar of mass production. For example, it is a particularly bulky and complex product among mass consumption goods, and this gives the car production process a distinctive character (Williams *et al.*, 1994).

While the lean production analysis was first developed in relation to motors, it has been advocated as broadly applicable across manufacturing. It is therefore important to consider some other leading sectors alongside motors. In this context there are three reasons for choosing the electricals sector. Firstly, putting aside the specialist suppliers of advanced military electronics, it has an established tradition of assembly line mass production of both consumer goods and manufacturing components. Secondly its labour force is significantly different from that of motors, especially in relation to the substantial employment of women workers – and in this respect it is the motor industry rather than electricals which is atypical of the pattern of employment in assembly-line manufacturing (Glucksmann, 1990; Lewchuk, 1996). Finally Japanese companies made earlier incursions into the UK in this sector and thus have longer established factories capable of pioneering distinctive forms of work organisation and employment relations.

Compared with motors or engineering, the food and drink sector has been comparatively neglected by social researchers, perhaps because of the importance of female employment in the industry and the relative quiescence of its industrial relations. Yet it is a sector where routine assembly work became entrenched at least by the early decades of the twentieth century, as companies moved increasingly into mass production for a mass consumer market. Furthermore, it is a highly concentrated and increasingly internationalised sector, though not one in which Japanese companies have been prominent. Thus it provides a distinctive context for innovations in work organisation and employment relations, which can fruitfully be compared with developments in motors and electricals. I will now consider each of these sectors in turn.

'Lean production' in motors?

The motor industry was built around tightly regulated assembly-line routines and, though car factories have always included non-line work processes, the line has come to epitomise semi-skilled mass production. Nevertheless, the industry has always been characterised by varied and evolving patterns of work and employment relations. Even as the industry became dominated by big firms, such features as payment systems, the extent of vertical integration and model mixes remained quite varied, while the competitive positions of contemporary firms and plants reflect differences in working hours, wage levels, product design and capacity utilisation as well as variations in the technical co-ordination and social control of the labour process (Tolliday and Zeitlin, 1986; Williams *et al.*, 1994; Shioma and Wada, 1995).

Between the wars British car firms developed semi-rationalised but labour-intensive flow-line operations to serve a middle-class market during a prolonged period of union marginalisation (Lyddon, 1996). Post-war they sought to adapt American production techniques to smaller volumes while retaining the advantages of devolved piece-rate based work organisation (Williams *et al.*, 1994), while car workers gradually built effective union organisation around the job-control issues generated by incremental work reorganisation and the cyclical insecurity of. the industry (Turner *et al.*, 1967). From the late 1960s corporate mergers and state intervention laid the basis for a crisis-ridden and contested process of sectoral restructuring which involved model rationalisation and plant closures but was primarily and one-sidedly preoccupied with the repudiation of piecework mutualities and tighter management control in the production process (Hyman and Elger, 1981). In the early 1980s this management offensive was reinforced, especially at state-owned BL, by Thatcherite state policies, while world overcapacity and the increasing competitive pressure of the Japanese producers were driving innovation and restructuring across the global operations of all the big firms.

In the early 1980s, with massive job losses and plant closures, managers in the British car plants gained increased management control over the allocation of labour, increased task flexibility and often increased effort (Beynon, 1984; Marsden *et al.*, 1985: 105–6; Grunberg, 1986). These changes involved de-manning and the extension of routine maintenance tasks among production workers, and pressures towards craft overlap for maintenance workers, but little sign of new forms of co-operative teamworking (Marsden *et al.*, 1985; Jurgens *et al.*, 1994). Despite overtones of 'macho-management', this involved tougher negotiations and more constraints on steward activity, rather than the dismantling of workplace trade unionism. At BL the toughness had clear political resonances, and the imposition of new working practices involved a high-profile management offensive: but the pace of change varied between factories and occupations, there were sporadic protests, and workplace unionism remained intact (Willman and Winch, 1985; Marsden *et al.*, 1985). In other motor firms a 'firmer implementation' of existing deals was the norm, though disputes resulted in all the large firms (Marsden *et al.*, 1985: 10).

Jurgens *et al.* (1994) place such findings in a wider European and American context. Unlike Womack *et al.* (1990) who, from their benchmark of lean production see the European industry as stagnating in classic Fordist mass production, they emphasise the extent of experimentation and uncertainty which characterised this period. Thus they chart a broad growth of emphasis on work reorganisation (especially teamworking) rather than automation, but also register the varied forms this took in different companies and national settings. Common denominators were efforts to integrate erstwhile indirect functions into the role of direct producers; reductions in supervisory levels with delegation of some responsibility to operators; and pursuit of team-based involvement strategies. Such changes were typically quite modest, primarily involving the horizontal integration of tasks but 'only timid and mostly symbolic' delegation of planning or control activities. Furthermore, this was accompanied by a tightening of corporate controls in the form of planned production parameters overlain by increasing use of benchmarking exercises to gear up productivity.

There was not, however, a uniform trajectory of change. While some companies, such as Ford, pursued a relatively uniform policy across their plants, other companies engaged in more varied and piecemeal experimentation. Furthermore, even Ford's operations were given distinctive inflections in different societies. The dominant bias of work reorganisation in German motor plants – influenced by an extensive craft-based vocational training system, an abundance of skilled workers, substantial high-value car production and union policies oriented towards work humanisation – was towards extensive deployment of skilled workers as line experts, pushing less skilled workers into subordinate roles. A different constellation of circumstances in the United Kingdom imparted a more traditional bias to work reorganisation, as the long-standing decentralisation of unions, coupled with their more recent weakening, left them capable of contesting participation initiatives which encroached on union representation, but unable to restrain management's pursuit of 'traditional strategies for rationalisation through industrial engineering and mechanisation' (Jurgens *et al.*, 1994: 116).

In the United Kingdom through much of the 1980s, this resulted in a modest and incremental implementation of features such as task-integration and self-inspection, sometimes facilitated by bargained compensation in terms of pay and grading but also punctuated by disputes, especially when management moved unilaterally to exploit their increased leverage and hence reinforced rank and file suspicions. Similar pressures for increased effort and interchangeability of labour continued through the decade, though the vigorous assertion of management power was increasingly interwoven with more explicit, if often superficial, efforts to mobilise worker commitment. For example, Ford pushed towards an omnibus operator grade, enlarged operator responsibilities for routine maintenance and quality assurance and increased mobility of labour. These moves, designed to generate continuous intensive working, were implemented within a tight system of financial control, work measurement and labour discipline (Starkey and McKinley, 1989: 97), resulting in disputes over disciplinary and regrading procedures, the determination of work rates and the reallocation of maintenance responsibilities. Ford managers sought to overcome the suspicions and opposition articulated by shop-floor unions through a long-term incrementalist strategy for building flexibility and commitment within the framework of management hegemony (Starkey and McKinley, 1989), but the real trajectory of change again involved the uneven and contested reworking of management control over the process of collective labour within mass production work (Darlington, 1994).

It is noteworthy that Jurgens *et al.* (1994: 181, 198, 251) found a long-standing pattern of informal flexibility about work pace and manning levels in the British factories, which outstripped that in most American plants but remained regulated by custom and practice. However, the way these issues became linked very directly to fears of job losses fed worker and union suspicions, and fuelled resistance to more formalised flexibility. In general job losses among skilled workers were relatively modest. Although management sought to exploit divisions between different trades they generally pursued a limited widening of responsibilities. It was not in their interests to sponsor the emergence of an electronics-based super-craftsman but rather to deploy training and skills parsimoniously. For production workers the pressures were greater as, against a background of continuing job losses, managers sought more flexibility in coping with fluctuating capacity utilisation and more complicated product mixes. Furthermore, managements increasingly deployed 'malicious productivity comparisons' (Jurgens *et al.*, 1994: 261, quoting a union official), sometimes linked to prospective investment decisions, to soften resistance and push through changes, though in reality lower labour costs in British plants remained a crucial part of the financial equation.

In these circumstances workplace unions moved away from a general hostility to participation and involvement schemes and rather sought to control them by exploring collectively co-ordinated forms of involve-ment. In part this reflected union recognition that a policy of boycotts was unsustainable, but it also reflected increased confidence that there was scope for collective grievances to be addressed in such settings. This mirrored management's realisation that involvement could not be imposed (Jurgens *et al.*, 1994). Thus a wary and ambivalent imple-mentation of involvement and team-working initiatives set the scene for developments during the 1990s. From this vantage point the lean pro-duction model could be seen as a chimera. Indeed, for all their emphasis upon the transferability of an organisational technology, even its propon-ents recognise that social integration into lean production is dependent upon a level of job security which seems incompatible with the cyclical character of Western economic development and which Japanese car producers are themselves finding difficult to sustain. Thus an emphasis on crisis-ridden experimentation, the persistent reproduction of variants which hardly amount to a 'break from Taylorism', and continuing forms of contestation (Jurgens *et al.*, 1994: 17) is likely to prove a better guide to the future than any expectation that these features are resolving into a fresh production paradigm.

Nevertheless Jurgens *et al.* recognise the increasing influence of the lean production model among European managers. On one hand the luxury car niche which helped sustain German and Swedish variants of work reorganisation is increasingly under pressure, while on the other the Japanese transplants into the UK, with their emphasis on 'on-the-job training', promise to emancipate corporate management from the limitations of national training systems (Mueller, 1992). Indeed, an in-creasingly popular interpretation of the partial recovery of the British motor industry relates it to the 'lean' operations of the major Japanese inward investors who arrived from the mid 1980s, and the influence of similar methods in the non-Japanese firms during the 1990s (Mueller, 1992; Wickens, 1993; Rhys, 1995). We have yet to establish a full account of the operations of the Japanese greenfield operations (Nissan in Sunderland, 1986; Honda in Swindon, 1989 and Toyota at Burnaston and Shotton, 1992) and might also expect to find important differences between them, as they operate in distinctive locations (contrast Swindon and Sunderland) with different corporate policies (such as Honda's dis-tinctive arrival via a joint venture with Rover and establishment of an engine plant, but also its repudiation of union recognition at Swindon). Nevertheless several important themes have already been identified, primarily from research on Nissan.

Firstly these firms *have* been able to construct patterns of flexible team-working and worker involvement which go beyond those of the established British motor plants. They have established tight work sched-ules with minimal buffer stocks, common grades for manufacturing employees, flexibility based on 'on the job' training, employee monitor-ing of defects and involvement in problem-solving activities. Secondly, however, these assembly plants continue to be built around modern, tightly paced assembly-lines, and such firms as Nissan themselves emphasise the rigours of track work and factory discipline (Wickens, 1987: 176). Furthermore, common grading and team-working involve only limited flexibility, primarily among a small cluster of standard tasks (Garrahan and Stewart, 1992), while worker innovation operates in the margins of 'a very strictly controlled production process' (Mair, 1994: 259). As Garrahan and Stewart (1992: 88–91) emphasise, the main innovative features of Nissan's work organisation – low buffer stocks, on-line inspection and rectification, maximisation of line speeds coupled with devices to signal 'help' – all contribute to the mobilisation of worker productivity through work pressure. In this sense it is quite misleading to counterpose lean and mass production, and it is perhaps not surprising that Nissan's personnel director talks instead of 'lean mass production' (Wickens, 1993). A crucial issue then becomes the basis and character of workers' commitment to this form of intensive and attentive mass production.

Nissan was clearly able to capitalise upon the experience of regional economic decline to mobilise powerful financial and political support for their operations, to present themselves as a break with the industrial past, and to operate a stringent selection procedure through which they recruited a young, 'green' workforce with limited industrial experience, all features conducive to workforce consent (Garrahan and Stewart, 1992; Stephenson, 1996). However, Garrahan and Stewart also emphasise that the very process of day-to-day operations is pivotal to the mobilisation of worker commitment (a theme also registered by Mair, 1994: 257–8). The ideological framing and practical structuring of work obligations and worker involvement by management, through processes like competition between teams and supervisory appraisals of individual performance, serve to monitor and reinforce conformity to management expectations. Furthermore, the form taken by the 'single union deal' with the AEU (now AEEU) in Sunderland has effectively excluded the union from day-to-day representational activity, so that 'problems' are addressed almost exclusively within a managerial framework.

In this context workers' responses to the costs and advantages of work at Nissan appear to range from the active enthusiasm of a minority, through widespread instrumental conformity, to resentful compliance or quitting by the most critical workers. This suggests that there will be limits to the successful mobilisation of mutual surveillance and inter-group competition, but these limits will be conditioned both by the evolving experience of the workforce (expansion increases job security and training or promotion prospects, though in 1993 Nissan cut hours and shed 400 jobs through voluntary redundancy) and the extent to which grievances become collectively articulated. These points are emphasised by Stephenson's (1996) comparative study of experience at Nissan and Ikeda-Hoover, a major components-supplier sited adjacent to Nissan. This contrasts the Nissan experience with the growth of active trade unionism at Ikeda, built around campaigns on issues such as health and safety and arbitrary supervision. Stephenson suggests that collective organisation developed at Ikeda both because a cluster of older female sewing-machinists brought earlier work and union experience to the new plant, and because the jobs at this sub-contractor involved both heavy work pressure and authoritarian management.

Thus the Japanese 'transplants' in the United Kingdom, building on their (varied) corporate histories of work reorganisation in Japan and the scope afforded by greenfield sites, have introduced production operations and employment relations which involve both tighter production schedules and the more active involvement of workers in monitoring production and modifying work routines. While this is best understood as a significant recasting of working practices around assembly-line mass production rather than as a paradigm-shift into post-Fordism (Wood, 1993; Williams *et al.*, 1994), the managements of other British car plants soon turned to the language of 'lean production' to reinforce and redirect their pursuit of change in the workplace. In particular they developed team-working and total quality programmes under this banner, though they were formulated, negotiated and implemented somewhat differently at different sites and companies.

At Rover such changes culminated in 1992 in the company-wide agreement of a 'New Deal' which committed workers to 'total flexibility and continuous improvement' in return for enhanced job security (IRS, 1992, 1993). While the company had engaged in rather limited and short-lived experiments in briefings and quality circles in the late 1980s (Smith, 1988), this involved more systematic team-working and quality initiatives. A distinctive feature was the election of team-leaders, which raised questions about union channels of representation, though in practice the managerial remit of such team-leaders was underlined both by a continuity of personnel and by the limits placed upon employee involvement. In this context stewards retained some leverage over manning levels, though management achieved significant reductions of inventories and (mainly indirect) workers while stewards found it increasingly difficult to monitor line speeds and quality group proposals.

Research at the Cowley plant in the mid-1990s documents major productivity gains following the 1992 agreement, but also shows that work reorganisation had remained uneven and relatively modest, with patchy job-rotation, a 'relatively constrained form of team working', 'a limited role for team leaders', and minimal operator involvement in continuous improvement (Scarborough and Terry, 1996: 30; see also Hayler and Harvey, 1993). While management interpret this as evidence that they have moved beyond the 'fear factor' to mobilise workers' skills and commitment, and stewards emphasise the sheer intensification of labour, Scarborough and Terry qualify both of these assessments. They suggest, firstly, that such features as improved logistics, increased capacity utilisation and better design for manufacturability also enhanced productivity. Secondly, change has been negotiated against the background of the drastic shrinkage and reorganisation of Cowley production, which has persistently underlined the precariousness of plant survival. Finally, management have not actually pursued a project of lean production dependent upon generalised worker expertise and commitment. Rather, they have pursued a process of de-bureaucratisation which has enhanced line-management discretion in interpreting market demands and defining production priorities, resulting in a markedly uneven and somewhat limited pattern of work reorganisation while eroding traditional levers of union influence.

At Vauxhall there was a particularly decentralised process of plant-by-plant negotiations which resulted in a series of factory agreements, which accepted team-working on the basis of appointed rather than elected team-leaders, but afforded stewards a more explicit role in their implementation (OMIRP, 1993; Carr, 1994; Murukami, 1995). This reflected both a more plant-focused and critical union approach and difficulties which management had experienced at one plant, when their pursuit of productivity gains by 'galloping the line' precipitated both uncontrolled labour turnover and organised opposition (OMIRP, 1993). Under these agreements changes in working patterns have generally remained more modest and unions have retained more influence over the critical issue of work pace, though this has not precluded areas of experimental innovation.

The implications of these changes for working practices and worker experience remain contested and uncertain. However, one valuable benchmark is provided by Garrahan and Stewart's (1995) research on workers' own assessments of developments at two major companies during 1992 and 1993. A clear majority of their informants reported significant changes in their experience of work, most often identified as involving team-working. For about a quarter of these workers (more often in automated areas than assembly) it meant an increase in skills, but for the rest it meant no change or even reduced skills. Meanwhile there was only a marginal increase in the range of tasks performed, but large majorities across all the factories found the work more tiring, both mentally and, even more so, physically. This suggests that the 'lean production' rhetoric, in which assembly work now relies upon creativity and problem-solving expertise and work becomes 'smarter not harder', finds little echo in the experience of these workers.

This supports the view that team-working facilitates reduced manning while deploying workers on a limited cluster of defined tasks, though there is often a 'redefinition of existing skills and task activities as new skills' (Garrahan and Stewart, 1995: 529). There is, then, a substantial gap between the rhetoric and the reality of work reorganisation in the established motor firms, and the implementation of the new management techniques continues to be marked by conflicts and contradictions.

From flow-line to lean production in electricals?

Electricals was a key sector in the development of mass production during the inter-war period. The leading firms in 'light' consumer goods manufacture combined mechanisation, flow-line assembly and the 'scientific' regulation of pay and work pace to maximise productivity, often on the basis of a predominantly female direct workforce and greenfield sites (Glucksmann, 1990). This meant increasingly fragmented and controlled work processes and the particular subordination of women workers in an entrenched gendered division of labour, but also continuing variety in personnel practices (ranging from paternalism to authoritarian casualisation) and differing combinations of payment systems, mechanisation and line work in different factories. This is consistent with Kelly's (1982) analysis of the post-war experiments in job redesign which led to a varied and evolving range of flow-line arrangements in the electrical engineering sector. He suggests that such experimentation, primarily a response to product-market changes and uncertainties, nevertheless remained largely within the job design repertoire developed by the Taylorist tradition. Thus consumer electricals was built around tightly organised assembly-line production, but was also characterised by continuing experiments in work reorganisation which represent variations around the theme of flow-line mass production.

It is against this background that the innovative features of the Japanese (and also South Korean and Taiwanese) inward-investors, on both brownfield and greenfield sites, can be assessed. Many of them located in the old coalfield regions of South Wales and central Scotland and, more recently, Durham. It has been suggested that in South Wales they were organised to maximise productivity 'not only through superior quality (and hence less time wasted on rejects and rectification) and through higher work speeds on individual tasks but through more rapid transfer of workers between tasks' (Morgan and Sayer, 1985). This task flexibility was pursued by minimising job descriptions and demarcations, cutting numbers of indirect workers and increasing management discretion over job allocation (with agreements pledging total flexibility between 'any kind or type of work within the employee's known abilities'). More recently Morris *et al.* (1993) have argued that many of these transplants have developed sophisticated total quality and JIT production systems. Moreover, while these JIT systems were often incomplete they created taut production schedules, because the remaining buffer stocks are found at the beginning or end rather than during the production process (Morris *et al.*, 1993: 59).

In emphasising not only the flexibility and tautness of such work organisation, but also its potential vulnerability, these studies highlight the issues of worker compliance and commitment. This leads them to emphasise the importance of sophisticated selection and appraisal procedures, simplified pay structures, team-based peer pressure, strictly enforced disciplinary procedures and single union deals as the institutional supports for worker commitment to accurate and intensive working. In particular selection processes have been geared to recruit workers with 'positive attitudes' rather than specific competencies, while policies for direct communication with the workforce and for narrowed forms of union recognition have been designed to reinforce such attitudes. While the distinctive regional inheritance, of working-class communities and masculine work cultures based on the development and crises of coal and steel, may have encouraged union recognition (in contrast to the practice of electricals transplants in some other regions), its influence has been attenuated by the recruitment of a largely female workforce, and, increasingly, location away from the mining districts. Furthermore national recession, regional decline and Thatcherite state policies have amplified the scope for innovation, especially for incomers on greenfield sites offering potentially secure employment. Under such circumstances workers and stewards may welcome 'rescue' by incoming firms, while the regional TUC has underwritten aspects of the new employment relations.

A further twist to the analysis of worker compliance and commitment has been provided by Sewell and Wilkinson (1992) who emphasise that JIT and TQM can be implemented through procedures and technologies which not only depend upon intense effort and application but also create the necessary levels of disciplined performance. Thus, following Foucault, they emphasise the panoptic character of the control systems through which operators are held accountable for shortfalls and defects in their performance. Their argument is that the rapid and visible monitoring of performance under JIT and TQM makes it possible for management to require immediate remedial action, both to correct performance and to rectify faulty components, so engendering self and peer monitoring of conduct. This powerfully reinforces labour discipline and facilitates an 'attack on the informal system and the black arts of making out'.

Such an argument sustains the emphasis on novelty but in a way sharply differentiated from any celebration of worker empowerment. Other evidence, however, suggests that this overstates both the innovative character of work organisation and the completeness of worker subordination in such plants. Firstly, Morris *et al.* (1993) themselves register major similarities between the work in these plants and earlier instances of mass production. The bulk of assembly work in such factories involves not only tightly controlled but also highly repetitive and routinised labour; the flexible allocation of workers between tasks does little to change this; and 'continuous improvement' initiatives usually involve pressures for speed-up from industrial engineers rather than the application of worker expertise. Furthermore, other research suggests that the implementation of both TQM and JIT procedures remains decidedly uneven within such Japanese electricals transplants, reflecting different commercial circumstances and management priorities (Taylor *et al.*, 1994; Elger and Smith, 1998a). This is consistent with Danford's documentation of a variety of 'fairly standard forms of flow line work organisation conditioned by sector trends and traditions' (1995: 2–3; 1998). In his research it was a *brownfield* buy-out, an auto-components manufacturer which had been reorganised into buffer-less flow-line cells which demanded continuous-paced working, which was closest to the ideal-type Japanese model.

Secondly, a central feature of both old and new plants has been an entrenched gendered division of labour between male machine operators and female manual assemblers, the former enjoying both grade and shiftwork premia though performing highly routinised machine-minding (Morgan and Sayer, 1985; Taylor *et al.*, 1994; Danford, 1998). Furthermore, despite some challenges by women workers and trade unionists, this gendered hierarchy has been little changed, as employers enjoy the advantages of recruiting low-paid and highly productive women operators while male workers gain preferential access to multi-skill training. Indeed Danford found that the reorganisation at the auto-components plant had sharpened the gendering division between automated and hand-assembly areas.

Finally, several critics have questioned the claim that a combination of slack labour markets, state support and the locational, recruitment, bargaining and surveillance policies of the transplants deliver enduring and effective supports for management priorities, be they innovative forms of total quality management or rather more mundane forms of tight management and intensive working. This is a theme in several case-studies of the incomplete, conditional and interrupted character of harmonious relations between management and workers at many transplant sites (Broad, 1994a, 1994b; Grant, 1994, 1996; Palmer, 1996). Employees commonly see key elements of their employer's production and personnel policies as inappropriate and/or inconsistent (classically in relation to petty discipline or in relation to the limits of any real involvement in work reorganisation), fuelling significant shop-floor dissatisfaction, though this may be directed more at some members of management than others and the dissatisfaction may also attach to existing forms of trade union representation. Such dissatisfactions are sometimes manifested in patterns of absenteeism and labour turnover, sometimes in small acts of disobedience or dissent (such as talking on the line).

Such problematical features of worker commitment and labour discipline have evoked a range of management responses, involving adjustments in recruitment policies (the widely noted shift from young workers to mature female recruits) and disciplinary processes (both reinforcement and judicious curtailment of surveillance and control) (Elger and Smith, 1998a). In this context Danford (1998, 1999) argues that the pressures of internationalised sectoral competition and the leverage of Japanese management have brought significant moves towards tighter control, fuller utilisation of capital and labour and intensified work pressure. This is primarily grounded in the way they have been able to capitalise on the wider economic and political context of the 1980s and 1990s, rather than in either the emancipatory character of new forms of work organisation or the panoptic possibilities of the electronic monitoring of worker performance. This implies that the tightening of labour discipline and intensification of labour in such workplaces remain open to challenge, though in current circumstances this has more often taken the form of low key disgruntlement than overt conflict.

Overall, then, these studies document the subordination of labour within highly standardised and tightly regulated work processes, often associated with significant innovations in personnel policy and per-formance monitoring but commonly still linked to fairly conventional flow-line production procedures. Against the vision of panoptic surveil-lance, they also register significant limitations to management's cap-acity to construct a compliant and committed workforce, signalled by continuing tensions and the often tacit negotiation of class and gender relations on the shop-floor. This pattern of experience has not fore-stalled enthusiasm for Japanese production concepts among the man-agements of British electricals companies, but it helps to explain both the patchwork character of the resulting innovations and the continuing importance of other sources of inspiration for flow-line work reorgan-isation, such as American transnationals.

The experience of one high-profile British electricals company, Lucas, underlines the piecemeal and contradictory character of the diffusion of Japanese innovations. Their programme of work reorganisation was part of a corporate recovery programme involving large-scale redundancies, the sale or closure of several factories and radical reorganisation of the surviving divisions. A key objective was to establish flexible team-working and just-in-time production, with the elimination of many indirect tasks and relocation of maintenance, inspection and support functions within production modules dedicated to the small-batch processing of complete products (Turnbull, 1986: 199–200). Turnbull argues that these innovations were intended to reduce stock-in-progress, manning levels, down time and set-up times; to subject workers to 'continual controlled pressure'; and to generate a distinctive team and productivity ethos cross-cutting established shop and trade identities. The result was work intensification but little individual or collective upskilling (Turnbull, 1988: 8–12). Management adopted a 'tough' approach to implementation, with threats of dismissals and closures and the side-lining of shop-stewards at critical junctures. Not surprisingly, this created obstacles to the mobilisation of effective worker commit-ment, while traditional forms of workplace trade unionism remained relatively resilient. Research at another Lucas factory (Elger and Fairbrother, 1992; Taylor *et al.*, 1994) suggests that these innovations, even though driven from the centre in crisis circumstances, were very unevenly implemented both between and within sites, while workplace unionism remained capable of influencing aspects of site restructuring. Indeed, the decline of indirect workers, the dispersal of staff, the ending of piecework and the development of modules not only posed challenges to union organisation at this plant, but also stimulated an active (but incomplete) process of union renewal.

While the Lucas experience seems fairly typical, it is also evident that considerable experimentation has continued within the rather heterogeneous electricals sector, and there are certainly examples of more radical initiatives, though the limits within which these have developed and the contradictions which they have faced once more suggest a pattern of experimentation around flow-line production techniques. One example involved 'flexible volume production' at a Scottish electronics plant (McKinlay and Taylor, 1996). Here 'self-managed teams' were responsible for recruitment, work allocation, coaching and peer assessment, in ways which engendered considerable commitment and self-discipline among employees at the pilot production operation. Once production took off in earnest, management sought to gear-up productivity through the team process and workers' responses became much more problematical. Firstly, many of the original enthusiasts saw the team-working ethos as under threat, and invoked team principles to criticise management. Secondly, management pressures on the teams (such as attempts to increase the stringency of peer assessment) prompted team members to distrust and subvert such procedures (through the tacit trading of scores). Thirdly, divergencies between team norms over such matters as the policing of absenteeism undermined the legitimacy of the process and encouraged teams to minimise their involvement in such activities. While management sought to modify and repair the mechanisms of self-policing, this study underlines the highly problematical character of team-based self-subordination and the contradictory pressures which create such fragility.

While experiments in work organisation continue to play an important role in this sector, the rhetoric of polyvalent high-trust team-working glosses over fundamental limits to such modes of working in the context of existing market and employment relations. Indeed, the dominant pattern of work design in the sector remains one of increased flexibility at the margins through job enlargement and intensification, coupled with management efforts to enhance their control over the resulting flexibility.

Food and drink: restructuring mass production

Food and drink developed as a mass production sector from divergent origins in small-scale, usually male-dominated, handicrafts on one hand and labour-intensive luxury food provision on the other, inheriting a mixed production process which combined quasi-craft, process, assembly and packaging work. Furthermore, UK manufacturers retained a more differentiated product range associated with more labour-intensive production than their US counterparts (Smith *et al.*, 1990). The sector nevertheless became characterised by increasingly large-scale production, marked by a sharply gendered division of labour in which women assembled and packaged the product (Glucksmann, 1990; Smith, 1991). Today it is dominated by large oligopolistic firms (though the giant retail firms have increasing leverage over even the large manufacturers), and British companies remain a major force in the context of international mergers and increasingly internationalised production.

Many food firms have undertaken a prolonged process of rationalisation of both product lines and production processes since the mid-1970s, with more capital-intensive production but also flexibility and team-working initiatives across both process and assembly operations. Cadbury's, a leading confectionery manufacturer, exemplifies these developments (Smith *et al.*, 1990). Tightly-managed labour-intensive assembly had long been pivotal to its labour process, and this was embedded within a factory paternalism which translated into relatively settled industrial relations during the post-war period. In this context a tradition of incremental mechanisation coexisted with the ingenious application of industrial engineering especially to gear up the pace of women assemblers. By the 1970s, however, intensified market competition prompted a search for productivity gains through major capital investment linked with the streamlining of the product range. While this was reinforced by fears that wage costs might escalate, the very effectiveness of labour-intensive methods also meant that gains from capital investment could only be assured by a more radical recasting of work relations.

By 1978 job cuts and increased workforce flexibility were enshrined in strategic corporate planning, and though work organisation issues were generally addressed at a late stage of equipment commissioning, these principles were effectively embodied in new plants. Thus the new investments provided a 'mechanism for transforming organisational and work cultures in favour of management' (Smith *et al.*, 1990: 168). This outcome was pursued through debate and negotiation among evolving alliances within corporate management, and through a shifting mixture of confrontation, manipulation and negotiation in relation to the workforce and unions. In general management played skilfully upon weaknesses of steward organisation, existing divisions within a heterogeneous workforce, and the growing insecurities of the early 1980s, to implement most of the changes they desired. Their pursuit of labour flexibility in the context of capital investment meant the recasting of working practices, but the established gender division of labour was largely reinforced rather than eroded.

Male maintenance workers, previously organised as centralised craft specialists, were reduced in numbers and redeployed into operating plants, where they had to embrace increased responsibility and cross-trade working, though day-to-day practice fell short of management's ambitions.

For male process operators the new plant meant much reduced manning levels, the elaboration of 'totally integrated' team-working in conjunction with continuous shift-working, and a move from manipulative to monitoring tasks. This involved a wider portfolio of tasks, including record-keeping, assistance with maintenance and cleaning, but training opportunities were constrained by tight manning levels and the role of tacit expertise was circumscribed by the use of pre-programmed controls. In constructing this pattern management gained critical leverage from their capacity to manipulate staffing of the new plant and select exceptionally committed workers, allowing them to entrench managerial prerogatives ahead of formal agreements. Meanwhile, the women workers at the centre of Cadbury's labour-intensive operations faced competition from, and redeployment around, a new generation of pick and place machinery. This meant a much smaller complement of direct workers, organised in teams on a uniform grade, trained through regular job-rotation, and deployed according to management requirements. This implied job enlargement and enhanced responsibilities, but also fewer rest pauses and loss of the indirect jobs which allowed an escape from line pacing. In practice, though, the limitations of the equipment meant that planned staffing levels were exceeded and significant task specialisation remained.

Thus a wave of new investment which began in the 1970s involved both the substantial displacement of labour and a management drive to redeploy labour in ways which involved wider task clusters more responsive to managerial direction. The overall result was the recasting of a heterogeneous division of labour in which skill enhancement was confined to a minority of craft workers and senior operators while labour generally became more intensive and malleable within evolving work routines. In summary 'flexibility had little to do with extending skills or worker satisfaction, and a lot to do with undermining the remaining areas of craft control in maintenance, extending managerial authority over labour mobility and ensuring greater utilisation of expensive capital equipment' (Smith, 1991: 154). This was largely accomplished through and around a process of consultation and negotiation which reflected the weakening of trade unionism but left an uneven pattern of collective representation intact.

Similar trends can be discerned across the sector, where a mix of corporate mergers, product rationalisation and capital investment drove a combination of plant closures and radical plant refurbishments, placing great pressures on workplace union organisation and affording management considerable leverage in work reorganisation (Smith, 1991; Knell, 1993; Darlington, 1994). From the mid-1980s, companies used a growing range of 'new management techniques', including multi-tasking, team-working, quality initiatives and communications briefings. However, recent studies underline the partial and contradictory character of such policies, the persistence of tightly regulated work routines, the limits of worker involvement, and the continuing importance of the politics of workplace industrial relations (Heaton and Linn, 1989; Scott, 1994; Pollert, 1996).

Scott traces these features in two contrasting workplaces, one with a history of strong workplace unionism against a backdrop of high unemployment (Frozen Foods) and another which excluded unions in a more buoyant labour market (Chocolate Works). In both cases managers sought to devolve more responsibility to workers by increasing areas of discretion, flexibility and involvement in continuous improvement, and also promoted direct communications with the workforce, by-passing stewards in the former and reducing the supervisory hierarchy in the latter. However, the reorganisation of manual tasks remained modest, often involving more responsibility without enhanced skills or autonomy, while management continued to exercise established forms of authority and discipline in controlling such matters as time-keeping and rest periods. Furthermore they often took decisions which contradicted their own rhetoric (like setting up a quality team then revising quality standards downwards to maximise output), fuelling scepticism or distrust on the shop-floor.

At Frozen Foods, shop-floor criticism developed into active opposition to management policies and a defence of traditional patterns of job control. The management (helped by contemporary legislation) provoked and won a strike, decisively weakening the union. As experienced stewards left, management imposed compliance on the workforce in a form far removed from the pretensions of 'human resource management'. Even more telling was the uneven and contradictory implementation of such policies at the Chocolate Works. Here a 'unitarist' rhetoric prevailed, but failed to turn instrumental compliance into active commitment. In each case, then, management altered the balance of power, but not the pattern of commitment, on the shop-floor. Scott draws unfavourable contrasts between these experiences and the modest incremental changes achieved through 'pluralistic' bargaining at his third case-study site. While significant union concessions were involved, this comparison suggests that established union–management relations offer more scope for real change than management strategies which purport to transcend negotiable conflicts of interest.

However, Pollert's (1996) research on team-working in a major confectionery plant with a long history of relatively conciliatory unionism develops a more critical appraisal of changes in such an environment. In this study management sought to devolve key responsibilities to team leaders within a framework of financial accountability, and to involve workers through quality circles and briefing procedures. In practice, however, team-working more often involved increased pressure than job enhancement: the team-leaders were overloaded, work tasks were little changed, and the cost-cutting imperative eroded training and quality commitments. Furthermore, despite being a flagship factory, the experience of job losses coloured workers' perceptions of the meaning of involvement and commitment.

Within an entrenched gendered division of labour team-working was experienced differently by men and women. It had some logic in the male-dominated, capital-intensive parts of the process, with relatively stable team composition and some variety of tasks despite the constraints of micro-processor controlled processes. In the female-dominated labour-intensive areas, however, job rotation simply meant 'repeating broadly the same operation' elsewhere on the line, and the spuriousness of team groupings was underlined by regular redeployment across teams.

Such work reorganisation created new foci for union intervention, as when Repetitive Strain Injury became a union issue or team-leaders (re)-turned to the unions for representation of their collective interests. Meanwhile senior managers remained ambivalent between incorporating and marginalising tactics, while middle managers often turned to stewards for help in addressing the tensions and pitfalls in teamworking. Thus workplace unionism was not marginalised. Unions retained leverage over certain aspects of change, though they remained on the defensive under the weight of management initiatives while inter-plant performance comparisons sustained pressure for further concessions.

In this sector the experience of work reorganisation was clearly differentiated in its effects, not only between men and women and different occupational groupings, but also between those plants which survived and those that underwent a process of attrition and closure (Darlington, 1994). Yet even new plants provide little support for diagnoses of generalised upskilling or worker empowerment. Thus research on a capital intensive, highly automated soft-drinks plant typical of the new inward investment of the late 1980s (Knell, 1993) found strong parallels with the South Wales electricals firms in terms of personnel management, with a single-union deal and the recruitment of green workers on the expectation that they would be 'willing to accept new methods' of multi-skilled team-based working. In practice, however, the shift-based teams of male 'technicians' found that the plant required little skilled input, some skilled workers left in frustration, and a more differentiated workforce evolved as semi-skilled workers were recruited in their place. In consequence the operation of this plant, the location of which was little influenced by human capital considerations, reinforced the predominance of low-wage unskilled labour in its local labour market.

Conclusion: a distinctive national pattern of work reorganisation?

My discussion of the car, electricals and food sectors has demonstrated that much of the work reorganisation undertaken in these key sectors of British manufacturing represents new permutations upon an established pattern of assembly-line or flow-line production. On one hand this has involved some fresh variants of team-working and task-rotation, with the allocation of more tasks to direct workers, the revamping of supervisory structures around team-leaders and/or the tighter gearing of production flows, but on the other hand such experiments generally involve more mundane changes than the rhetoric associated with them. Furthermore, they often occupy a place within a longer pattern of variations and adjustments in job design, driven by efforts to match the exigencies of production and employment relations with evolving competitive pressures and market demands. In the United Kingdom, then, work reorganisation in mass production manufacturing has involved limited shifts in patterns of competence and control within and between established occupational groups, largely involving modified variants of existing expertise. Underlying these modest developments have been management preoccupations with reduced labour and other costs, managerial prerogatives over the disposition and intensity of labour and a real but limited concern to tap workers' 'tacit skills'. What, then, are we to make of this record of work reorganisation, which offers little sign of either the multi-skilled craftician of flexible specialisation or the empowered team-worker of lean production?

Firstly, it throws a valuable light on claims that the 1980s witnessed a 'productivity miracle' in British manufacturing. While economists have clearly documented a substantial gain in manufacturing productivity in this period, its scope and basis remain controversial (Nolan, 1989; Glyn, 1992; Blackaby and Hunt, 1993). Different yardsticks place the figures in contrasting lights: while the proponents of a 'miracle' emphasise improvement from the 1970s and relative gains against European competitors, the sceptics argue this involved a return to a pre-1974 trajectory and still leaves the United Kingdom lagging in absolute terms. However, both agree that manufacturing productivity growth in the 1980s reflected job-shedding, rather than sustained capital investment or capacity growth, and that the pattern of low investment resumed after a brief surge in the late 1980s. This focuses attention on the significance of organisational change and the implications of a changed balance of power between management and unions. The proponents of a 'productivity miracle' tend to interpret this in terms of the qualitative transformation of work relations as legislation emancipates management from the 'shackles' of union regulation. However, my overview reinforces the arguments of the sceptics, that on the one hand the effects of state policies on management–union relations have been rather indirect, involving a delayed and uneven process of union marginalisation, while on the other such marginalisation has tended to *reinforce* existing management priorities to enhance the malleability and intensity of labour alongside modest capital investment, much more than experimentation with enskilling or autonomous team-working (Nolan and O'Donnell, 1995).

The theorists of flexible specialisation could reasonably argue that we need to look at other sectors and smaller firms to test *their* prognosis, but they generally accept that flexible specialisation is thin on the ground in the United Kingdom, and instead focus their attention on an apparent divergence between developments in the United Kingdom and elsewhere. This saves flexible specialisation from the test of British experience by emphasising British backwardness and exceptionalism. However, wider international studies raise questions about the extent to which developments elsewhere conform to the model of flexible specialisation. Furthermore, it is far from clear that the patterns of work reorganisation pursued by manufacturers in the United Kingdom have proven unsuccessful for capital.

Hirst and Zeitlin (1989a, 1989b) develop a strong version of the backwardness argument, counterposing the British experience to that of innovative regions in several other advanced capitalist societies. They acknowledge that the productivity of British manufacturing increased in the early 1980s, but see this as a one-off consequence of demanning and the closure of old capacity. For them the balance of payments deficits from the late 1980s once more reveal the underlying decline of British manufacturing competitiveness, fuelled by a crisis of infrastructural investment but fundamentally a consequence of failure to develop the new forms of flexible specialisation. They attribute this failure to a whole ensemble of restrictive and short-sighted institutions, ranging from managements obsessed with short-term financial returns, through the subaltern status of engineers and the sectional protective reflexes of British trade unionism, to the *laissez-faire* stance of the British government. These combine to limit organisational innovation and to prolong the survival of out-dated and inefficient standardised mass production arrangements, while overseas competitors have established new productivity and quality norms through flexible manufacturing.

Such arguments from international comparisons usefully highlight the significance of uneven development, both between national economies and between regions. They also mesh with an increasing recognition that any failings in the performance of British industry cannot simply be blamed on trade unions or shop-floor 'restrictive practices' (Nichols, 1986b). In particular the productivity trajectory of manufacturing owes much to distinctive features of the organisation and competencies of British management, involving tensions between specialised staff functions; limited training, especially in production management; and the subordination of production engineering to financial priorities. The pattern has also been reinforced by a largely abstentionist state policy on training which, minimally qualified by limited attempts at co-ordination and interventions designed primarily to control the unemployed, has persistently delegated responsibility to employers. They in turn have displayed a long-standing ambivalence towards training: many firms have sought to narrow training while responding to shortages by 'poaching' skilled labour from others.

However, Hirst and Zeitlin's analysis of uneven development depends on a highly problematical contrast between an archaic and crisis-ridden mass production and the emergent synergies of flexible specialisation, when it has become increasingly evident that the supposed exemplars of flexible specialisation in Italy and Germany fail to conform to their model. Thus commentaries on the 'third Italy' identify the powerful role of large final processors and retailers and the continuing importance of low pay and substantial insecurity among sub-contractors (Amin 1991), while discussions of Baden-Wurttemburg emphasise the dominance of large firms, the extent to which they subordinate smaller enterprises within and beyond the region and the absence of clear up-skilling (Braczyk, 1995). Such findings suggest that more attention must be given to the varied logics of different trajectories of restructuring in specific national economies, regions and sectors, rather than reading these off from an idealised conception of flexible specialisation.

In this context Nolan and O'Donnell (1991, 1995) outline elements of a more appropriate characterisation of the pattern of developments in the United Kingdom. They suggest that the trajectory of British manufacturing should be analysed in terms of the *active facilitation* of certain forms of production organisation, and not simply in terms of the constraints which foreclose change. In particular they argue that British workers have 'been unable to close off routes to profitability based on low wages, job segmentation and labour intensification' (Nolan and O'Donnell, 1991: 11). This has meant that transnational firms 'have come to see Britain not as a base for highly skilled, high value-added production, but as an ideal location in which to carry out labour intensive, assembly and sub-assembly work' (Nolan and O'Donnell, 1991: 12). Thus many of the features often construed as constraints on flexible specialisation are better seen as concomitants of the long-standing dominance of a rather different trajectory of *profitable* accumulation. This applies not only to the structure and culture of management and the organisation of training and skills, but also to such features of British trade unionism as fragmentation, decentralisation, bargained co-operativeness and bloody-mindedness (Hyman and Elger, 1981).

From this vantage point 'Britain stands out as a specialist producer of relatively low tech, low value-added products and as a low wage, low productivity, low investment economy' (Nolan and O'Donnell, 1991: 9). However, this should not be seen primarily as the result of a generalised failure to innovate, but rather as a product of the restructuring and locational decisions of manufacturing corporations, guided by distinctive costs and benefits. For example, inward-investing firms are often concerned with issues of market access and may be attracted by the prospect of recruiting 'green labour', but the existence of considerable pools of relatively cheap but *experienced* labour has certainly encouraged the location and retention of labour-intensive production in the UK. Ford's decisions in locating several of its more labour-intensive sub-assembly plants in the United Kingdom (Roots, 1986) and the employment profiles of the inward-investing electricals firms in South Wales

(Morris *et al.*, 1993) and Telford (Elger and Smith, 1998b) represent examples of the resulting bias towards semi-skilled assembly. At the same time, of course, such corporate calculations are embedded in evolving international corporate policies, so we need to track the varied and changing ways in which manufacturing operations in the United Kingdom are inserted into wider corporate structures and commodity chains (Gereffi and Korzeniewicz, 1994; Smith and Elger, 1996). Thus the US semi-conductor firms investing in Scotland have gained market access and capitalised upon a cheap but technically sophisticated labour force by investing in relatively capital-intensive development and production, using both semi-skilled and skilled technical labour (Henderson, 1989), while commercial vehicle plants in the United Kingdom are developing team-working and customised assembly explicitly on the basis of semi-skilled workforces, with the marginalisation of craft workers (Thompson *et al.*, 1995).

The advocates of lean production, like the theorists of flexible specialisation, deploy a model of institutional backwardness in their discussion of the organisational differences and productivity differentials between Japan and the West, *but* they emphasise that a combination of market pressures and corporate learning is now driving a wider adoption of lean production. In this context state encouragement of inward investment, a weakened labour movement and a tradition of decentralised bargaining can be seen as facilitators of the spread of this new model. Once more, though, this reads developments through the distorting mirror of spurious ideal-types. Firstly, it glosses over the problematical and changing features of Toyota's production arrangements, reflecting both the costs borne by employees and the problems which model diversity, recruitment and pollution pose for management (Nomura, 1993; Berggren, 1995; Benders, 1996). Once these features are recognised there is no longer an unproblematical model to disseminate. Secondly, it collapses the spectrum of production arrangements and contingencies which characterise the operations of contemporary manufacturers (within sectors, between sectors and across commodity chains) into a simple contrast between lean and mass producers (Williams *et al.*, 1994; Thompson *et al.*, 1995). It therefore provides no language for understanding the variegated patterns of uncertain experimentation and the uneven patterns of compliance, negotiation and contestation which have characterised contemporary work reorganisation.

It is these features of experimentation and low-key contestation which need to be integrated into broad characterisations of the logic of relatively cheap labour-intensive branch plant production and the continuing importance of the core features of assembly-line mass production, if we are to understand both the variety and the limits of work reorganisation in British manufacturing during the 1980s and 1990s.

CHAPTER 10

A historical construction of the working class

IAN ROBERTS

Introduction

In what follows I wish to concern myself with the relationship between sociology and the working class. It may indeed appear to some that for sociology the working class is a sacred object. Its omnipresent nature belies its apparently infinite capacity for mutation. For some it has appeared as the rabble or the mob, others have stressed the historical and cultural changes underlying its transformation into the proletariat (Thompson, 1965; Bauman, 1982). It has been seen variously as a social problem to be controlled, a social problem to be helped (these two views are by no means mutually exclusive), a threat to cultural standards or as the subject and object of history, an agency for the transcendance of alienation bringing an end to the prehistory of humankind. At each pole of analysis the movement of this class, either flowing naturally from advances in the living standards of its members or developing actively in pursuit of its historical role, is never neutral with respect to the existent social system. It is either the grave-digger of capitalism or the newly arrived citizen of a consequently more integrated post-capitalist mass society. Curiously, however, whilst most theorisations of the working class have begun with their insertion into a structured social system; occupying the lower levels in the social hierarchy, such involuntary location is often seen to emphasise the specific type of consciousness or world view of the working class. This often goes well beyond indicating the material (and therefore necessarily historical) context of consciousness and rather predicates a quintessential essence of those belonging to the class. In what follows I want to lay bare some of these constructions as they have appeared in accounts of working-class communities in the post-war period.

The working class as a social problem

Although the working class has remained a focus of attention for British sociologists in the post-war period there is little agreement as to the nature of the class. Whilst a number of positions have developed, when considered together one thing that most of them have in common is the impression they give that the working class just can't win. The beliefs and behaviour of individuals within the class appear to be analysed in relation to a prescribed agenda. They are either abnormal and ignorant (Paneth, 1944; Spinley, 1953), have impaired ego due to role restrictions (Kerr, 1958), display low cultural horizons (Zweig, 1961) or are 'incurious, inarticulate, almost inanimate' (Greenslade, 1976).

Implicitly their salvation would seem to lie in adopting middle-class attitudes and behaviour. On the other hand insofar as they have been seen to be making these changes they are seen as becoming enmeshed in a faceless culture (Hoggart, 1957) or impoverished in the presence of unexampled wealth (Seabrook, 1988). Where workers begin 'to think and act like capitalists' (Taylor, 1982), their actions become increasingly permeated by sectionalism both at work and in the wider community (Lane, 1974). One is tempted to throw one's hands in the air and exclaim, 'Who are these people?' with their internally inconsistent values (Mann, 1970), are they stupid? Apparently they cannot even control their bowels properly (Spinley, 1953)! The dehumanisation, or the losing of the subject apparent in many of these value-free studies is for me summed up in the outlook of the author who concludes that: 'For them, life is not so much a mystery, more a non-event' (Greenslade, 1976: 151).

It seems that the working class do indeed constitute a 'problem' for sociology. However, it may be the case that sociology has become a problem for the working class. In order to investigate more fully the roots of this particular problem it is necessary to look more closely at several specific monographs and ask, in as irreverant tones as possible, 'Where do these people get their ideas from?'

One of the features of many studies upon the working class that strikes me is the unfamiliarity of the descriptions of life and the way in which behaviour is reinterpreted in what is often an uncritically middle-class paradigm. A good example of the application of this context is Marie Paneth's study *Branch Street*. Published in 1944 and having the subtitle *A Sociological Study*, this work is not in fact sociology but rather represents a purely subjective report upon the setting up, and eventual demise, of a play scheme in a 'slum' area of London. In spite of having little to recommend it, the study was precised in Josephine Klein's (1965) *Samples from English Cultures*, thereby bestowing a degree of respectability upon the monograph. The assumptions interwoven in the text I found profoundly disturbing and yet their very visibility ensures that this book surely cannot be taken too seriously? For example, after a two-evening introduction to the play scheme Paneth was asked to take over responsibility for it. She goes on:

I was rather keen on it. I like to tackle a difficult group. I lay awake at night and tried to imagine who these children were and what was wrong with them. I knew nothing about them. Why were they so exceptionally aggressive and lewd? They were dirtier and more miserable looking than the others I had seen hitherto and they certainly distrusted us. . . . I pity them. I feel that the whole world has let them down. I feel responsible for what is done to them, for the harm and the misery which they suffer. Above all, I cannot bear the idea that they shall grow up like that. (Paneth, 1944: 13–14)

A sweeping diagnosis indeed! On the one hand the author suggests that she knows nothing about them, but on the other wonders what is wrong with them and cannot bear the idea that they will grow up like that. Again at another point the author relates her experience of taking four of the girls from Branch Street on a camping trip:

Those fifty hours with them had given me literally a wild headache, so great had been the strain of the mental effort needed to follow their quick changes of mood and attitude; so disgusting and depressing beyond words that which I had seen. They had been nice only during the short spells of expectation. Once they had got what they were hoping for, achieved the state of fulfilment, then their anger and cynicism, their untrustworthiness, unreliability and aggressiveness immediately got hold of them again. (Paneth, 1944: 86)

A sociological study? The uncritical inclusion of words such as 'nice' buttressed around the taken-for-granted life-style of the author as an absolute standard, allied to the lack of any attempt to capture in a sympathetic form the subjective understandings of the agents themselves, should put us on our guard. Far harder to evaluate, however, is the secondary analysis of such work where the original account is stripped of its more manifest failings and is generalised into respectable sociology:

To sum up the Branch Street infant's experience . . . we see that he does not grow in a soil which allows to take root such ideas that there is a time and place for everything, that good things arrive regularly though one may have to wait or even cry for them, that foresight and effort will please the parent and be rewarded by them. The absense of this kind of learning is to be connected with the absence of striving, the intollerence of frustration, the inability to wait for gratification, which marks the adult personality. (Klein, 1965: 11)

In many of the early community studies there is a great concern with child-rearing practices and the implications that these hold for the adult personality. Thus, for example, we are told in several studies that working-class children are fed on demand: 'Although mothers know that the welfare centre insists upon adherence to a strict time schedule in feeding they rarely follow this advice' (Spinley, 1953: 46). Similarly Kerr points out in her study that,

Although nurses and doctors give instructions about regular feeding hours, on the whole babies are fed when they appear to be hungry or start to cry. Mrs I. said that the hospital told her to feed Winnie every three hours and that if the baby is asleep she should be woken for the feed. Her nephew Gilbert, aged 23, who was present said that in his view a baby should not be woken to be fed but should be fed when it cries. 'The baby knows when it is hungry not the clock.' (Kerr, 1958: 55)

Clearly such a view was deemed deviant in the 1940s and 50s and was associated with abnormal personality development or, in the more sanitised versions, a tendency towards instant as opposed to deferred gratification. This is an interesting issue for, as subsequent changes in child-rearing practice over recent years demonstrate, the issue of time-table *vs* demand feeding is clearly a relative one, and yet in these studies social 'science' uncritically incorporated the middle-class, or at least the medical professional, point of view as an absolute against which working-class deviation could be held up in an unfavourable light. Again the importance of instant and deferred gratification as class-related psychological traits outlived the supersession of the relativity of the empirical substance in which they were supposedly grounded. Indeed, even at the time, the opposition of timetable feeding of the middle-class to the demand feeding of the working class perhaps owed more to an image of what acceptable middle-class practice should be rather than that practice itself. For in their study of Nottingham the Newsons (1963) found that of their sample of working-class and middle-class families 'over half favoured feeding on demand whereas only 6 per cent kept rigidly to the clock; the others were all more or less flexible in their response to the child's needs'.

Not only in relation to feeding is the working-class child reared in an 'abnormal' manner. Spinley gives a catologue of individual traits and behaviour based on interviews and observations with 'my slum friends', as she refers to her respondents. We are told that:

The baby is not rigidly toilet trained. (p. 48)
Throughout childhood and adolescence he will have little or no control over his
    sphincters. (p. 49)
He does not have during childhood and adolescence enough sound sleep. (p. 52)
He witnesses much conflict in his home. (p. 57)
He resents and fears the authority of the police. (p. 60)

The implicit deviance evident in these points is amplified in the sup-porting text offered by the author, thus,

He fights dirty. At school children are told the middle class rules – no below the belt, don't hit a man when he's down, don't hit a girl – but in their own areas these rules don't apply and the boy who tries to abide by them is always beaten. If he arranges to abide by the rules in a fight he finds that he gets into the street to be taken unawares by a foul kick. Boys learn to get the first kick in and so well aimed that it brings the opponent to the ground, then the thing to do is damage him as much as possible while he is at a disadvantage. Nor does it matter if the opponent is smaller; it is smarter to fight with someone smaller than with someone stronger. If a girl angers a boy she is struck, although boys say that they do not hurt girls, they just, 'Knock them about a bit.' (Spinley, 1953: 64)

We are informed that the cumulative affect of all these individual factors is profound:

With all these factors operating in the life of one child a rather clear picture is formed of the resulting personality. . . . It is here contended that the following personality characteristics may be expected in a child of this area: A basic insecurity; a serious sexual disturbance which is associated with feminine identifications; an inability to form close affectional ties; an absence of a strong and efficient super-ego; an inability to postpone satisfaction and an absence of conflict over pleasures; a highly sensitive ego and marked narcissistic trends; a ready aggressivenes; a tendency to 'leave the field' when circumstances are experienced as unpleasent; a rebellious attitude towards authority. (Spinley, 1953: 79)

In these early post-war studies the texture of the substantive accounts is often at odds with the value-free claims of authors' scientific stances. The above accounts are imbued with language and concepts derived from psychology with a focus upon the pathology of these 'strange' people accepted as an unproblematic issue. For those eschewing the psychological smoke-screen, the value judgements from a standard of implicit common sense based on an uncritical valorisation of middle-class culture are often more transparent. This is especially so where accounts of working-class and middle-class people appear side by side. Take for example two of the case studies from a total of 200 assembled in *English Life and Leisure*, a book written by Seebohm Rowntree and George Lavers, published in 1951:

Case 16
Mrs. D. is a young housewife of 26. Her husband is an architect. They are very much in love and are anxious to get a house of their own (they are now in a furnished flat) because they want to start a family. They hope to have three children.

Mrs. D. is a very gentle person who would do anything for any one. She has not been a regular churchgoer but was married in church and has started going occasionally. As far as can be told, her life has no vice or unpleasantness of any kind, and a church could hardly make her better!

She is a teetotaller and non-smoker. Is of course innocent sexually, and does not gamble. She likes the radio, cinema and theatre, but her main recreation is looking after her husband.

Case 9
Mrs. W. is distrustful of her fellow humans for most of them look down on her and show it. She might be any age between 40 and 55, but says she is 39. She is enormously fat, to an extent that defies description, and though she lives in a large, well-fitted council house in a large town, she is a complete slattern. She goes about with her clothes unfastened, bare feet thrust into muddy carpet slippers, long black hair uncombed, dirty hands and dirty face. Two men live with her, to one of whom she is married, and her children are divided between them. She is now pregnant again and it is astonishing that either of the men – both decent working-class types – could copulate with such a monstrous creature. (Rowntree and Lavers, 1951: 5 and 9)

Again it should be stressed that the authors hold to a view of social science which is seen to be objective and value-free, as the following passages from the introduction make clear:

The bulk of the interviewing was undertaken by G. R. Lavers, but to supplement his work, and as a check on any personal bias that might be inherent in
it, a substantial number of case histories were obtained for us by Professor F.
Zweig, Miss Susan Garth (a free-lance journalist), Miss M. E. Walker (in Leeds)
and Miss R. Raymond (in London). . . . We have, of course, approached every
facet of our subject with carefully objective minds, and our widely different
personal backgrounds have helped to supress our individual enthusiasms and
prejudices, for we have been a check each upon the other. (Rowntree and
Lavers, 1951: xiii–xiv)

In relation to these early post-war studies we should be careful not
to be too critical of the individual substantive comments, in particular
individual expressions of class bias and sexism. For it would be wrong
to view perspectives from one epoch by the standards of another. The
point is, then, not the narrow one of personal bias, but rather that
perceptions of working people and their pathologies were constrained
within the perspectives of a social science which bore the imprint of the
position of social scientists within a class-divided society. We can then
believe the claims of Rowntree, Lavers, Zweig *et al.* to be producing an
account which to their collective view is objective. Yet such objectivity
in the end amounts to a legitimation of the world view of those who do
the studying and the writing, the familiar and the immediately compre-
hensible. The life of an architect's wife 'has no vice or unpleasantness
of any kind', for her account can be believed in its entirety. The 'enormously fat slattern' on the other hand cannot even be trusted to impart
her true age.

'Communities' and 'affluence'

The exploration of the working class as a social problem, the concern
with the exotic (defined in relation to a middle-class life-style) and
the deviant is particularaly prevalent in the earliest post-war studies.
Gradually, however, studies which attended to more 'normal' features of
working-class life began to emerge. It is perhaps more than a coincidence
that these emerged at a time when absolute poverty was begining to
decline in the first stirrings of the affluent society. Also at a time when
the first tranche of post-war working-class grammar school educated
pupils were entering the professions including academia. This new sociology of the working class can perhaps best be divided into two traditions.

The first of these traditions focused upon 'community studies', upon
attempting to understand working-class communities from within. A
second and to some extent more powerful tradition began to form around
the problem of the affluent society and the place of the worker within
it. It should not be thought that there were no intersecting themes between these two traditions, for in reality the community studies became
enmeshed within the material changes occurring in their locales. Thus a
concern with residential relocation figured in several community studies

and the move from the 'traditional' urban village towards the new estates on the periphery of cities was seen as symptomatic and expressive of a new life-style of the affluent worker.

One of the earliest and most influential of the community studies was Young and Willmott's *Family and Kinship in East London* (1957). According to Brian Jackson, this study was of great importance because it 'changed the focus from untypical problem families or male-centred discussions of collective bargaining and the creation of trade unions, to the ordinary world of women and home' (Jackson, 1968: 5). The study is indeed welcome relief from the overt condescension of Paneth, Spinley, etc. It offers a particularly useful analysis of family structure and the importance of the mother/daughter bond in the process of everyday life. Yet the study has a number of defects which it shares with others of this genre. The account of the move from Bethnal Green to Greenleigh is predicated upon too stark a picture of a before and after kind. The time period allotted after the move to Greenleigh is not long enough to assess the potential for the evolution of community. This problem is compounded by the restriction of the analysis to adults as occupying one particular place in the life cycle, and the consequent lack of consideration of the role of children as the builders of community on new estates through their enforced group membership in school and more informal relationships outside.

Such accounts of a once-and-for-all transformation in the nature of the working class consequent upon a geographical move from traditional inner-city areas to peripheral estates is a theme that is celebrated in many works, including those more recent than Young and Willmott's. The theme is variously constructed but invariably includes notions of loss and cultural decline. Thus in a study of the history of Sunderland one observer commented:

The question was asked 'what went wrong?' If in 1939 and earlier, before the break up in the pattern of working class life, the heroic women ruled the roost, how do you account for the transition to the notorious bingo-women who neglect their children and who have allowed family life to go to pot on the large new housing estates in Sunderland and elsewhere. (Hopkins, 1974: 25)

There is now just enough evidence emerging to question analyses such as these. The idea of a breakdown of community and attendant moral decline consequent upon geographical relocation has been criticised by Willmott himself (1963), emphasising the extended duration necessary to witness the evolution of community. It could be argued that this sharp focus upon supposed fundamental change following geographical relocation is merely one expression of a more general tendency that occurs in many of the contexts where students of society have studied the working class, namely that even when sympathetic social commentators have studied working-class life their analysis is usually grounded in single contexts. That is their studies are concretely built up either around a particular, usually short, epoch and/or restricted to a particular modality of life, e.g. community or industry. The result is that generalisations are framed upon the basis of single concrete contextualisations. Therefore any changes that occur, any movements that take place, serve to transgress the framework deployed. This of course can be annoying for the individual theorist but more often than not is merely rationalised as a fundamental change in the essential qualities of working-class people. It should be stressed that the changes which initiate such closure and the construction of alternative essence need not have anything to do with the working-class people themselves but may reflect in some cases the biography of the researcher. Thus the sense of loss and moral decline in the works of Hoggart, Jackson and Marsden and Jeremy Seabrook perhaps reflect the movement away from the class of origin by the authors themselves. Social distance, temporal difference and geographical distance, all of these moves serve to frustrate understandings built upon a general characterisation drawn from a single concrete context and, as we have already observed, unfamiliarity breeds condescension.

In Young and Willmott's account the theme of fundamental transformation is enhanced due to the lack of any consideration of the world of work, and this is also true of the earlier organicist accounts of Hoggart and Roberts. Such lacunae cannot be justified in studies that purport to deal with community. Certainly within the northern industrial cities studied by Hoggart and Roberts the long shadow of work and/or its absence is cast over many other areas of life. Is the negation of such a reference in Hoggart's *Uses of Literacy* indicative of his lack of direct experience of the world of work?

Herein lie many of the problems associated with the sympathetic accounts of working-class life presented by organicists and the community studies type of approach, namely that the width and depth of their interpretive schemes are restricted to the extent of their own personal experience. The upshot of this, especially where the theorists are ex-grammar school pupils, is that the power of definition and denotation bestowed upon academics is rarely matched with a sophisticated interpretive endeavour which can engage directly with the subjects of the study. Rather the past experience of the authors is uncritically valorised, reified and then projected as an absolute with which to gauge subsequent deviation. The result is to a lesser or greater degree either a combination of past romanticism with present condescension or a useful statement of a very particular phenomenon.

Perhaps an example of the latter approach is Jackson and Marsden's study *Education and the Working Class* (1966). For a book with such a general title the actual focus of the study is rather narrow, with the majority of attention being devoted to the working-class grammar school pupil. Their treatment of the problems confronting such pupils and their families is useful, grounded as it is in their own experience – they include themselves in their sample.

This is in contrast to Brian Jackson's later study, *Working Class Community* (1968), where we are treated far more to an account focused on institutions, 'Brass Bands', 'At the Club', 'In the Mill', etc. The chapter on schooling deals mainly with grammar school girls and there is little attempt to understand the experience of the majority in this sphere. Because of such foci there is more evidence of disjunction between the institutions considered than continuity. This is not to say that such studies are unwelcome. They do provide a welcome relief to the pathological frameworks of the first wave of post-war studies. Their emphasis upon the normality and intelligibility of working-class life is their strength. Unfortunately, however, this framework is usually short-range and brittle, with many of the researchers, some of whom are the least ideologically self-conscious of commentators, endorsing a partial interpretive framework, one which valorises past potential and devalues the present.

The concerns of the second wave of community studies overlapped to a large degree with those of the theorists that Goldthorpe has denoted as organicists. They both saw working-class life as distinctive and valuable and this led them to fear the secular developments of affluence and privatisation which they saw as tending to destroy those older qualities that they so valued. Sharing their analysis of secular developments, but not always their evaluation of its effects, were the embourgeoisement theorists. There are several versions of embourgeoisement theorisation, both Marxist (Marcuse, 1964) and liberal (Lipset, 1964). The specifics of individual presentations vary, but a common theme is that because of secular changes, greater affluence, the changing nature of work, etc., the working class are becoming more akin to the middle class in behaviour and outlook. As one grounded version of this theory put it,

working class life finds itself on the move towards new middle class values and existence . . . the change can only be described as a deep transformation of values, as the development of new ways of thinking and feeling, a new ethos, new aspirations and cravings. (Zweig, 1961: ix)

Whatever was new among the working class we shall return to at a later point, but first we should note that there was nothing new about the theory of embourgeoisement. Goldthorpe *et al.* (1969) trace the origins of the theory back to the concerns of Engels' writing in the 1870s and 80s, emphasising the appparent craving for respectability and willingness of British workers to embrace bourgeoise social values, life-styles and political ideas. Understood in this way, the problem with embourgeoisement is that it seems to be taking rather a long time to work itself out empirically. Moreover in Engels' formulation the process was seen as an explanation of an exceptional and temporary development, the affluence of the British worker built upon the colonial exploitation of the first industrial nation. It is therefore perhaps more useful to stress the individual phases of embourgeoisement theorisation than to emphasise a unitary continuity of the phenomenon.

The first wave of post-war embourgeoisement theory was far more part of a general theory of how mature capitalism works than were earlier more particular versions of the thesis (e.g. Carr-Saunders and Caradog-Jones, 1927, 1937). Yet the historical timescale for the development of this general theory was relatively short. The optimism expressed in the liberal version of the theory was an abrupt transformation from the extreme pessimism expressed by many liberal thinkers towards the end of the Second World War. Thus, commenting in 1943 on the prospects for the US economy in the post-war period, the economist Samuelson expected a 'nightmarish combination of the worst features of inflation and deflation . . . there would be ushered in the greatest period of unemployment and industrial dislocation which any economy has ever faced' (1943: 51). A similar outlook led Joseph Schumpeter to suggest in 1945 that: 'The all but general opinion seems to be that capitalist methods will be unequal to the task of reconstruction. (It is) not open to doubt that the decay of capitalist society is very far advanced' (quoted in Armstrong *et al.*, 1984: 23). Thus it is no coincidence that the specific form of embourgeoisement thesis which developed in the post-war period only crystallised once the long boom was well under way, in spite of the claims of some to have identified 'the logic of industrialism' (Kerr, 1960). Most of the presentations were written at the general theoretical level, with both liberal and Marxist versions relying upon a straightforward economic and/or technological determinism with little direct evidence of the actions of individual agents. One notable exception to this was Zweig's *The Worker in an Affluent Society* (1961). The study began as an investigation into the intersection of family and industrial life but became more broadly focused upon social change and post-war development.

The work is interesting for the presentation of its own methodology. It is far more consciously 'scientific' than many of the community studies. A triangulation of methods is used with five principal approaches. Firstly, survey methods were deployed interviewing respondents using a standardised schedule. Secondly, a 'test' for cultural horizons was developed. Thirdly, responses to sets of provocative sayings and proverbs were analysed. Fourthly, 'qualitative material' was used, and finally historical records and statistics of individual firms were included. Despite, or perhaps because of, this 'scientific' approach much that we are presented with resembles the kind of analysis we were treated to in the post-war 'pathology' studies. (This should not surprise us given Ferdynand Zweig's contribution to Rowntree and Laver's study.) Thus we are informed by the author that most people readily gave their consent to be interviewed, however, 'It was mostly shy or backward types who refused to come to my office' (Zweig, 1961: xiv). We are not told what are the basis of such evaluations, given that these people refused to see the author. More serious, however, are the failings of the analysis apparent throughout the text where interesting findings are continually devalued through the insertion of gross value judgements. Thus we are informed that married men are more fully developed personalities than single men (p. 159), that working people display 'flock-like behaviour' not only in patterns of acquisition but also more generally in terms of attitudes. Clearly in the latter case such interpretation devalues the coherence of experience of those being studied.

Zweig identifies a process of homeostasis in working-class life which, when coupled with an observed lack of alienation and developing trend to acquisitiveness, has an affect upon the working-class 'man' which 'loosen the sense of identity with his own class, to which he is bound no longer by the links of common hardships, handicaps and injustices, and the constant call to arms in class warfare' (Zweig, 1961: 69). The evidence for such claims are interesting, for whilst theories of embourgeoisement at the general level display economic and technological determinism, Zweig's presentation is, at least at important points, idealist. Thus at one point it is suggested that drunkenness among the working class is declining and temperance is on the rise, furthermore that the benefits of temperance can be seen in car and home ownership. This is seen as the working class conforming to a more middle-class attitude and way of life – the moral rise of the working class is accentuated. Nowhere does Zweig consider that the series of causation may be the reverse, i.e. that home and car ownership takes resources previously spent on drink. Or that the tendency towards car and home ownership is the upshot of the material process, not so much affluence *per se* but rather an unprecedented period of economic stability.

At many points throughout the book the author devalues what he cannot comprehend, that which fails to conform to his own vision of the world. Nowhere is this more apparent than in his treatment of that well-worn theme of cultural horizons. His test for cultural horizons, which sounds so scientific in the introduction, turns out to be a list of ten 'great' names. The test involves identifying what these people were famous for, thus Karl Marx = philosopher/social theorist, Einstein = scientist, etc. After completing these 'tests' the author concludes pessimistically upon the cultural horizons of the working class, several of whom thought Nijinski was a race horse. However, he seems to take for granted that all sections of the middle class would have scored far higher in these tests. We are informed that 'the working man's culture is much more present day minded than that of other classes' (p. 93) and that their cultural horizons are generally low. He goes on to suggest a possible connection between a low cultural horizon, as established by the test, and a low IQ, for those who scored the lowest also had 'expressed themselves very poorly and their vocabulary was rather scanty.' But:

Sometimes, however, even among these men one could meet a wit and intelligence which was rather surprising. They had native reserves of intelligence which had not been tapped and which might perhaps have been developed by stimulation from the outside. (Zweig 1961: 94)

Such observations in a book purporting to witness a grounded case of embourgeoisement indicate that the process, in the author's eyes, could not be too far advanced. The echoes of past pathological accounts of working-class essence are clearly audible in this study. Ironically such echoes are boosted to a volume comparable to their original level in the work of a theorist who could be seen to represent a second wave of organicist writing, namely Jeremy Seabrook.

In a number of studies Jeremy Seabrook has, following Richard Hoggart, expressed a consistent message that the working class has become impoverished amid a world of material wealth. The prospect identified by Hoggart in *The Uses of Literacy* (1957) has aparently reached its apogee, the death of socialism and the acceptance of capitalism by working class people is total. Thus we are treated to a characteristic vision of what working-class people have become in Seabrook's book *Unemployment* (1982) where we meet Dave in the Wheatsheaf pub in Sunderland:

'I'm very right-wing. There's too many people in the nick who ought to be at the end of a rope. You go and do a bank, spill blood like it was milk, only eight or ten years. It's ridiculous. I've got no time to worry about mankind, I'm too busy worrying about myself. I think everybody is selfish, everybody is out for himself. All our brothers! What brothers? I don't believe it. What happens in Asia, Africa, that's their fucking bad luck. And when they come here, give them handouts, offer them houses. It's asking for trouble if you can't house your own people. I don't believe in unions – the only union I believe in is a guy and a chick coming together for a good fuck: I don't worry about the bomb either; the only big bang I'm concerned with is the one I might get tonight.'

Such accounts are repeated in most of Seabrook's works (1978, 1985, 1988). The degradation that they show arguably goes beyond the illustration of the material reality of working-class life in Britain after the collapse of the long boom, as Huw Beynon has argued in addressing the purpose behind Seabrook's genre:

In the 1930's, Orwell . . . was concerned to shock the middle class; his aim was to show them how wretched were the lives endured by the workers whose energies were at the very foundation of society. Seabrook, in contrast, details how wretched are the workers themselves, and how their lives have come to perpetuate the capitalist order. (Beynon, 1982: 289)

Seabrook, of course, is in theory sympathetic to those caught in such a dehumanised existence, but in his writing has taken great pains to reproduce what Beynon has argued is at best a partial picture of working-class life. For example, had Seabrook come to the Wheatsheaf at Sunderland on a Sunday night rather than a Monday he could well have talked to me and an assortment of miners, shipbuilding workers, etc.

who regularly attended a trade union studies group there, but this would not have fitted very well into his account. What we are left with is a view of the world and working people which is clearly pathological: 'Prosperity, which was to have raised their eyes above the pitiful horizon of blinkered insufficiency, has plunged them rather into the consolations of forgetfulness' (Blackwell and Seabrook, 1993: 10). The recurring theme of pathology is clearly a strong one which emanates from writers with various political views. How are we to understand the significance of this theme in the context of the crisis in class theory?

Conclusion

The attack by Saunders (1989) on the salience of retaining social class as a useful indicator of social difference is premised upon the suggestion that other sources of stratification and identity have clearly assumed a greater importance. What I believe an examination of the historically emerging portrayal of the working class displays is the need to appreciate both the continued perceptual gulf that exists between the normality of life as it is lived, the double-tongued signs which such life indicates, and the way in which such accounts must be located reflexively within the the changing structures and processes of class society itself. These concerns impact both on methodologies and the reflexive situation of those who do the writing and those who are written about. The recurring theme of pathology in studies of the working class illustrates well both of these issues. If we look to a comparison between the pathology that is evident in accounts of the working class in the first wave of community studies and the accounts of Seabrook we can illustrate these dimensions.

In the first wave of community studies the deployment of paradigms drawn from psychology and psychiatry dominated. The assumption of pathology and middle-class superiority was present in the very conception of these projects. Its basis confirms very directly the class divisions that existed between those that were writing and those that were written about. The yawning gulf that separates the researchers from the researched is evident to an extent that makes the embourgeoisement thesis championed in the inter-war period by Carr-Saunders and Caradog-Jones appear patently ridiculous. In such a context we could hardly expect the deployment of a sophisticated attempt at *verstehen*, appreciating the world from the actor's point of view.

The world of the 1980s and 1990s is of course in many respects very different from the world in 1945. The long boom announced its appearance and eventual demise. The welfare state and expansion of the education system was to some extent built upon this economic wellbeing. High levels of absolute social mobility were recorded, including those academically-minded working-class scholars like Seabrook himself.

Therefore the pathology that emerges in his accounts of contemporary working-class life cannot surely be of the same sort as that of the first wave of community studies. Seabrook apparently lets people speak for themselves and yet he chooses his respondents carefully. Community and political activists are avoided, as is the world of work. We are not given any account of the possible tension between what is said and how life might actually be lived on a day-to-day basis. Seabrook rarely takes the trouble to stay in one place long enough to appreciate such a possible tension. He rather goes from town to town capturing quotations which validate notions of increasing degradation and then moves on to do the same elsewhere. Working-class life is represented as it is captured only in presented discourse. People are speaking for themselves but within the constraints of the interview situation or as snippets overheard on bus journeys, etc. Seabrook's loss of roots in the working-class childhood of his past are replicated in his rootless sociology. His presentation of pathology is not, then, the absolute rendering of social distance that we encounter in the first wave of community studies but rather is the sad regret of the rootlessness that social mobility so often brings. Both portrayals of the pathology of the working class, then, are to be related to the dynamics of the wider class-divided society, the former in the historically more rigid structural conditions of the immediate post-war period, the latter in the context of a society displaying higher levels of absolute social mobility.

In respect of more recent times, then, the notion of the ladder analogy of social mobility outlined by Raymond Williams seems apposite. Social mobility remains an individual experience. The fact of such mobility does not alter the basically class-divided nature of society, although the phenomenal dilemmas of living that people confront do clearly change. The reflexive study of the historically evolving portrayal of working-class life does not suggest that class has dissolved. On the contrary, the gap between those who do the writing and those who are written about seems to be widening.

CHAPTER 11

Sexual segregation and community[1]

FRANK ENNIS

Introduction

The notion of community is associated with concepts of social cohesion and order. The community represents, or is held to represent, the quintessence of all that is considered good in human relations. This is no accident. Tönnies, the founding figure of the sociology of community, in the detailing of Gemeinschaft relations, praised this socio-cultural form for the benefits that it brought to society as a whole and the individual in particular (Tönnies: 1957). He identified the community as constituted from relationships which were enduring and intimate, where a person knew their place in society, understood their own worth. The community is characterised by Gemeinschaft relations which represent for the individual emotional cohesion, depth, continuity and fullness (Bell and Newby, 1971: 24). As a consequence of Tönnies' delineation of the nature of community, subsequent investigations, whether conducted at a theoretical or an empirical level, have been concerned with embellishing this basic structure.

Those who followed in the wake of Tönnies have all considered community as an organic structure, wherein the groups and individuals who are part of it act to generate social cohesion and stability. Community is always viewed positively, always assessed in terms of its contribution to stability between groups and individuals. Yet all this activity has generated little which provides the basis for an objective assessment of this cultural construct. Stacey raised the question of whether the 'concept was a useful abstraction' (1969: 134). Cohen pointed out that 'all definitions of community contain or imply theories' (1985: 11), while Bell and Newby warned against the incorporation of normative prescription in community studies (1971: 252).

The source of this problem is not difficult to determine. Tönnies not only provided the framework for investigation but supplied the initial 'normative prescription' which writers and researchers have accepted unquestioningly. The task for most researchers has been to identify the elements which generate stability in a particular social structure. What that has meant is that empirical work has invariably sought to flesh out the organic structure of any particular community under investigation.

That is not to say that there have not been theoretical developments. The nature and functioning of the organic structure which is held to be community has been elaborated and embellished by other writers. The Chicago School adopted a social ecology approach whose basic premise was that society could be considered a living organism, each part interacting with other parts for the benefit of the whole. The structural-functionalism school of thought as exemplified by Parsons presumed that the individuals and institutions within any social system will gravitate towards an equilibrium state and that they act to ensure that stability and social cohesion is maintained. This is made possible because all of the individuals within the system have agreed values, beliefs and objectives. Consequently all individuals and groups within the system act in order to sustain the system (Parsons, 1951).

This perspective, which informed much social anthropological thought in the early and middle parts of the twentieth century, provided the basis for the examination of industrial communities. Though more developed than Tönnies' Gemeinschaft, the similarity of concerns is evident. Structural-functionalism rests on an organic analogy which presumes that human society can be evaluated as if it were a living organism.

Though the structural-functionalism has been discredited (see Lee and Newby, 1983), the basic premise for community outlined by Tönnies – the notion of community as an organic structure – still provides the agenda for research. The yardstick for developing a sociology of community is the Gemeinschaft as detailed by Tönnies. The aim of researchers is to determine the significance of homogeneity, locality and the family – the critical elements of the organic structure – in generating social cohesion.

While this article will throw up questions about the validity of the organic structure approach in setting an agenda for research and will suggest that many community studies are based on no more than the application of a normative prescription, it must be borne in mind that researchers have perhaps simply taken on board what their informants – i.e. members of the community – have told them. What many community studies do demonstrate is the great value that people place on the family and those social relations which generate neighbourliness and sociability. The family, the neighbourhood and the workplace are critical areas of interaction in everyday life – frequently one or more of these areas is viewed positively by informants. The lack of a critical purview may arise because such representations emanating from the study of everyday life appear to confirm the viability of this 'normative prescription'.

The subject matter of this article will be working-class communities in the north-east of England. Reference here is made to communities generated as part of the industrialisation of the north-east in the second half of the nineteenth century. These communities were thus identified by their association with the dominant industry which provided the economic wherewithal for their existence. The source material will be derived from oral history archives found in the north-east. Two of these archives, the Miners History Project (MHP)[2] and Easington District Council – Past and Present Archive (EDC) were collected with a view to recording the remembrances of those who had lived in mining communities which it was believed were about to disappear. The majority of the recollections relate to the experiences of those who lived in mining villages. A third archive covers the experiences of women who worked in shipbuilding on the Tyne and Wear during the Second World War (WIS).[3] A fourth source of oral history data was the result of research into the Jarrow March (JMT).[4] In addition, interview material collected in the course of doctoral research between 1982 and 1986 (DR) is utilised. What is important about all of this material is that it has been provided by people who lived in industrial communities for all or most of their lives. Consequently, the data provides information on the experience of living in these communities during the twentieth century.

The particular focus for this article will be on gender roles within these communities. This is a critical area. The organic structure approach identifies the family as an archetypal sub-system for community. Tönnies states that the family is the 'prototype of all unions of Gemeinschaft'. He developed this further by stating that the prototype of the family persists in all Gemeinschaft associations. The fundamental social relationship was as that 'between master and servant, or, better, between master and disciple'. Tönnies saw the family as based on patriarchal control – i.e. power and authority are vested in the male. The family functions as a unit which socialises its members in the values and beliefs of the community and acts to constrain the behaviour of members under the authority of the male head. This focus on the family as a unit in which women and men act out different roles means that the allocation of gender roles is subsumed by considerations of the functioning of the family as a unit. Such a perspective neglects a proper consideration of the sexual division of labour in understanding the operation of social structures. The presumption is that men and women undertake their respective tasks for the benefit of social cohesion and stability. This precludes consideration of how the norms, values and beliefs operate to maintain a gender division. Most importantly, a perspective derived from an agenda set by notions of an organic structure does not allow for the fact that the segregation of the sexes may in fact be a critical organising principle of community structure. It is to these issues we now turn.

Organic structure and gender differentiation

Community studies have not neglected consideration of the sexual division of labour. The different tasks undertaken by women and men have been documented. This is part of the agenda for determining the operation of the organic structure of a particular community. All groups and individuals are presumed to make a contribution to the stability of social relations. Every act is assessed with respect to the notion that the maintenance of social cohesion is the objective for all. Yet such studies, with their focus on family as a sub-system within an organic structure, do not give proper emphasis to the significance of the sexual division of labour.

The organic structure approach, derived from Tönnies as modified by structural-functionalist schools, can be discerned in the study of industrial communities. A clear example of this is provided by *Coal is our Life*, the study of Ashton, a mining community in the Yorkshire coal field. The authors did not state the theoretical premises from which their research methodology was derived. Reading the report, it is apparent that the authors utilised the organic structure approach, appropriately modified by concepts derived from structural-functionalism as the basis for their research methodology.

The authors begin by utilising the industrial structure of the locality as the criterion for determining the socio-cultural boundary. The spatial limits of the industrial structure are thus held to determine the community's socio-cultural identity. It becomes possible to define the spatial limits of the community. Dennis *et al.* set the parameters for their evaluation thus:

Ashton is a predominantly working-class town owing its development to the growth of its collieries. The latter have drawn people and houses around them, the main pit is almost in the centre of the town. But the collieries have exercised a centripetal influence in other ways. Most of the men in Ashton are miners. The cohesive results of these facts are well-known. First, there is the inapplicability of the miner's skill to the other trades. Secondly there is the long history of acrimonious disputes for which the coal industry is notorious. Common memories of past struggle have undoubtedly helped to bind a community such as Ashton. (Dennis *et al.* 1956: 14)

Having defined the spatial characteristics of the town dominated by the collieries, the authors state that it is the common experience that men have of working in coal-mining which provide the basis for homogeneity in the community and is hence a critical factor in generating social cohesion. The miners (and the community) have acquired, it is argued, a common set of values and beliefs because of their common past. It is the 'cohesive results' of the men working together in one industry. The cohesion is based on the isolating character of the miner's skill and the 'long history of acrimonious disputes'. It is the male experience which the authors identify as the key integrating factor in this community.

Women are considered as a marginal group in Ashton. Though Dennis *et al.* describe their experiences, their influence on community norms is considered minimal. The role for a woman according to 'the consciously accepted the division of labour' is to 'keep in good order the household provided for by the money handed to her each Friday by her husband' (Dennis *et al.*, 1956: 181). That role also requires women to take responsibility for child care. Here the objective is clear. A mother is to 'rear boys to be miners and girls to be their wives' (*ibid.*: 235). The authors in their conclusions on the role of the family echo the propositions of Tönnies and the structural-functionalists in stating that 'the function of the family is as a mechanism for perpetuating the social structure, not only in terms of the production of the social personalities required by ... [the] community' (Dennis *et al.*, 1956: 245).

When women act in a manner which does not conform to this role, they are identified as a disruptive force:

> While the nature of the work and the history of the industry in Ashton have thrown men together in this way, they have exerted an opposite or centrifugal force on women. The coal industry provides no paid work for them. In an area where there is no alternative they have to do without it. Ashton, however, lying as it does in the reach of the coal zone of the West Yorkshire industrial region, is within reach of alternatives. (Dennis *et al.*, 1956: 14)

In this interpretation it is men through the integrating influences of their work experience who provide the cohesive 'centripetal' forces in Ashton, while women are identified as disruptive. In the case of Ashton this is because women can take up employment outside the community. The implication here is that in order for cohesion and stability to be maintained women should not take up employment outside the community. It is no accident that the authors come to this conclusion. As Johns remarks, Dennis, Henriques and Slaughter have internalised the male miner's eye view of the community (Johns, 1980: 15). The consequence of this is that: 'The relations of production at work are lovingly described; the relations of production in the home and community are ignored with equal determination' (Frankenburg, 1976: 37). The authors, in adopting the miners' perspective, see women as an object or the enemy of the male – 'a passive object for whom he is driven to underground work' (*ibid.*). The authors place little value on the work of women even in the domestic role.

With an understanding of the community as moving towards equilibrium and a belief that the community's institutions function in order to integrate the groups and individuals which constitute the community, the inevitable focus of the authors has been on the public, i.e. male-dominated sphere. Hence mining work, trade unions, working-men's clubs are examined for their positive effects in generating social cohesion and stability. The authors do not, as Frankenburg observes, examine the consequences of this male solidarity for women:

> The responsibility of women for housekeeping and childcaring, the solidarity of the male peer group reinforced by shared work hazards, shared pit language, shared clubs and shared interest in Rugby League, led to a situation in which men reacted against exploitation not as a class against capitalism, but as a gender group against women – or rather within the framework of sex solidarity against a specific woman chosen and caged for this express purpose. (*ibid.*: 40)

While not all writers adopt the perspective of informants so readily, a continuing feature of such studies is the implication that the proper place for women is in the domestic environment. Thus, Williamson in his account of the Northumberland mining village, Throckley, states that without women this community (and others) would have been no more than 'labour camps' (1982: 118). While superficially this is intended to re-assess women's historical role and to re-evaluate women's work it can be construed as re-affirming that 'a women's place is in the home'. The basic assumption implied here is that the only way a mining village can be satisfactorily organised is in the manner he described. The pattern is familiar – a community based on family units, divided on gender lines, where men function as breadwinners and women as housekeepers. It presumes the inherent incapacity of men to provision themselves and implies that the ascribed role for women is proper and apt.

Because Williamson identifies women as essential to the community in terms of their activities in the private sphere, he does no more than reinforce the typical view of the role of women in these communities. Women's activities became the badge of community. Their subordination, however praised, however celebrated, becomes an essential part of the organic structure.

By starting from the perspective of community as an organic structure in which groups and organisations are considered as acting, consciously or unconsciously, towards equilibrium, in the interests of social cohesion, issues relating to the nature and origins of the gender division within community are subsumed by a perspective of the family as the basic unit of the community.

What we can argue is that what Dennis *et al.* and Williamson describe is a socio-cultural unit the critical feature of whose organisation is the gender division. Neither study examines the significance of this in terms of the structuring and organisation of the community. It can be argued that the gender divide is the key feature in the structuring of community and that within the community there are only two fundamental groups – women and men. Role differentiation within the family reflects a wider gender division within the community as a whole rather than constituting a basic unit of society. The family in this case is not the prototype of community relations as Tönnies argued but rather a reflection of the wider division which characterises the community and society as a whole. The family is not the site from which this division is produced, but instead the site of its operation.

Maintaining the boundaries

The functionalist view of community argues states that it is the needs of the family which causes gender differentiation (see Parsons, 1951). Women and men adopt roles which are the most appropriate for them to fill for the benefit of the family and the wider community. What is absent in considerations of these structures is understanding of the means by which this division is maintained. It can be argued that though the community may generate stability, the question is whether the notion of organic structure is an adequate explanation of how gender roles are determined. Is the maintenance of ascribed roles for women and men the consequence of autonomic behaviour, a result of the community and the family functioning in the manner of an organism? In this section we examine the means by which the woman's role is sustained in and by the community.

Typical cultural terms for gender roles were elaborated by a Consett steelworker. Writing in the 1930s, in an overly romantic celebration of his work, he defined male/female relations thus: 'we are as the lords of creation and it is for the women to do the serving and tending' (Watson, 1978: 239). The 'lords of creation', working-class men are invested with this deistic authority through making steel:

> To labour at the furnace is a man's job. There is no problem of sacrificing one's masculinity as there is with clerical work, machine minding, and the like. When the flames from a cast of iron leap up at us like an inferno, when we are weary of the dull grind of incessantly shovelling hot wet sand, I and my mates may curse the day we were born, but the time comes when the iron is safe and at rest and one is free to go home; then it is sweet to have pitted one's strength against the elemental forces. (*ibid.*: 226–7)

Despite the extreme imagery employed by Watson this extract lays bare the premises which govern male/female relationships: men affirm their masculinity in their struggle with 'elemental forces' while women remain in the background 'serving and tending'. In the north-east, in the traditional working-class community, the legitimacy of that claim was acknowledged by the attention to serving men which women and family members gave in mining villages:

> Me mam used to look out of the window for the bus coming down. And as soon as she saw the bus the dinner had to be . . . [served]. Then she'd start to lift the dinner. (DR, 1985)

> I've been in a house where a man was getting up at teatime. He was going to have eggs for his tea. And there was somebody put at the foot of the stairs to say when he was coming so that the egg would be just three-and-a-half minutes when he came. He shouldn't have to wait for it. It shouldn't be spoiled. (DR, 1985)

The subservience of women to men's needs in such cases is the consequence of the power and authority vested in men as 'head of the family'. Men were socialised from an early age to expect service from women, as this anecdote demonstrates:

> There's one thing you have to understand in a place like Ashington or Bedlington where you're very 'colliery' the little boys come to school absolutely helpless.

The little girls can fasten their pants up and fasten their slippers and do all that sort of thing. But the little boys they've been looked after. They are the men. (DR, 1985)

In the traditional working-class community the boundaries are clear-cut. Transgression of boundaries invokes the operation of cultural constraints:

If a married woman went out and worked, Oh she would have been talked about. But mind, I've gone to the 'blast' [beach] and carried bags of coal, up off the beach. (EDC, 1976: 50)

If a man had been seen pushing a pram before 1940 he would have been a laughing-stock. And to do housework, that would have been humiliating. (JMT, 1982: 5)

Women working in employment outside the home attracted moral censure. Men who did housework or child care faced ridicule. The different manifestations of cultural constraints reflect the different evaluations put upon these 'intrusions'. Housework, etc. for men was considered demeaning (hence laughable), employment for women threatening to the moral order (hence censurable). We are reminded here of the low status associated with women's work – housekeeping and child care. Even in the 1930s, unemployed men with time on their hands did not share responsibility for management of the home with their partners (see Ennis, 1982: 68–9).

Instances of domestic co-operation between wife and husband do emerge occasionally from archival material:

as soon as the meals were finished he used to wash the dishes . . . he would work and wash . . . he would do all sorts. . . . We never went out without one another. . . . If I couldn't get out for the bairns well he would stop in so we made the arrangement, that one didn't go out without the other. I mean I worked just as hard as him. (WIS, 1984: 22)

While this is evidence of the stereotypical female/male roles being re-negotiated, it is not a total re-working. The husband 'helped' rather than shared – such arrangements were based on individual, personal inclination rather than socio-cultural premises.

As men were breadwinners the amount of money that women received from the family purse depended upon the attitude of their partners. The organic structure did not include any predetermined rules for the division of the 'family wage'. As a 'lord of creation' the husband determined the allocation. This could mean that socialising with workmates was more important than supporting his family, as a Jarrow woman explained:

There'd be more mothers than me would be ambitious for their family. And wanted them to go to the secondary school. . . . All my four girls went to school till they were 16 and that was another struggle . . . cos . . . the Dad drank. I didn't get the money I should have got. . . . He must have been making an awful lot of money then. I was only getting about £6 a week then. He was a rivetter. And he was one of those, he went out. He liked his pocket full of money. (JMT, 1982: 10)

What this indicates is the superordinate position that men held in the communities. That position in some cases was reinforced by physical coercion. This, as a Jarrow woman who worked as a welder during the war explained, was considered a man's 'right':

the lads in the shipyard . . . somebody would get married and they'd say 'How long have you been married?' 'A fortnight.' 'Have you not given her a good hiding yet?' (WIS, 1983: 7)

Even when the man was unemployed he retained that 'right':

My father used to hit my mam. It was the way of life. . . . Right up the street the men used to stand in bands. It was more that they didn't have a job and poverty that got them down. But it was the women and kids who were suffering with the men. But somehow or other they thought they were very badly done by, but the women and kids suffered more. (WIS, 1983: 7)

In this case, the woman justified her father's actions by explaining that he 'felt responsible for his family and he couldn't work to support them. He felt a failure' (*ibid.*). Unemployment was offered as the reason here. But in Ashton it was employment and its frustrations which were identified as the cause (Dennis *et al.*, 1956: 249).[5] In Consett, service from women – with the potential for coercion in default – was derived from the male's position as 'a lord of creation'. The frame of reference for the female/male relationship was not in fact determined by the structures of unemployment, employment or deistic potential. The referential framework of those relations is founded on a cultural separation between the public and the private – the former being identified as the male realm, the latter female. Their most familiar representation is in the family unit – with the male as breadwinner entering the public world and the female as breadserver operating within the private. What is critical is the value set on male activities in the public realm and the view that women should 'serve and tend' men.

While, for the majority of women, these examples of the family relationship may demonstrate the exception rather than the rule, the pre-eminence of men in the community was not in doubt. Such behaviour coloured women's assessments of their partners. A man who did not drink heavily, who did not offer violence and who was generous with his wages was valued positively by women. But this did not mean that such men lost their superordinate status. This was a consequence of male dominance in the public sphere. For the life for a working-class woman was one spent mainly in the 'private sphere of the home, family and neighbourhood' (Roberts, 1984: 2). This restrictive nature of this space and the inherent inequality was recognised explicitly by some female informants. A wartime welder commented:

it's never really bothered me being equal. You know, I'm married. I've got a family. I've got a home and I'm content with my lot. Mind, if I was young I might be different. . . . If I had my youth back. . . . Yes if I had the opportunity. You see in my day . . . when I was in my 'teens', they didn't have the opportunity to do that kind of thing. Now they get the opportunity and I think if I had my time over again, in this age, I would be the same as the rest . . . that go for a career . . . if I had the education . . . and I had . . . say, degrees. University degrees the same as anybody else – well I think I would expect to be paid the same you know. (WIS, 1983: 3)

While this assessment of opportunities is undoubtedly over-optimistic, in her assessment of her past she acknowledges that marriage, home-making and child care were the only available long-term options open to her and other north-eastern women. Though women moved from the private sphere into the public in wartime, the constraints placed on them operated still:

I went down to Jarrow to see the film – called *The Wicked Lady*. It came out during the war, and was at the Empire in Jarrow. And the last bus up to Prim-rose was half-past nine but it didn't come out until quarter to eleven . . . I was by myself. . . . My mother had put the bairn to bed. My mother knew where I was but my father didn't even know I was out. He thought I had gone to bed. . . . Anyway I came round the corner and stopped at the gate. And he looked and as I say it was blackout . . . he peered right up to my face and he says 'What are you doing out?' I says 'I've been to the pictures.' That was the one and only time I went to the pictures during the whole of the war . . . I got in the house and he says 'Coming in at quarter past eleven at night while your husband is fighting at the front', he says 'Not under my bloody roof you don't.' And I never went out any more. . . . I was married, and I was still being told what to do, but I was living in his house you see. That was the attitude. (WIS, 1983: 7)

Patriarchal control of the movement of women in public space – male space – is evident here. That patriarchal power was (and is) founded on a rigid separation along gender lines which not even the woman's marital status nor her independence as a wage-earner (electrician in Hawthorn-Leslie's, Hebburn) could confound. Beyond these restraints which came from the family, the wider community could not countenance a woman going beyond the bounds of her ascribed role:

When the war was over I saw an advert in the paper for a welder – working in a garage. Well I'd enjoyed welding and thought I could do some more and earn money. But the man at the garage just laughed when I turned up and said that he wouldn't employ a woman. (WIS, 1983: 22)

The employment of women in the shipbuilding industry had been con-sidered as only temporary, undertaken for the duration of the war. For most women this work was a satisfying experience. It was stimulating and they had the satisfaction of a wage packet. Though reluctant to give up the work they accepted the view of the community that they had to return to the domestic sphere, as this observation demonstrates:

I think I would have gone out myself [to take up paid employment] but my husband liked his home comforts, he wanted me there when he came in from work. Because when the bairns grew up (by then I had two) and when I think they were 11 or 12 years old I had got a part-time job. But it meant I wasn't in for him coming in for his tea and he didn't like that. He wanted me to sort of have his tea ready and see that the bairns were well looked after. They were anyway you know, I wouldn't leave them running the streets. But he liked his home comforts and he used to say 'Oh you stop at home and I'll go out to work'.[6] (WIS, 1983: 3)

The difficulty for women in reacting against the limitations imposed upon them by this community structure was that the role they fulfilled was of vital importance to the community. They were engaged in the physical and social reproduction of the community's values and beliefs, as Roberts states:

Women's dual role as family financial manager and moral guide cannot be underestimated. She acted within tight financial and social constraints. However good her managerial abilities, she was necessarily restricted by the family's income; she was further restricted in her choice of action by the moves of her family, her kinship group, and her neighbourhood. She was, of course, limited by her actual physical environment, her home; finally, she would generally be hampered by frequent and prolonged childbearing. (1984: 125)

Conceptual definitions of this kind as the basis for self-assessment are rare in archival material. Most informants (women and men) justify their acts using a narrative form. The structure which defines and constrains is rarely addressed. It is the acts which are described and behind them lies the moral text which unspokenly validates them. Thus the ingenuity and inventiveness which women displayed in fulfilling their role is described in terms of what was done:

Three uncles. I had three lodgers with me. I had him and my boy. I used to start on a Thursday morning, I used to bake eight loaves of white bread, four loaves of brown, a dozen tea cakes, spice and rice. I used to do a big lump of ham, pease pudding. You have no idea what I used to make. I stood there from first thing on a Thursday morning 'till twelve o'clock on a Thursday night baking. (EDC, 1976: 15)

For another informant, it was the statement 'we had a dinner every day' which is critical (JMT, 1981: 6). Providing this in the 1930s during the time of hardship (her husband was unemployed for nine years) became a symbol of personal worth, personal worth whose features are defined by the space in which she operated. As Murcott has observed, providing 'a proper meal' is a key requirement for fulfilling the female role:

Effectively a proper meal is a cooked dinner. This is the one which women feel is necessary to their family's health, welfare and, indeed, happiness. It is a meal to come home to, a meal which should figure two, three or four times in the week, especially on Sundays. (Murcott, 1983: 80)

For this informant, her work was validated by the remembrance of those times by her five children:

(we) often talk about it now. They often sit and talk the lot of them. How they used to like their dinners y'know. We used to all sit round the table together. Happy days. They were happy days. We were quite happy. (JMT, 1981: 6)

The physical demands placed on women in pursuit of their role fulfil-ment were matched by emotional demands made upon them at the centre of the family's attention. A necessary role requirement was that women be continually present in the home. Breaks, relief from this situation were rare. One informant described how she and her neigh-bour both found relief through working in Clelland's shipyard during the Second World War:

I never missed nothing. I kept them clean and looked after their bellies. See that they were fed. I mean in those days it was all home-made bread . . . I did all that – washing and everything. I've seen me go to bed at one o'clock in the morn-ing – dead beat . . . I didn't like coming home to all those jobs you know, but I liked the shipyard – I loved the work there. We used to go out in the morning. She used to shut her front door and I used to shut mine. And we both used to say 'Thank God we're leaving our troubles behind'. . . . We forgot about our troubles and worries. (WIS, 1984: 11)

In the assessment of their lives women fall back on making a virtue of necessity. As described earlier, women entered marriage and the role of housewife/mother not through choice but as a consequence of socio-cultural constraints which map out a narrow path for their careers. What is significant in this self-assessment is that women evaluate the opera-tion of their lives by stressing the 'hard work' involved in fulfilling their role expectations. Women's acceptance of their role was in part deter-mined by the limitations placed upon them by the wider community and by their own recognition of the importance of what they were required to do. Another integral part of this acceptance was the view that men and women were inherently different, that the space in which they each played out their roles was one which because of this inherent difference necessarily excluded the presence of the other. Earlier it was shown that men considered that female space was an inappropriate one for them to occupy. Women shared this perception of male space, as a woman who worked as a caulker/burner during the Second World War in South Shields stated:

I didn't think shipyards was made for women . . . before I went in I thought oh it's bad. Because I mean men – sometimes they are inclined to forget them-selves aren't they? . . . You know coming out with their language and that. (WIS, 1984: 15)

This woman's acceptance of the notion of a male space – a space where men amongst men can and should behave in a different way to the way in which they behave in the company of women – is another element in women's acceptance of their role within the community. While both women and men internalise the notion of separateness, what is critical is how this was constructed. Following Tönnies, writers have argued that this is an inevitable outcome of the functioning of the organic community. What is suggested here is that the exclusion of women from male concerns and the consequent sexual segregation is an essential organising feature of the community – a 'normative prescription' for the organisation of society rather than the product of either 'nature' or 'function'. The experience of women working in shipbuilding during wartime demonstrates that the 'prescription' can be changed:

> The disruption of war . . . [exposed] the conceptual and material frailty of the boundaries between the masculine public domain of war and work and the feminine private domain of home and family. The family unit was atomised by conscription, women's war work, child care provision outside the home and evaluating a situation accentuated by bomb damage to housing stock. Further, following the blitz in 1940, the provision of communal feeding in Local Authority British Restaurants and in industrial canteens and by the expansion of the school meals service encroached upon, drawing into the public domain that function par excellence – wifely service in the provision of meals – which underpinned the ideology, indeed spirituality of the family and the power relative within it. (Allatt, 1983: 48)

Those areas – child care, cooking, maternal presence – which are the hallmarks of the private sphere were drawn into the public sphere. The primary purpose was to release women as workers for the industrial labour force in order that the conflict be resolved favourably. Their private functions were taken over as a matter of public concern. What this demonstrates is that the determination of what constitutes the public and private changes over time and can be radically altered according to the requirements of specific situations.

Sexual segregation in north-eastern communities is not the consequence of the functioning of an organic structure which is in turn the consequence of the particular circumstances which led to the establishment of these communities. Though initially these communities may have come about because of the location of a particular industry or industries, the exclusion of women from these industries was a deliberate act, engendered by a cultural divide whose source is the wider society. The boundary is maintained arbitrarily, as the experience of women workers in the wartime shipbuilding industry demonstrates. Cultural pressures operate to confine women to the domestic sphere, whereas men operate in the public sphere. This divide is supported by community members who internalise the notions of defined female and male spaces in which it is believed that it is appropriate for women and men to operate.

Sexual segregation: a methodology for the sociology of community?

What has been demonstrated here is that the sociology of community has been undertaken with an agenda which flows from Tönnies' original definition of the community. Those who have followed have utilised the notion of an organic structure as the framework for their investigations. That framework is subjective, containing 'a normative prescription' which sociologists have sought to elaborate and embellish in order that they might demonstrate adequately the functioning of a socio-cultural unit which is considered to provide the paradigm of human organisation.

This is apparent in the work on Ashton by Dennis *et al.* The primary concern of their work is to demonstrate the operation of the organic structure within a mining community. The key focus of their work is the work and leisure experiences of men. The shared values and beliefs on which the presumed homogeneity of the community is based is in the male, public realm. They do not consider the possibility that there exists a different view worthy of investigation amongst that other part of the community – the women who live in this segregated world. Women and the family are presented as adjuncts to men. What is most striking about the first edition of this study is that the authors do not outline any theoretical or methodological premises on which their work is based. Yet this 'community study' is so clearly an attempt to develop Tönnies' organic structure. The study itself lives up to Bell and Newby's typification of community studies as a mixture of 'normative prescription and empirical description'.[7]

The limitations of that approach have been indicated. The organic structure approach means that little weight is given to the importance of sexual segregation as a key feature of community structure, in particular the failure to recognise that the family unit as defined by an organic structure approach neglects adequate consideration of the subordination of women.

The examination of archival material relating to community structure in the north-east of England suggested that a basic principle of community structure is sexual segregation. The exclusion of women did not stem from the unseeing functioning of an organic structure. Instead cultural mechanisms operate to maintain the divide and in particular to exclude women from activities which were the preserve of the male.

A research agenda which takes as its starting-point the premise that sexual segregation is a critical organising feature of community offers the possibility of a more comprehensive examination of the operation of community. It also offers the chance to create a link between the organisation of community and the wider society of which the community is a part.

Notes

1 This article is based on doctoral research conducted between 1982 and 1986. The results of that research can be found in Ennis (1986) 'Time, Person and Place in the North-East of England', unpublished PhD thesis, University of Durham.

2 The full collection of tapes and transcripts is kept at Beamish Museum who kindly allowed this material to be used.

3 This archive now kept at Newcastle Central Library was the product of research undertaken by the author, Ian Roberts and Professor Richard Brown, Department of Sociology and Social Policy, University of Durham. Funding was received from the Nuffield Foundation.

4 The results of this research can be found in Ennis (1982) 'The Jarrow March of 1936 and the Symbolic Expression of Protest', unpublished MA thesis, University of Durham.

5 According to the authors 'women were oppressed by the relationships imposed by the miner's work and dependence on wages' (Dennis *et al.*, 1969: 9).

6 Of course this notion that there was a choice as to who could take up employment was not available at that time. Although women did enter the marketplace in greater numbers post-1945, the opportunities to take up employment which provided a family wage were limited. This was not a real choice for the woman or the man.

7 In the Introduction to the second edition (1969) Henriques tries to make amends for this lack, but the offerings are very thin.

CHAPTER 12

Not working in the inner city: unemployment from the 1970s to the 1990s

MARGARET M. CURRAN

Introduction

Unemployment is a major source of deprivation in an increasingly unequal society. In the 1980s and 1990s the gap between the richest and poorest households in the United Kingdom has widened dramatically. The share of income which goes to the bottom 10 per cent of households has fallen substantially from 4.2 per cent in 1979 to only 3 per cent in 1992–3, whilst the top 10 per cent now command more than a quarter of all household income. As the gap between rich and poor has widened, the unemployed have replaced pensioners as the dominant group amongst the poorest households. The official interpretation is that:

The changing composition of the bottom of the income distribution has been caused by . . . increasing unemployment and self employment as well as an improvement in the income position of pensioners. (Department of Social Security, 1995)

The impact of rising unemployment during this period has been compounded by the consistent trend of government policy to reduce the 'income position' of the unemployed. A stream of policy changes, including the withdrawal of earnings-related supplements, the taxation of benefits, the substitution of Social Fund *loans* for Supplementary Benefit Exceptional Needs *payments*, and the forthcoming introduction of the Job Seekers Allowance, has combined to reduce the resources made available to unemployed people through the benefit system.

The low incomes of unemployed people and their households represent only the tip of the iceberg of the true cost of unemployment to individuals and to society as a whole. For unemployed people the consequences of life without a wage extend well beyond both their status in the labour market and the immediate and pressing threats of poverty, debt, rent arrears or mortgage repossession. The psychological impact of unemployment has received considerable attention from researchers from the pioneering study of Marienthal in the 1930s (Jahoda *et al.*, 1972) to a variety of studies in the 1980s and beyond (for example

Ullah, 1987; Warr, 1987; Burchell, 1993; Gershuny, 1993). A review of this extensive literature is beyond both the scope and the purpose of this paper. It is sufficient to note both Burchell's acknowledgement that 'there is indeed good, well documented evidence that, on aggregate, the unemployed suffer worse psychological health than the employed' and his caution against the simplistic conclusion that psychological ill health is a condition of all of the unemployed and none of the employed (Burchell, 1993: 188). The links between unemployment and physical health are also complex. There is evidence that unemployment is associated with raised mortality rates in both unemployed men and their wives, with particularly high risks of dying through lung cancer, heart disease and suicide (Moser *et al.*, 1987). However, as one review concludes, 'precisely how unemployment kills is still not known' (Office of Health Economics, 1993: 9).

The impact of unemployment spreads beyond the individual both to their personal and social relationships and to the wider community. The Social Change and Economic Life studies in the 1980s found that unemployment was associated both with limited adaptation of the domestic division of labour (Gallie *et al.*, 1993) and with marital dissolution (Lampard, 1993). Although there was 'little sign of the withdrawal into passivity and social isolation that was highlighted in the earlier studies' unemployed people tend to be in segregated social networks which offer weak support in both psychological and material terms (Gallie *et al.*, 1993: 262).

The broader impacts of unemployment on localities and communities are extensive. Although the links between unemployment and crime are complex and contested it cannot be coincidence that a moral panic about crime in general, and street crime in particular, arises when and where there is a high rate of unemployment amongst urban youth. The less newsworthy effects of unemployment on local communities can be devastating:

The impoverishing effect of unemployment on a community is not fully shown by the rate in any month or even year. It is the slow decay over time that leaves many long out of work, others prematurely retired from the labour force and many families faced with only one in two or three generations bringing home a wage. The poverty can generally be seen in both public and private services: poor schools and medical services with insufficient or less qualified staff, [and] limited shopping facilities forcing the poor to pay more. (Sinfield and Showler, 1981: 20)

Unemployment and its consequences are clearly not evenly distributed in either social or spatial terms (Green, 1995). In the early 1990s the media paid considerable attention to the impact of unemployment on formerly affluent, formerly secure sections of the community as the recession hit the middle classes, the suburbs and the South East. There has even been talk of the end of the 'North–South Divide'. However unemployment is still 'a most unequal tax' (Showler and Sinfield, 1981) and unemployment rates remain highest where they have always been highest: amongst the working class, in the inner cities and in the North.

This brief review demonstrates, if demonstration were needed, that unemployed people and their communities pay dearly for the unemployment which Norman Lamont, then Chancellor of the Exchequer, described in 1991 as a price 'well worth paying' to get inflation down. The rest of this paper explores the experience and consequences of unemployment in particular working-class communities in Newcastle upon Tyne, the 'capital city' of North-East England. The starting point lies in research conducted in 1979 by Richard Brown, Jim Cousins and the author, and published by our research sponsor[1] as *Working in the Inner City* (Cousins, Curran and Brown, 1982). The core of the project was the collection of detailed work, and non-work, histories from over 700 residents of three small areas of Newcastle upon Tyne. The aim here is to examine the role of unemployment in the work histories of our survey respondents in the decade from 1969 to 1979, and then address the question 'what happened next?' The experience of survey respondents in the 1970s provides the context for an analysis of evidence from other, secondary, sources, about the circumstances of residents of the same areas in the recessions of the 1980s and 1990s – and in the brief 'boom' which separated them. The evidence suggests that those areas of the city whose residents were disadvantaged in the (comparatively) good years of the 1970s, may well emerge from the second recession in a decade with minimal connection with the world of work.

Areas, methods and sources

The work histories which will be discussed were collected in 1979 in a study of three contrasting small areas of Newcastle upon Tyne: an inner city 'zone of transition' (Elswick), a more traditional settled working-class inner city area (Walker) and an outer city area of working-class council tenants (Denton). The areas selected were not complete wards but were defined as groups of 1971 Census enumeration districts, some of which crossed ward boundaries. The survey areas do not therefore correspond with the boundaries of the current wards which bear the same names. However, in both geographic and social terms Elswick, Walker and Denton wards provide the closest equivalents to the survey areas which can be identified in current statistical sources.

In each survey area we sampled half of all households, and attempted to interview all household members who were economically active, i.e. working or available for work. Our interviewers achieved a response from 81 per cent of households and from 71 per cent of identified economically active individuals. Interviews were completed with a total of 764 economically active residents: 434 [57 per cent] men and 330

[43 per cent] women. The core of the interview was a series of questions about respondents' work and non-work histories in the decade between 1969 and their interviews in the first half of 1979. The discussion in this paper centres on the role of unemployment in these work histories. (For more general analyses see, for example, Cousins, Curran and Brown, 1982; Cousins and Curran, 1982; Brown, 1982.)

The work history data were coded and filed in two distinct but related ways. The main record for each respondent included a summary of their work history including the number, occupational and industrial range of the jobs they had held and whether they had experienced repeated or long-term periods of unemployment. In a second separate data set the unit of analysis is not the individual but a phase in an individual's work history: a discrete period of employment, unemployment or economic inactivity. The record of each period carried details of the preceding and succeeding periods. This means that we can examine how each period of unemployment began, how it ended, and the kind of change in status which it brought about. The dates of these work history periods were also used for a year by year analysis of respondents' transitions between jobs and statuses.

The age structure of the group and, to a lesser extent, the inability of respondents to provide full work histories, leads to lower sample numbers in the earlier years of the decade. The number of respondents for whom work history information is available rises from 511 in 1969 to 764 in 1979. (Figures each year are for February, the month when fieldwork began.) A chronological analysis of respondents' experience of finding and losing jobs throughout the 1970s is used here to track the impact of rising unemployment on their work histories.

The original research design placed some emphasis on the potential differences between the two contrasting inner areas and the outer city area. However the similarities between the employment experiences of residents of the areas proved to be more striking, in many respects, than their differences. We concluded that:

employment related deprivation and disadvantage . . . are not confined to a small distinctive minority of those in manual and routine white collar work, neither are they confined to the inner city . . . .we are dealing with a normal part of urban working class experience. (Cousins, Curran and Brown, 1982: 112)

Where the similarities between the three areas are of more significance than their differences, residents' work histories are analysed together as examples of urban working-class experience.

The discussion of developments in the 1980s and 1990s addresses the key concern of this paper, unemployment in the inner city, by focusing on the two inner-city areas: Walker and Elswick. It is based entirely on ward level analysis of secondary sources: the 1981 and 1991 Censuses of Population, and local analyses of the Employment Department count of unemployed claimants.[2]

Unemployment in the 1970s: incidence and consequence

In February 1979 when the Newcastle survey fieldwork began, the national rate of registered unemployment was reported to be 5.7 per cent, falling to 5.1 per cent in May as fieldwork ended. In the Northern Region unemployment rates were considerably higher: 8.7 per cent and 7.9 per cent respectively. The rate of unemployment in the survey sample was higher still: taking the three areas together we calculated a registered unemployment rate of 10.3 per cent. Because of the high rate of non-registration, particularly amongst women seeking part-time work, this is a serious underestimate of the proportion of respondents who had no job and wanted to work.

On the broader definition of availability for work which was used in the study, 13.6 per cent of the survey sample were unemployed. The men and women who said that they were available for work were active in seeking employment: 95 per cent of the registered unemployed and over 80 per cent of those who were not registered had used some method to try to obtain employment. Many had used most if not all of the means available: registering with Jobcentres (not then a condition for receiving benefit), using private agencies, answering newspaper adverts, approaching employers and making enquiries through friends and relatives. This active job search underlines the genuine availability for work of the non-registered unemployed; in the remaining discussion all respondents who said that they were available for work are described as unemployed.

The 'snapshot' view of the survey respondents early in 1979 showed an unemployment rate of 13.6 per cent: more than one in eight. The summaries of their work histories show that experience of unemployment and job loss during the previous decade was much more widespread. Between 1969 and 1979:

- over a third [38%] had been unemployed at some time
- a quarter had been made redundant
- almost one in six [16%] had spells of unemployment totalling more than twelve months
- almost one in ten [9%] had been unemployed for a continuous period of over a year.

These experiences were most common in the less settled inner area (Elswick) and amongst men, and least common in the outer city area and amongst women. The unemployment rates for men in 1979 were 20 per cent in Elswick, 13 per cent in Walker and 10 per cent in Denton. However unemployment and redundancy were not unusual for either men or women in any of the areas. Experience of each of these forms of labour market deprivation was commonplace even amongst the women living in Denton, the outer area with the lowest unemployment in the survey. Although this group were less disadvantaged than inner-city women,

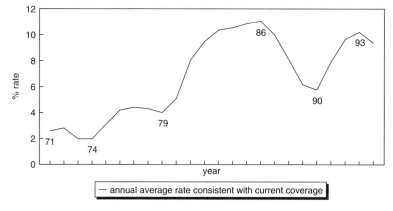

Figure 12.1 **UK unemployment rate 1971–94**

Source: Employment Department.

or men in any area, their histories since 1969 showed that 22 per cent had been unemployed, 9 per cent had been made redundant, 10 per cent had spells of unemployment totalling more than twelve months, and 5 per cent had been unemployed for over a year. In this sense unemployment was a 'normal' part of urban working-class experience in the 1970s, and it transcended both gender and the boundaries of the inner city.

The profile of the respondents who had been unemployed in each year from 1969 to 1979 was remarkably stable:

- about half had left their previous job involuntarily, through redundancy, dismissal or the end of a temporary job
- about half had worked previously in personal service, semi-skilled or unskilled manual occupations, whilst the proportion of the employed in these occupations was closer to a third
- the proportion who came from manufacturing jobs varied from year to year, but the average of a third was very similar to the proportion of the employed who were in manufacturing.

All of the reported experience of being out of work happened in a period when the general level of unemployment appears in retrospect to have been relatively low. The 1970s marked the transition between comparatively full employment in the 1960s and the deep recession of the early 1980s. There was a peak in 1971–2, but unemployment was still comparatively low in the first half of the 1970s. In the wake of the oil crisis, the unemployment rate rose sharply from the beginning of 1974, reaching a peak late in 1977. The survey interviews in 1979 coincided with a 'blip' in the course of two years of slowly falling unemployment which preceded the steep increase in the early 1980s (Figure 12.1).

The peak in unemployment in 1971–2 and the increases from 1974 were associated with a number of features of respondents' experiences

Table 12.1   **Jobs ended and jobs started 1970–8**

Year[1]	Involuntary job endings (per 100 econ. active[2])	% job endings followed by unemployment[3]	% job starts lasting <1 year	% job moves to lower social class[4]
1970	4	21	23	15
1971	5	20	28	15
1972	9	22	39	22
1973	5	19	35	17
1974	7	19	29	17
1975	5	36	33	18
1976	8	30	42	19
1977	8	40	46	21
1978	7	50	n.a.	25

Notes:

1 All years reported have over 100 job starts and over 100 job ends. Fewer than 50 were reported in 1969 and 1979.
2 Economically active = employed or unemployed (February).
3 As % of all job ends followed by employment or unemployment.
4 Includes both direct job changes and changes via unemployment. Registrar General's social classes are ranked from I to V with no manual/non-manual division of III. Experience of the higher social classes (I and II) was confined to a very small minority of respondents.

in the labour market (Table 12.1). The swings in the economic cycle resulted in both direct and indirect impacts on the work histories of individual men and women. In particular rising unemployment:

* increased their chances of losing a job involuntarily, through redundancy, dismissal or the end of a fixed-term job
* increased the chances that the end of a job would be followed by unemployment: the proportion of all job terminations followed by unemployment reached 50% in 1978 and rose to 60% of the (47) job terminations reported in 1979
* reduced the duration of those jobs which were started: the proportion lasting for less than a year rose from 29% in 1974 to 46% of jobs started in 1977. (Since fieldwork was in spring 1979, the durations of jobs begun in 1978 were short: 85% less than a year.)
* diminished the 'quality' of job changes which they were able to make: whether they moved directly from job to job or via a period of unemployment, their chances of moving to a job in a lower social class increased.

In summary, the work histories of these working-class residents of a northern city in the 1970s showed that the experience of being without a job was widespread. Furthermore, the impact of economic change on their working lives extended well beyond the immediate and obvious risk of unemployment. During the unemployment peaks of 1972 and the progressive increase in unemployment from 1974 the jobs which they were able to obtain became more short-term and insecure and they slipped further down the social class scale. Analysis which is not presented here demonstrates the flexibility of their work histories which were 'characterised by substantial mobility between jobs, occupations, socio-economic groups, social classes and industries' (Cousins, Curran and Brown, 1982: 30). The residents of these areas of Newcastle evidently included significant numbers of the recurrently unemployed 'blue jeaned philanthropists of the late 20th century' whose 'virtuous flexibility enables the market economy to work' (Daniel, 1990: 234).

The 1980s and 1990s: claimants counted and the hidden unemployed

The residents of the Newcastle survey areas entered the labour market of the 1980s from a position of considerable flexibility but very little strength. The remaining part of this paper moves on from the detailed analysis of the work histories of the survey sample in the 1970s to explore the evidence which can be gleaned from statistical sources about what happened, in the areas where they lived, in the 1980s and 1990s. All of the information presented relates to residents of the electoral wards which most closely correspond, geographically and socially, to the 1979 survey areas. The correspondence is not exact and this statistical information is not directly comparable with the survey data for reasons of geography, sample coverage, sample selection, etc. Its value lies in the picture it can provide of the kinds of labour market experience which were likely to face the residents of the 1979 survey areas in the 1980s and 1990s.

The discussion will focus on the two inner city areas: Elswick and Walker. The concentration on the inner urban areas reflects a desire for clarity in addressing the key concern of this paper: unemployment in the inner city. It does not mean that the experiences of residents in the outer city area were in any way less problematic in the 1980s and 1990s than they had been in the 1970s. On the contrary, the evidence suggests that their experiences of unemployment and deprivation in the labour market continued to be different in degree, but not essentially in kind, from those of the inner-city residents.

The 1970s and 1980s saw massive changes in the national and local economies. Nationally unemployment rose from 1979 to a peak rate in 1986 which would be recorded as over 10 per cent on even the current basis of the unemployed claimant count. In Tyne and Wear, the county and conurbation of which Newcastle is a part, half of all manufacturing jobs and two thirds of primary sector jobs were lost in 20 years from 1971 to 1991. The 100,000 lost jobs in manufacturing and 25,000 jobs in mining and other primary industries were not replaced by 50,000 new service sector jobs, many of which were part-time (Tyne and Wear Research, 1994a). In the 1990s total employment in the county has apparently been more stable but the structural changes have continued with the end of both coal-mining and shipbuilding on Tyneside and a continuing shift from full- to part-time employment. Nationally and locally, unemployment soared in the early 1980s, then fell to a low point in 1990 before increasing again in the 1990s (Figure 12.1). These broad trends provided the context for changes in unemployment in the inner-city areas from the 1970s to the 1990s.

Information about unemployment in small areas can be obtained from two standard sources: the decennial Censuses of Population and the monthly count of unemployed claimants. The census has the great advantage of allowing analysis of both self-defined unemployment and of other categories of non-employment. Census data will be used here to explore the rates of unemployment and of premature withdrawal from the labour market in 1981 and 1991. The deficiencies of the monthly count of unemployed claimants are well rehearsed and 'it is clear that the general public, many politicians, the media and various pressure groups do not trust the [claimant] unemployment figures or find them convincing' (Royal Statistical Society, 1995: 39). The claimant count does indeed bear all the scars of a by-product of a constantly changing administrative system which has itself become a political football. However, for all its faults, it is a uniquely current indicator of differences in one measure of unemployment between small geographic areas. The absence of any alternative source in the ten years between censuses leads most local labour market analysts to favour cautious use over outright rejection.[3] The extent to which the claimant count undercounts unemployment will not be discussed in detail here, but assessment of a range of sources suggests that 'for every three unemployed claimants [in Tyne and Wear] in 1994 there was probably a fourth person excluded from the official count who had no job and wanted to work' (Tyne and Wear Research, 1995: 20). Because of the effects of benefit regulations women who are seeking work are particularly liable to be excluded from the claimant count. With these caveats, the claimant count will be used to update the assessment of unemployment in the inner-city areas to the mid 1990s.

At the beginning of the period covered by the survey respondents' work histories the 1971 Census recorded unemployment rates in both the inner-city wards which were well above the average for Newcastle, itself well above the national average. In Walker, the traditional riverside industrial area, more than one in ten of the residents who regarded themselves as part of the labour force were seeking work. In Elswick, the ward in the West End of the city with a more unsettled population, the unemployment rate was more than one in eight. By 1981, two years after the survey fieldwork, the rate of unemployment in Newcastle had

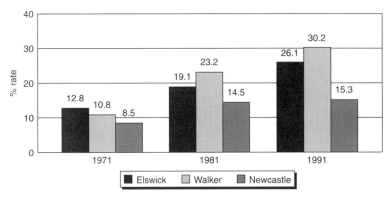

Figure 12.2   **Unemployment in Inner City Wards 1971–91**

Source: Census – reported in City of Newcastle upon Tyne [1993].

increased substantially and the loss of jobs in traditional industries had increased unemployment in Walker to more than 50 per cent above the city average, overtaking that in Elswick. By 1991 three out of ten of the 'economically active' residents of Walker and more than a quarter of those in Elswick were looking for work. These unemployment rates were respectively double and 70 per cent above the average for Newcastle (Figure 12.2).

The 1991 Census thus reveals levels of unemployment in the inner city areas which are, by any standards, extremely high. The census also reveals substantial numbers of people who are 'jobless' but did not describe themselves as unemployed on the census form.

The first category of 'hidden unemployment' is perhaps not very well hidden from the seasoned observer of government policies for the unemployed. Government training and employment schemes have taken a number of forms from the early days of Job Creation Schemes and Youth Opportunities Programmes to the current Youth Training and Training for Work schemes whose variants now appear under more catchy local titles like 'Tyneskill Choices'. The 1991 Census was the first to identify such schemes as a separate category of economic activity. These programmes are generally targeted at younger people, whom both the census and the claimant count record as having the highest rates of unemployment. Table 12.2 shows that the proportion of young inner-city men describing themselves as unemployed rose from 35 per cent in 1981 to around 40 per cent in 1991. When the 'hidden unemployment' represented by government schemes is included in the total, it becomes apparent that in the inner-city areas half of the young men and a third of the young women who were in the labour market did not have a job.

The second category of 'hidden unemployment' is reflected in the level of economic activity. Nationally the proportion of men of working

Table 12.2   **Youth unemployment and government schemes**

Economically active residents aged 16–25	1981 % unemployed[1]	1991 % unemployed[1]	1991 % on schemes	1991 Total %
Men: Elswick	35	42	9	51
Men: Walker	35	39	11	50
Women: Elswick	18	27	7	34
Women: Walker	25	28	9	37

Note:
1 Self-defined as 'unemployed and looking for a job' or waiting to start a job.

Source: 1981 and 1991 Censuses (Small Area Statistics) Crown Copyright.

Table 12.3   **Labour market participation of residents: percentage economically active**

	ELSWICK 1981	ELSWICK 1991 [change]	WALKER 1981	WALKER 1991 [change]
MEN aged:				
16–64	84	76 [–8]	90	79 [–11]
45–54	88	79 [–9]	93	80 [–13]
54–59	84	69 [–15]	85	64 [–19]
60–64	73	44 [–29]	66	37 [–29]
WOMEN aged:				
16–59	63	52 [–11]	62	53 [–9]
45–54	67	58 [–9]	66	61 [–5]
55–59	56	41 [–15]	53	50 [–3]

Source: 1981 and 1991 Censuses (Small Area Statistics) Crown Copyright.

age who were working or seeking work fell from over 90 per cent to under 87 per cent between 1981 and 1991, whilst women's economic activity rate increased from less than 61 per cent to almost 68 per cent. In the City of Newcastle men's economic activity rate started from a lower base (88 per cent) in 1981 and fell more rapidly to just 82 per cent in 1991. Women's economic activity, which had been higher than the national average at almost 64 per cent in 1981, increased slowly and fell behind the national average in 1991 at less than 66 per cent (Tyne and Wear Research, 1994). In the two inner-city wards, Elswick and Walker, both men's and women's economic activity rates fell during the 1980s (Table 12.3).

Economic activity rates may change for a variety of reasons including changing age structures and increases in further education or full-time child care. Changes which are concentrated in the older age groups will also include the effects of early (pensionable) retirement. However, in the inner-city wards they are more likely to reflect a tendency for those without work to stop regarding themselves as 'unemployed and looking for a job'.

As Table 12.3 shows, the 1980s saw a dramatic decline in labour market participation by both men and women aged between 45 and retirement age in the inner city wards. The effects are most striking for men: a fifth of men in their later forties and early fifties, a third in their late fifties and well over half of men in their sixties but below retirement age do not regard themselves as part of the labour market. Four out of five of these economically inactive men described themselves as unable to work because of long-term sickness or disability. The adverse health effects both of Tyneside's traditional heavy industry and of long-term unemployment are undeniable, but it seems likely that many of these men are 'discouraged workers' who have left the labour force prematurely partly for health reasons and partly because of their poor assessment of the chances of finding work. These men occupy 'an indeterminate status between full economic activity and total economic inactivity . . . too old to work but too young to be retired' (Casey and Laczko, 1989: 510). Whilst the fall in women's participation was slower, the drop in their economic activity is significant, particularly as it occurred when women's participation in the labour market was generally increasing.

In summary, the evidence from the Censuses of Population shows that the general rise in unemployment between 1981 and 1991 was felt particularly strongly in the two inner-city wards. Their rates of unemployment diverged even further from the average in a city whose unemployment is consistently well above the national average. 'Unemployment' is not, however, the whole story. The extent of the lack of work in these communities is disguised for the young by government training schemes and for older workers by withdrawal from the labour market.

Local analyses from the claimant count offer little cause for optimism about unemployment in the inner-city wards, either in the brief 'boom' of the late 1980s or in the economic 'recovery' in the 1990s. Both Elswick and Walker wards have consistently recorded average unemployment rates of over 20 per cent since 1986, when the available data series began and when unemployment began to fall. In 1994 Elswick and Walker had average claimant unemployment rates of 29 per cent and 26 per cent respectively; around double the average for the City of Newcastle, itself well above the regional and national rates. The rates of recorded unemployment amongst men, who are less likely than women jobseekers to be excluded from the claimant count, were still higher. Despite the effects of government schemes diverting the unemployed into training, and of discouraged jobless workers leaving the labour force, an average month in 1994 saw almost four out of ten economically active men in Elswick and a third in Walker claiming unemployment benefits (Tyne and Wear Research, 1995). These areas thus remained characterised by the low proportion of their residents who were 'working in the inner city' or, indeed, elsewhere.

Conclusion

In the 1970s, unemployment rates were low by subsequent standards. In the Northern urban working-class communities studied in this paper, rates of unemployment were around double the national average, with about one in ten members of the labour force registered as unemployed. The experience of being without a job was much more widespread than the snapshot provided by an unemployment rate might suggest. In these communities, at the end of the 1970s, the number of people who were or had ever been unemployed was sufficiently great to make it clear that unemployment was a common part of urban working-class experience.

As unemployment increased in the 1980s and again in the 1990s the inner cities were particularly hard hit. Even in the brief 'boom' of the late 1980s at least one in five members of the labour force living in these areas of Newcastle upon Tyne was an unemployed claimant. By 1994, over a quarter were unemployed in an average month. The true extent of the lack of work is disguised by training schemes for the young and an indeterminate status between long-term unemployment and early retirement for older workers. 'Youth' for these purposes continues at least until the mid-20s, and 'older' labour market behaviour begins in the mid-40s. Even in the 20 years between these extended fringes of the labour force, between 30 per cent and 40 per cent of men in the inner-city areas were unemployed at any one time in 1994 and many more will have experienced life without work. All of the available evidence, including the Newcastle survey results cited above, shows that persistently high counts of 'the unemployed' reflect still greater numbers of people experiencing life as part of the changing 'Unemployed Flow' (Daniel, 1990). In the 1980s and 1990s, in the communities studied in this paper, only a small minority of households will have escaped the experience of unemployment. In these urban working-class communities 'not working' has virtually become the norm.

At the level of individual experience, the consequences of long-term exclusion from the world of work are potentially devastating as problems caused by material poverty may be compounded by a lack of physical and psychological wellbeing. The Social Change and Economic Life studies (Gallie, Marsh and Vogler, 1993) demonstrated the substantial stresses which unemployment places on marital, family and social relationships. These studies also found that unemployed people, in contrast with those in earlier studies, had not become passive social isolates, although the networks in which they functioned were segregated and unable to offer strong support. These findings illustrate the impact, both positive and negative, of the concentration of unemployment in particular communities. The positive aspect for the individual is that within a community where unemployment is the norm there is little stigma attached to being unemployed. Unemployment is not, in this sense, a cause for personal isolation. The negative aspect is that whilst unemployed social networks may dominate in a particular locality, their separation from networks which include people in employment reinforces their exclusion from the world of work and, perhaps, from 'social citizenship' (Morris, 1994).

Some commentators regard this kind of exclusion as the defining characteristic of the contested category of the 'underclass':

The underclass are those who fall outside this class schema, because they belong to family units having no stable relationship at all with the 'mode of production'. (Smith, 1992: 4)

Morris [1994] provides a thorough review of the debate about the 'underclass' and its emergence from a Victorian view of the 'dangerous classes' to current political concerns about the emergence of a 'culture of dependency' amongst the benefit-claiming residents of areas like those discussed in this paper. The debates around the definition of the underclass will not be rehearsed here. The essence of the concept is implicit in much current debate about the significance of social inequality for social and economic policy. Concerns about the 'danger' of the underclass undermining social values have considerable resonance in current UK political debate, whilst an address to social exclusion is central to emerging social policy in the European Union. The crucial point on which sociologists and policy-makers might agree is that social exclusion has implications both for the excluded and for the society which excludes them.

Turning to the more specific impact of unemployment on the labour market, the Newcastle study showed that in the 1970s the impact of recession on working lives extended well beyond the immediate and obvious risk of unemployment. Jobs became shorter-term and more insecure, and those who were able to find work often had to accept a reduction in their occupational status. Little seems to have changed in the 1980s, when an analysis from the Labour Force Survey identified a strong association between unemployment and non-standard, i.e. temporary or part-time, employment (Payne and Payne, 1993).

The growth of various forms of insecure employment in the 1990s has been considerable, and the combination of actual and perceived insecurity has been blamed for the persistent absence of the 'feelgood factor'. It has even been suggested that 'the social psychology of job insecurity might have to take over from the social psychology of unemployment as the research topic for the 1990s' (Burchell, 1993: 211). Whilst the suggestion of a takeover may be excessive, the poverty and marginalisation of urban working-class communities in the 1990s is certainly compounded when the little work that *is* available to their members is intermittent, insecure and badly paid. New forms of employment, including contracts with no guaranteed hours, fixed-term contracts and low part-time hours, give employers flexibility for cost control and strategic planning. For employees they offer an unpredictable income, and levels of insecurity which make the planning of a career, of major life changes like household formation, or even of a modest holiday, virtually impossible. Work which offers so little security and control to individuals, families and communities already marginalised by their experience of unemployment, does little to promote their sense of inclusion in a broader society.

To conclude, the evidence presented in this paper suggests that the inner-city areas whose residents were disadvantaged in the comparatively good years of the 1970s, now have only a fragile connection with the world of work, with the kinds of job to which the young might aspire and from which the old might retire. Economic and social inequalities which made the Northern urban working classes particularly vulnerable to the efffects of unemployment have made 'not working' a common experience throughout the 1970s, 1980s and 1990s.

Notes

1 The work histories were collected in a study carried out between 1978 and 1982 as part of the Department of the Environment's Inner Cities Research Programme, with additional analyses financed by the (then) Social Science Research Council.
2 I am grateful to my colleagues at Tyne and Wear Research for their assistance in accessing these data sources.
3 The Labour Force Survey which provides a measure of unemployment on the internationally agreed (ILO) basis is a sample survey with results subject to significant margins of error at county and Metropolitan District level and unavailable for smaller areas.

REFERENCES

Abrams, P. and Brown, R. K. (1984) *Work, Urbanism and Inequality* (2nd edn), London: Weidenfeld & Nicolson.

Abel-Smith, B. and Townsend, P. (1965) *The Poor and the Poorest*, Occasional Papers on Social Administration, no. 17, London: Bell & Sons.

Abrams, P. (1982) *Historical Sociology*, Shepton Mallet: Open Books.

Abercrombie, N. and Urry, J. (1983) *Capital, Labour and the Middle Classes*, London: Allen & Unwin.

Allatt, P. (1983) 'Men and war: status, class and the social reproduction of masculinity', from E. Gamarnikow, D. Morgan, J. Purvis and D. Taylorson (eds) *The Public and the Private*, London: Heinemann.

Allen, S. (1982) 'Gender inequality and class formation', in A. Giddens and G. Mackenzie (eds) *Social Class and the Division of Labour*, Cambridge: Cambridge University Press.

Allen, S. (1983) 'Production and reproduction: the lives of women homeworkers', *Sociological Review*, 31(4).

Allen, S. (1987) 'Gender, race and class in the 1980s', in C. Husband (ed.) *'Race' in Britain*, London: Hutchinson.

Allen, S. (1989) *Gender and Work in Mining Communities*, paper presented to BSA Annual Conference, Plymouth.

Allen, S. (1993a) *Counting Women's Labour*, paper presented at Fifth International Interdisciplinary Congress on Women's Studies, University of Costa Rica.

Allen, S. (1993b) *Citizenship: Minorities and Gender*, paper presented to the conference on Class, Status and Party at the Fin de Siècle, University of Leicester.

Allen, S. and Truman, C. (1992) 'Women, business and self-employment: a conceptual minefield', in S. Arber and N. Gilbert (eds) *Women and Working Lives: Divisions and Change*, Basingstoke: Macmillan.

Allen, S. and Truman, C. (eds) (1993a) *Women in Business: Perspectives on Women Entrepreneurs*, London: Routledge.

Allen, S. and Truman, C. (1993b) 'Women and men entrepreneurs: life strategies, business strategies', in S. Allen and C. Truman (eds) *Women in Business: Perspectives on Women Entrepreneurs*, London: Routledge.

Allen, S. and Wolkowitz, C. (1987) *Homeworking: Myths and Realities*, Basingstoke: Macmillan.

Amin, A. (1991) 'Flexible specialisation and the small firm in Italy: myths and realities', in A. Pollert (ed.) *Farewell to Flexibility*, Oxford: Blackwell.

Amsden, A. H. (ed.) (1980) *The Economics of Women and Work*, Harmondsworth: Penguin.

Anderson, Bridget (1993) *Britain's Secret Slaves: An Investigation into the Plight of Overseas Domestic Workers*, London: Anti-Slavery International.

Anthias, F. (1990) 'Race and class revisited – conceptualising race and racisms', *Sociological Review*, February.

Anthias, F. (1991) 'Parameters of difference and identity and the problem of connections', *International Review of Sociology*, April.

Anthias, F. (1992) 'Connecting "race" and ethnic phenomena', *Sociology*, August.

Anthias, F. (1995) 'Cultural racism or racist culture? Rethinking racist exclusions', *Economy and Society*, 24(2).

Anthias, F. and Yuval-Davis, N. (1992) *Racialized Boundaries: Race, Nation, Gender, Colour and Class and the Anti-Racist Struggle*, London: Routledge.

Appelbaum, R. and Henderson, J. (1995) 'The hinge of history: turbulence and transformation in the world economy', *Competition and Change*, 1(1).

Armstrong, P., Glyn, A. and Harrison, J. (1984) *Capitalism Since World War II*, London: Fontana.

Asad, Talal (1993) *Genealogies of Religion*, Baltimore: Johns Hopkins University Press.

Atkinson, A. B. (1974) 'Poverty and Income Inequality in Britain' in D. Wedderburn (ed.) *Poverty, Inequality and Class Structure*, Cambridge: Cambridge University Press.

Austrin, T. (1978) 'Industrial Relations in the Construction Industry', University of Bristol, unpublished Ph.D. thesis.

Austrin, T. and Beynon, H. (1980) *Masters and Servants – Paternalism and its Legacy on the Durham Coalfield*, ESRC Working Paper, University of Durham.

Baldamus, W. (1961) *Efficiency and Effort*, London: Tavistock.

Ballard, R. and Kalra, V. S. (1994) *The Ethnic Dimensions of the 1991 Census: A Preliminary Report*, Manchester: Manchester Census Group.

Banks, J. and Webb, D. (1977) *Ideas or People: The Vocational Dilemma for Sociology Graduates*, London: British Sociological Association.

Baritz, L. (1960) *The Servants of Power*, New York: Wiley.

Barker, D. L. and Allen, S. (eds) (1976) *Sexual Divisions and Society: Process and Change*, London: Tavistock.

Barnes, J. A. (1981) 'Professionalism in British Sociology', in P. Abrams, R. Deem, J. Finch and P. Rock (eds) *Practice and Progress: British Sociology 1950–1980*, London: Allen & Unwin.

Barnett, R. J. and Muller, R. E. (1974) *Global Reach: The Power of the Multinational Corporations*, New York: Simon & Schuster.

Bauman, Z. (1982) *Memories of Class*, London: Routledge & Kegan Paul.

Bell, C. and Newby, H. (1971) *Community Studies: An Introduction to the Sociology of the Local Community*, London: Allen & Unwin.

Benders, J. (1996) 'Leaving lean? Recent changes in the production organization of some Japanese car plants', *Economic and Industrial Democracy*, 17.

Berger, John and Mohr, Jean (1975) *A Seventh Man: The Story of a Migrant Worker in Europe*, Harmondsworth: Penguin Books.

Berger, P. L. (1964) *The Human Shape of Work*, New York: Collier-Macmillan.

Berggren, C. (1993) 'Lean production: the end of history?', *Work, Employment and Society* 7(2).

Berggren, C. (1995) 'Japan as number two: competitive problems and the future of alliance capitalism after the burst of the bubble boom', *Work, Employment and Society* 9(1).

Beteille, A. (ed.) (1969) *Social Inequality*, Harmondsworth: Penguin.

Bevan, S. and Thompson, M. (1992) *Merit Pay, Performance Appraisal and Attitudes to Women's Work*, Sussex: Institute of Manpower Studies.

Beynon, H. (1982) 'Jeremy Seabrook and the British working class', in *The Socialist Register 1982*, London: Merlin.

Beynon, H. (1984) *Working for Ford*, 2nd edn Harmondsworth: Penguin.

Beynon, H. (1997) 'The Changing Practices of Work', in Brown, R. K. (ed.) *The changing shape of work*, London: Macmillan.

Beynon, H. and Austrin, T. (1994) *Masters and Servants. Class and Patronage in the Making of a Labour Organisation*, London: Rivers Oram Press.

bin Salleh, H. (1991) *Social Development Issues in Primary Commodity Production in Malaysia*, Kuala Lumpur: Malaysian Institute of Economic Research.

Binns, D. (1991) *Administration, Domination and 'Organisation Theory'*, London, Polytechnic of East London: Occasional Papers on Business, Economy and Society, No. 4.

Binns, D. (1993) *Total Quality Management, Organisation Theory and the New Right: a Contribution to the Critique of Bureaucratic Totalitarianism*, University of East London: Occasional Papers on Business, Economy and Society, No. 11.

Blackaby, D. H. and Hunt, L. C. (1993) 'An assessment of Britain's productivity record in the 1980s: has there been a miracle?', in N. Healey (ed.) *Britain's Economic Miracle: Myth or Reality?*, London: Routledge.

Blackwell, T. and Seabrook, J. (1985) *A World Still to Win*, London: Faber & Faber.

Blackwell, T. and Seabrook, J. (1993) *The Revolt Against Change*, Chicago: Vintage.

Blauner, R. (1964) *Alienation and Freedom*, Chicago: University of Chicago Press.

Bolton, B. (1975) *An End to Homeworking?*, London: Fabian Society, Tract no. 436.

Borzeix, Anni (ed.) (1986) 'Retour sur l'entreprise', *Sociologie du Travail*, XXVIII(3).

Bourke, Joanne (1994) *Working-Class Culture in Britain. 1890–1960*, London: Routledge.

Bradley, H. (1996) *Fractured Identities*, Cambridge: Polity.

Braczyk, H. J. *et al.* (1995) 'The region of Baden-Wurttemburg: a post-Fordist success story?', in E. Dittrich *et al.* (eds) *Industrial Transformation in Europe*, London: Sage.

Brah, A. (1993) ' "Race" and "culture" in the gendering of labour markets: South Asian young Muslim women and the labour market', *New Community*, 19(5).

Braham, P., Rattansi, A. and Skellington, R. (eds) (1992) *Racism and Antiracism: Inequalities, Opportunities and Policies*, London: Sage.

Braverman, H. (1974) *Labor and Monopoly Capitalism: The Degradation of Work in the Twentieth Century*, New York: Monthly Review Press.

Bresheeth, H. and Yuval-Davis (eds) (1992) *The Gulf War and the New World Order*, London: Zed Books.

Broad, G. (1994a) 'The managerial limits to Japanisation', *Human Resource Management Journal*, 4(3).

Broad, G. (1994b) 'Japan in Britain: the dynamics of joint consultation', *Industrial Relations Journal*, 25(1).

Broadfoot, P. (1996) *Education, Assessment and Society*, Buckingham: Open University Press.

Brown, J. A. C. (1954) *The Social Psychology of Industry*, London: Penguin.

Brown, M. (1974) *Sweated Labour: A Study of Homework*, London: Low Pay Unit Pamphlet no. 1.

Brown, P. and Crompton, R. (1994) *Economic Restructuring and Social Exclusion*, London: UCL Press.

Brown, R. K. (1965) 'Participation, conflict and change in industry', *Sociological Review*, 13(3).

Brown, R. K. (1967a) 'Technology, technical change and automation', in S. R. Parker *et al. The Sociology of Industry*, London: Allen & Unwin.

Brown, R. K. (1967b) 'Research and consultancy in industrial enterprises', *Sociology*, 1(1).

Brown, R. K. (1973) 'Sources of objectives in work and employment', in J. Child (ed.) *Man and Organization*, London: Allen & Unwin.

Brown, R. K. (1976) 'Women as employees: some comments on research in industrial sociology', in D. L. Barker and S. Allen (eds) *Dependence and Exploitation in Work and Marriage*, London: Longman (also reprinted with a Postscript in D. Leonard and S. Allen (eds) (1991) *Sexual Divisions Revisited*, Basingstoke: Macmillan).

Brown, R. K. (1981) 'Sociologists and industry – in search of a distinctive competence', *Sociological Review*, 29(2).

Brown, R. K. (1982) 'Work histories, career strategies and the class structure', in A. Giddens and G. Mackenzie (eds) *Social Class and the Division of Labour*, Cambridge: Cambridge University Press.

Brown, R. K. (1988) 'The employment relationship in sociological theory', in D. Gallie (ed.) *Employment in Britain*, Oxford: Blackwell.

Brown, R. K. (1992) 'World war, women's work and the gender division of paid labour', in S. Arber and N. Gilbert (eds) *Women and Working Lives: Divisions and Change*, Basingstoke: Macmillan.

Brown, R. K. (1995) *How has the nature of work and employment changed in the region*, MIMEO.

Brown, R. K. (1995) *Understanding Industrial Organisations: Theoretical Perspectives in Industrial Sociology*, London: Routledge.

Brown, R. K. (ed.) (1997) *The Changing Shape of Work*, London: Macmillan.

Brown, R. K. and P. Brannen (1970) 'Social relations and social perspectives amongst shipbuilding workers – a preliminary statement', Parts I & II, *Sociology*, 4(1 & 2).

Brown, W. (1962) *Piecework Abandoned*, London: Heinemann.

Buck, N. (1993) *Comparative Income Distribution in Two Welfare Regimes: The Impacts of Household and Labour Market Change in Britain and Germany*, Working Papers of the European Scientific Network on Household Panel Studies, no. 84, Colchester: University of Essex.

Burawoy, M. (1979) *Manufacturing Consent: Changes in the Labor Process in Monopoly Capitalism*, Chicago: University of Chicago Press.

Burawoy, M. (1985) *The Politics of Production*, London: Verso.

Burchell, B. (1993) 'The effects of labour market position, job insecurity and unemployment on psychological health', in D. Gallie, C. Marsh and C. Vogler (eds) *Social Change and the Experience of Unemployment*, Oxford: Oxford University Press.

Burgess, R. G. (1989) 'Patterns and processes of education in the UK', in P. Abrams and R. K. Brown (eds) *UK Society*, London: Weidenfeld & Nicolson.

Burgess, R. G., Hughes, C. and Moxon, S. (1989) *Educating the Under Fives in Salford*, Coventry: University of Warwick.

Burns, T. and Stalker, G. M. (1961) *The Management of Innovation*, London: Pergamon.

Bush, M. L. (ed.) (1992) *Social Orders and Social Classes in Europe Since 1500*, London: Longman.

Bythell, D. (1978) *The Sweated Trades: Outwork in the 19th Century*, New York: St Martins Press.

Campbell, J. (1987) *Nye Bevan and the Mirage of British Socialism*, London: Duckworth.

Carew, A. (1987) *Labour Under the Marshall Plan: The Politics of Productivity and the Marketing of Management Science*, Manchester: Manchester University Press.

Carey, A. (1967) 'The Hawthorne studies: a radical criticism', *American Sociological Review*, 32.

Carr, F. (1994) 'Introducing team working – a motor industry case study', *Industrial Relations Journal* 25(3).

Carr-Saunders, A. and Caradog-Jones, D. (1927, 1937) *A Survey of the Social Structure of England and Wales*, Oxford: Oxford University Press; Oxford: Clarendon Press.

Carson, K. (1970) 'White collar crime and the enforcement of factory legislation', *British Journal of Criminology*, 10(4).

Casey, B. and Laczko, F. (1989) 'Early retired or long term unemployed?: the situation of non-working men aged 55–64 from 1979 to 1986', *Work, Employment and Society*, 3(4).

Chandler, A. D. (1962) *Strategy and Structure: Chapters in the History of Industrial Enterprise*, Cambridge, Mass.: MIT Press.

Chinoy, E. (1955) *Automobile Workers and the American Dream*, Garden City: Doubleday.

City of Newcastle upon Tyne (1993) *City Profiles: Results from the 1991 Census.*

Clark, A. (1993) *Diaries*, London: Weidenfeld & Nicolson.

Clark, M. M. (1988) *Children Under Five: Educational Research and Evidence*, London: Gordon & Breach.

Coates, K. and Silburn, R. (1970) *Poverty: The Forgotten Englishmen*, Harmondsworth: Penguin.

Cockburn, C. (1991) *In the Way of Women: Men's Resistance to Sex Equality in Organisations*, London: Macmillan.

Coffield, F. and Vignoles, A. (1997) *Widening Participation in Higher Education by Ethnic Minorities, Women and Alternative Students* (Report 5 of the Dearing Report on Higher Education), London: HMSO.

Cohen, A. P. (1985) *The Symbolic Construction of Community*, London: Tavistock.

Cohen, P. and Baines, H. S. (eds) (1988) *Multi Racist Britain*, London: Macmillan.

Cohen, R. (1987) *The New Helots: Migrants and the International Division of Labour*, Aldershot: Avebury.

Cohen, S. (1987) 'A Labour process to nowhere', *New Left Review*, 165.

Common, J. (ed.) (1978) *Seven Shifts*, London: E. P. Publishing.

Coombs, R. (1985) 'Automation, management strategies and labour process change', in D. Knights and H. Willmott (eds) *Job Redesign: Critical Perspectives on the Labour Process*, London: Gower Press.

Cousins, J. M. and Brown, R. K. (1975) 'Patterns of paradox – shipbuilding workers' images of society', in M. Bulmer (ed.) *Working Class Images of Society*, London: Routledge & Kegan Paul.

Cousins, J. M., Curran, M. M. and Brown, R. K. (1982) *Working in the Inner City: A Case Study*, Inner Cities Research Programme Report No. 8, Department of the Environment.

Cousins, J. M. and Curran, M. M. (1982) 'Patterns of disadvantage in a city labour market', in G. Day *et al.* (eds) *Diversity and Decomposition in the Labour Market*, London: Gower Press.

Cox, D. J. (1978) *Living and Studying with Capitalism: Some Comments on the Development of British Industrial Sociology*, Hatfield: Hatfield Polytechnic for the Organisation of Sociologists in Polytechnics and Cognate Institutions.

Cressey, P., Eldridge, J. and MacInnes, J. (1985) *Just Managing: Authority and Democracy in Industry*, Milton Keynes: Open University Press.

Crompton, R. (1993) *Class and Stratification*, Cambridge: Polity.

Crompton, R. and Mann, M. (eds) (1986) *Gender and Stratification*, Cambridge: Polity Press.

Crompton, R. and Sanderson, K. (1990) *Gendered Jobs and Social Change*, London: Unwin Hyman.

Crozier, M. (1964) *The Bureaucratic Phenomenon*, London: Tavistock.

Cunnison, S. (1966) *Wages and Work Allocation*, London: Tavistock.

Curran, M. M. (1982) *Work Histories and Changes in the Economy*, Urban Employment Study Working Paper, Department of Sociology and Social Policy, University of Durham.

Dalton, M. (1959) *Men Who Manage*, New York: Wiley.

Danford, A. (1998a) 'Work organisation and labour process inside Japanese firms in South Wales', in P. Thompson and C. Warhurst (eds) *Workplaces of the Future*, London: Macmillan.

Danford, A. (1998b) *Japanese Management Techniques and British Workers*, London: Mansell.

Daniel, W. W. (1990) *The Unemployed Flow*, London: Policy Studies Institute.

Danziger, N. (1995) *Danziger's Britain*, Flamingo, 1997.

Darlington, R. (1994) *The Dynamics of Workplace Unionism: Shop Stewards' Organisation in Three Merseyside Plants*, London: Mansell.

David, T. (1990) *Under Five – Under Educated?*, Buckingham: Open University Press.

Davies, N. (1997) *Dark Heart: The Shocking Truth About Hidden Britain*, London: Chatto & Windus.

Dawe, A. (1970) 'The two sociologies', *British Journal of Sociology*, 21.

Deem, R. (1996) 'Border territories: a journey through sociology, education and women's studies', *British Journal of Sociology of Education*, 17(1).

Delphy, C. (1993) 'Rethinking sex and gender', *Women's Studies International Forum*, 16(1).

Delphy, C. and Leonard, D. (1986) 'Class analysis, gender analysis and the family', in R. Crompton and M. Mann (eds) *Gender and Stratification*, Cambridge: Polity Press.

Dennis, N., Henriques, F. and Slaughter, C. (1956) *Coal is our Life: An Analysis of a Yorkshire mining Community*, London: Eyre & Spottiswoode.

Dennis, N., Henriques, F. and Slaughter, C. (1969) *Coal is our Life: An Analysis of a Yorkshire mining Community* (2nd edn), London: Eyre & Spottiswoode.

Department of Education and Science (1979) *Local Authority Arrangements for the School Curriculum*, London: HMSO.

Department of Education and Science/Welsh Office (1989) *Records of Achievement*, London: DES/Welsh Office.

DfEE (1996) 'Projections of demand for full-time and sandwich undergraduate study' as quoted in National Committee of Inquiry for Higher Education.

Department of Social Security (1995) *Households Below Average Income: a statistical analysis 1979–1992/93*, HMSO.

Dex, S. (1985) *The Sexual Division of Work*, Brighton: Wheatsheaf.

Dicken, P. (1997) *Global Reach* (3rd edn), London: Paul Chapman.

Donald, J. and Rattansi, A. (eds) (1992) *'Race', Culture and Difference*, London: Sage Publications.

Du Gay, P. (1995) *Consumption and Identity at Work*, London: Sage.

Durkheim, E. (1960) *The Division of Labour in Society*, Chicago: Free Press.

Edwards, P. *et al.* (1992) 'Great Britain: still muddling through', in A. Ferner and R. Hyman (eds) *Industrial Relations in the New Europe*, Oxford: Blackwell.

EEC (1987) *Non-Salaried Working Women in Europe: Women Running their Own Businesses or Working Independently – Women Involved in their Husband's Professional Activity*, Brussels: Commission of the European Communities.

Eldridge, J. E. T. (1971) *Sociology and Industrial Life*, London: Nelson.

Elger, T. (1975) 'Industrial organisations: a processual perspective', in J. B. McKinlay (ed.) *Processing People: Cases in Organisational Behaviour*, London: Holt, Rinehart & Winston.

Elger, T. (1990) 'Technical innovation and work reorganisation in British manufacturing in the 1980s', *Work, Employment and Society* 4, Special Issue.

Elger, T. (1991) 'Task flexibility and the intensification of labour in British manufacturing during the 1980s', in A. Pollert (ed.) *Farewell to Flexibility?*, Oxford: Blackwell.

Elger, T. and Fairbrother, P. (1992) 'Inflexible flexibility: a case study of modularisation', in N. Gilbert *et al.* (eds) *Fordism and Flexibility: Divisions and Change*, London: Macmillan.

Elger, T. and Smith, C. (eds) (1994) *Global Japanization? The Transnational Transformation of the Labour Process*, London: Routledge.

Elger, T. and Smith, C. (1998a) 'Exit, voice and "mandate": Management strategies and labour practices of Japanese Firms in Britain', *British Journal of Industrial Relations*, 36(2).

Elger, T. and Smith, C. (1998b) 'New town, new capital, new workplace? The employment relations of Japanese inward investors in a West Midlands new town', *Economy and Society*, 27(4).

Elson, D. and Pearson, R. (eds) (1989) *Women's Employment and Multinationals in Europe*, Basingstoke: Macmillan.

Emmett, I. and Morgan, D. H. J. (1982) 'Max Gluckman and the Manchester shop floor ethnographies', in R. Frankenberg (ed.) *Custom and Conflict in Britain*, Manchester: Manchester University Press.

Engels, F. (1892) *Socialism: Utopian and Scientific*, Chicago: Charles & Kerr.

Ennis, F. (1982) 'The Jarrow March of 1936 and the Symbolic Expression of Protest', unpublished MA thesis, University of Durham.

Ennis, F. (1986) 'Time, Person and Place in the North-East of England', unpublished PhD thesis, University of Durham.

EOC (1993a) *Annual Report*, Manchester: Equal Opportunities Commission.

EOC (1993b) *Women and Men in Britain 1993, Annual Statistical Review*, Manchester: Equal Opportunities Commission.

Finch, J. (1984) 'A first class environment? Working class playgroups as pre-school experience', *British Educational Research Journal*, 10(1).

Flanders, A. (1964) *The Fawley Productivity Agreements*, London: Faber & Faber.

Ford, Glyn (1992) *Fascist Europe: The Rise of Racism and Xenophobia*, London: Pluto Press.

Frankenburg, R. (1976) 'In the production of their lives . . . men (?)', from D. L. Barker and S. Allen (eds) *Sexual Divisions and Society: Process and Change*, London: Macmillan.

Friedman, A. L. (1977) *Industry and Labour: Class Struggle at Work and Monopoly Capitalism*, London: Macmillan.

Frobel, F., Heinrichs, J. and Kreye, O. (1980) *The New International Division of Labour*, Cambridge: Cambridge University Press.

Fry, D. and Ullah, P. (eds) (1987) *Unemployed People: Social and Psychological Perspectives*, Milton Keynes: Open University Press.

Galbraith, J. K. (1992) *The Culture of Contentment*, London: Penguin.

Gallie, D., Gershuny, J. and Vogler, C. (1993) 'Unemployment, the household and social networks', in D. Gallie, C. Marsh and C. Vogler (eds) *Social Change and the Experience of Unemployment*, Oxford: Oxford University Press.

Galton, M. (1998) 'Back to consulting the ORACLE', *Times Education Supplement*.

Galton, M., Simon, B. and Croll, P. (1980) *Inside the Primary Classroom*, London: Routledge & Kegan Paul.

Gamarnikow, E., Morgan, D., Purvis, J. and Taylorson, D. (eds) (1983) *The Public and the Private*, London: Heinemann.

Garnsey, E. (1978) 'Women's work and theories of class stratification', *Sociology*, 12(2).

Garnsey, E. (1984) 'The rediscovery of the division of labour', in K. Thompson (ed.) *Work, Employment and Unemployment*, Milton Keynes: Open University Press.

Garrahan, P. and Stewart, P. (1992) *The Nissan Enigma: Flexibility at Work in a Local Economy*, London: Cassell.

Garrahan, P. and Stewart, P. (1995) 'Employee responses to new management techniques in the auto-industry', *Work, Employment and Society*, 9(3).

Geary, J. F. (1995) 'Work practices: the structure of work', in P. Edwards (ed.) *Industrial Relations: Theory and Practice in Britain*, Oxford: Blackwell.

Gereffi, G. and Korzeniewicz, M. (eds) (1994) *Commodity Chains and Global Capitalism*, Westport: Praeger.

Gershuny, J. (1993) 'The psychological consequences of unemployment: an assessment of the Jahoda thesis', in D. Gallie, C. Marsh and C. Vogler (eds) *Social Change and the Experience of Unemployment*, Oxford: Oxford University Press.

Giddens, A. (1978) 'The prospects for social theory today', *Berkeley Journal of Sociology*, 22.

Giddens, A. (1990) *The Consequences of Modernity*, Cambridge: Polity Press.

Gilborn, David (1990) *'Race', Ethnicity and Education: Teaching and Learning in Multiethnic Schools*, London: Unwin Hyman.

Gilroy, P. (1987) *There Ain't No Black in the Union Jack: The Cultural Politics of Race and Nation*, Chicago: University of Chicago Press.

Glass, R. (1960) *Newcomers*, London: Allen & Unwin.

Glavanis, P. (1995) 'The "New Helots" in the European Union', in Iordanis Psimmenos, *Metanastefsis apo ta Valkania (Migration from the Balkans)*, Athens: Papazisis & Glory Books.

Glavanis, P. (1996) ' "Muslim voices" in the European Community: community, identity and employment', in P. Gholemis, G. Hadjimichalis and M. Vaiou (eds), *Forms of Informal Employment in the European Union*, Athens: POLITIS.

Glavanis, P. (1996a) ' "Global labour" in the Arab Gulf States: opportunity or threat to global/regional development and security', *Competition and Change*, 1(3).

Glavanis, P. (1998) 'Islam in Europe: the stranger within', *Innovation* (Special issue edited by Unas Samad on Migration and Multiculturalism: Muslims in Europe), Vienna, ICCR.

Glucksmann, M. (1986) 'In a class of their own? Women workers in the new industries in inter-war Britain', *Feminist Review*, 24.

Glucksmann, M. (1990) *Women Assemble: Women Workers and the New Industries in Inter-war Britain*, London: Routledge.

Glyn, A. (1992) 'The "productivity miracle", profits and investment', in J. Michie (ed.) *The Economic Legacy 1979–1992*, London: Academic Press.

Goldberg, D. T. (1993) *Racist Culture: Philosophy and the Politics of Meaning*, Oxford: Blackwell.

Goldschmidt-Clermont, L. (1982) *Unpaid Work in the Household*, Geneva: International Labour Office.

Goldschmidt-Clermont, L. (1987) *Economic Evaluations of Unpaid Household Work*, Geneva: International Labour Office.

Goldthorpe, J. H. (1966) *Orientation to Work and Industrial Behaviour Among Assembly-Line Operatives: A Contribution Towards an Action Approach in Industrial Sociology*, unpublished paper to the Conference of University Teachers of Sociology, London.

Goldthorpe, J. H. *et al.* (1968) *The Affluent Worker: Industrial Attitudes and Behaviour*, Cambridge: Cambridge: University Press.

Goldthorpe, J. *et al.* (1969) *The Affluent Worker in the Class Structure*, Cambridge: Cambridge University Press.

Goldthorpe, J. H. (1980) *Social Mobility and Class Structure in Modern Britain*, Oxford: Oxford University Press.

Goldthorpe, J. H. (1983) 'Women and class analysis: in defence of the conventional view', *Sociology*, 17(4).

Goldthorpe, J. (1988) 'Intellectuals and the working class in modern Britain', in D. Rose (ed.) *Social Stratification and Economic Change*, London: Hutchinson.

Goldthorpe, J. (1997) 'The "Goldthorpe" Class Schema', in D. Rose and K. O'Reilly (eds) *Constructing Classes*, London: Office For National Statistics.

Goodrich, C. L. (1920) *The Frontier of Control: A Study in British Workshop Politics*, London: Bell.

Gordon, P. (1989) 'Just another Asian murder', London: *Guardian*.

Gordon, P. and Klug, F. (1986) *New Right, New Racism*, London: Searchlight Publication.

Gorz, André (1970) 'The role of immigrant labour', *New Left Review*, 61.

Gorz, A. (1976) *The division of labour: the labour process and class struggle in modern capitalism*, Atlantic Highlands: Humanities Press.

Goulbourne, Harry (1993) 'Aspects of nationalism and black identities in post-imperial Britain', in Cross, Makolm and Raith, Michael (eds), *Racism, the City and the State*, London: Routledge.

Gouldner, A. (1954) *Patterns of Industrial Bureaucracy*, Chicago: Free Press.

Gouldner, A. (1955) *Wildcat Strike*, London: Routledge & Kegan Paul.

Grannovetter, M. (1985) 'Economic action and social structure', *American Journal of Sociology*, 91(3).

Grant, D. (1994) 'New style agreements at Japanese transplants in the UK', *Employee Relations* 16(2).

Grant, D. (1996) 'Japanization and New Industrial Relations', in I. Beardwell (ed.) *Contemporary Industrial Relations: A Critical Analysis*, Oxford: Oxford University Press.

Green, A. (1995) 'A comparison of alternative measures of unemployment', *Environment and Planning A*, 27(4).

Green, P. (1981) *The Pursuit of Inequality*, Oxford: Martin Robinson.

Greenhalgh, C. (1979) 'Male labour force participation in Great Britain', *Scottish Journal of Political Economy*, 26(3).

Greenslade, R. (1976) *Goodbye to the Working Class*, London: Marion Boyars.

Gregson, N. and Lowe, M. (1994) 'Waged domestic labour and the renegotiation of the domestic division of labour within dual career households', *Sociology*, 28(1).

Gross, E. (1992) 'What is feminist theory?', in H. Crowley and S. Himmelweit (eds) *Knowing Women*, Cambridge: Polity Press.

Grunberg, L. (1986) 'Relations in the economic crisis: a comparison of British and French automobile plants', *Sociology* 20(4).

Hall, S. and Jacques, M. (eds) (1986) *Modern Times*, London: Lawrence & Wishart.

Hall, S. (1988) 'New Ethnicities', in K. Mercer (ed.), *Black Film/British Cinema*, London: ICA Document 7.

Hall, S. and Jacques, M. (1988) *New Times*, London: Lawrence & Wishart.

Hall, S. (ed.) (1992) *The Empire Strikes Back*, London: Hutchinson.

Halsey, A. H. *et al.* (1997) *Education: Culture, Economy, Society*, Oxford: Oxford University Press.

Halsey, A. H., Floud, J. and Anderson, C. A. (eds) (1961) *Education, Economy and Society*, New York: The Free Press.

Hammersley, M. (1994) 'On feminist methodology: a response', *Sociology*, 28(1).

Hanson, P. *et al.* (1995) *Made In Europe*, London: IBM UK and London Business School.

Harastzi, M. (1977) *A Worker in a Workers' State*, Harmondsworth: Penguin.

Harding, S. (1992) 'The instability of the analytical categories of feminist theory', in H. Crowley and S. Himmelweit (eds) *Knowing Women*, Cambridge: Polity Press.

Hayler, T. and Harvey, D. (eds) (1993) *The Factory and the City: The Story of the Corley Automobile Workers in Oxford*, London: Mansell.

HESA (1996) *Students in Higher Education Institutions 1995/96*, Cheltenham: HESA.

Heaton, M. and Linn, I. (1989) *Fighting Back: the Shop Steward Response to New Management Techniques*, TGWU/Northern College.

Henderson, J. (1989) *The Globalisation of High Technology Production*, London: Routledge.

Hill, J. M. M. and Trist, E. L. (1953) 'A consideration of industrial accidents as a means of withdrawal from the work situation', *Human Relations*, 6, November.

Hill, J. M. M. and Trist, E. L. (1955) 'Changes in accidents and other absences with length of service', *Human Relations*, 8, May.

Hirst, P. and Zeitlin, J. (1989a) 'Flexible specialisation and the competitive failure of UK manufacturing', *Political Quarterly*, 60(2): 164–78.

Hirst, P. and Zeitlin, J. (eds) (1989b) *Reversing Industrial Decline? Industrial Structure and Policy in Britain and her Competitors*, Oxford: Berg.

HMSO (1995) *Training Statistics 1995*, London: HMSO.

Hobsbawm, E. (1964) *Labouring Men*, London: Weidenfeld & Nicolson.

Hobsbawm, E. (1984) *Worlds of Labour*, London: Weidenfeld & Nicolson.

Hoggart, R. (1957) *The Uses of Literacy*, London: Chatto & Windus.

hooks, b. (1984) *Feminist Theory from Margin to Center*, Boston: Southend Press.

Hope, E., Kennedy, M. and De Winter, A. (1976) 'Homeworkers in North London', in S. Allen and D. L. Barker (eds) *Dependence and Exploitation in Work and Marriage*, London: Longman.

Hopkins, C. (1974) *The Moving Staircase*, Durham: Wearside Printing Company.

Hughes, A. (1996) 'Traitor', *New Internationalist*, July.

Hughes, C., Burgess, R. G. and Moxon, C. (1991) 'Parents are welcome: head-teachers' and matrons' perspectives on parental participation in the early years', *Qualitative Studies in Education*, 4(2).

Hunt, P. (1980) *Gender and Class Consciousness*, London: Macmillan.

Hurstfield, J. (1978) *The Part-Time Trap*, London: Low Pay Unit, Pamphlet, no. 9.

Hurstfield, J. (1980) *Part-Time Pittance*, London: Low Pay Unit, Review, no. 1.

Hurstfield, J. (1987) *Part-Timers Under Pressure*, London: Low Pay Unit, Pamphlet, no. 47.

Hutton, W. (1995) *The State We're In*, London: Jonathan Cape.

Hyman, R. (1982) 'Whatever happened to industrial sociology', in D. Dunkersley and G. Salaman (eds) *The International Yearbook of Organisation Studies*, London: Routledge & Kegan Paul.

Hyman, R. (1987) 'Strategy or structure? Capital, labour and control', *Work, Employment and Society*, 1(1).

Hyman, R. (1988) 'Flexible specialisation: miracle or myth?', in R. Hyman and H. Streeck (eds) *New Technology and Industrial Relations*, Oxford: Blackwell.

Hyman, R. (1991) 'Plus ca change? The theory of production and the production of theory', in A. Pollert (ed.) *Farewell to Flexibility?*, Oxford: Blackwell.

Hyman, R. and Elger, T. (1981) 'Job control, the employers' offensive and alternative strategies', *Capital and Class*, 15.

IRS (1992) 'Lean production and Rover's "New Deal"', *IRS Employment Trends* 514, June.

IRS (1993) 'TGWU's response to lean production at Rover', *IRS Employment Trends* 534, April.

Jackson, B. (1968) *Working Class Community*, London: Routledge & Kegan Paul.

Jackson, B. and Marsden, D. (1966) *Education and the Working Class*, Harmondsworth: Penguin.

Jahoda, M., Lazarsfeld, P. and Zeizel, H. (1972) *Marienthal: The Sociography of an Unemployed Community* (first published 1933), London: Tavistock.

Jaques, E. (1951) *The Changing Culture of a Factory*, London: Tavistock.

Jaques, E. (1961) *Equitable Payment*, London: Heinemann.

Jacques, M. (ed.) (1989) *New Times: The Changing Face of Politics in the 1990s*, London: Lawrence & Wishart.

Jennett, C. and Stewart, R. G. (eds) (1987) *Three Worlds of Inequality, Race, Class and Gender*, Melbourne: Macmillan.

Jermier, J. M. (1991) 'Review of Knight and Willmott eds (1990)', *Administrative Science Quarterly*, December.

Jewish Women in London Group (1989) *Generations of Memories: Voices of Jewish Women*, London: Women's Press.

Johns, A. V. (1980) *By the Sweat of their Brow*, London: Croom Helm.

Joyce, P. (ed.) (1996) *Class*, London: Routledge.

Jurgens, U. *et al.* (1994) *Breaking from Taylorism: Changing Forms of Work in the Automobile Industry*, Cambridge: Cambridge University Press.

Kamata, S. (1983) *Japan in the Passing Lane*, London: Allen & Unwin.

Karabel, J. and Halsey, A. H. (eds) (1977) *Knowledge, Ideology and Power in Education*, Oxford: Oxford University Press.

Kelly, J. (1982) *Scientific Management, Job Redesign and Work Performance*, London: Academic Press.

Kerr, C. (1960) *Industrialism and Industrial Man*, Cambridge, Mass.: Harvard University Press.

Kerr, M. (1958) *The People of Ship Street*, London: Routledge & Kegan Paul.

Klein, J. (1965) *Samples From English Cultures*, vol. 1, London: Routledge & Kegan Paul.

Knell, J. (1993) 'Transnational corporations and the dynamics of human capital formation: evidence from West Yorkshire', *Human Resource Management Journal*, 3(4).

Knights, D. and Willmott, H. (eds) (1990) *Labour Process Theory*, London: Macmillan.

Kolakowski, L. (1978) *Main Currents in Marxism*, Oxford: Oxford University Press.

Kumar, K. (1985) *Prophesy and Progress*, Harmondsworth: Penguin.

Kumar, K. (1995) *From Post-Industrialism to Post-Modern Society*, Oxford: Blackwell.

Lampard, L. (1993) 'An examination of the relationship between marital dissolution and unemployment', in D. Gallie, C. Marsh and C. Vogler (eds) *Social Change and the Experience of Unemployment*, Oxford: Oxford University Press, pp. 264–98.

Lane, T. (1974) *The Union Makes Us Strong*, London: Arrow Books.

Lavalette, M. (1991) *Some Very Peculiar Practices: Work Organisation and Safety in the North Sea Oil and Gas Industry*, University of Aberdeen, Department of Occupational and Environmental Medicine.

Lee, D. and Newby, H. (1983) *The Problem of Sociology*, London: Hutchinson.

Lewchuk, W. (1996) 'Men and mass production: the role of gender in managerial strategies in the British and American auto industries', in H. Shiomi and K. Wada (eds) *Fordism Transformed*, Oxford: Oxford University Press.

Linhart, R. (1978) *The Assembly Line*, London: Calder.

Linhart, Robert (1981) *The Assembly Line*, London: Calder.

Lipset, S. M. (1964) 'The changing class structure of contemporary European politics', *Daedalus*, 63(1).

Littler, C. R. (1982) *The Development of the Labour Process in Capitalist Societies*, London: Heinemann.

Littler, C. R. (1990) 'The labour process debate: a theoretical review', in D. Knights and H. Willmott (eds) (1990) *Labour Process Theory*, London: Macmillan.

Lockwood, D. (1966) 'Sources of variation in working-class images of society', *Sociological Review*, 14(3).

Lockwood, D. (1986) 'Class, Status and Gender', in R. Crompton and M. Mann (eds) *Gender and Stratification*, Cambridge: Polity Press.

Lupton, T. (1963) *On the Shop Floor*, Oxford: Pergamon.

Lupton, T. (1966) *Management and the Social Sciences*, London: Hutchinson.

Lyddon, D. (1996) 'The Myth of Mass Production and the Mass Production of Myth', *Historical Studies in Industrial Relations*, 1.

MacFarlane, Alan (1987) *The Culture of Capitalism*, Oxford: Blackwell.

McKinley, A. and Taylor, P. (1996) 'Power, surveillance and resistance: inside the "Factory of the Future"', in P. Ackers *et al.* (eds) *The New Workplace and Trade Unionism*, London: Routledge.

Mair, A. (1994) *Honda's Global Local Corporation*, London: Macmillan.

Mann, F. C. and Hoffman, L. R. (1960) *Automation and the Worker*, New York: Holt.

Mann, M. (1970) 'The social cohesion of liberal democracy', *American Sociological Review*, 35(3).

Mann, M. (1986) 'A crisis in stratification theory?', in R. Crompton and M. Mann (eds) *Gender and Stratification*, Cambridge: Polity Press.

Marcuse, H. (1964) *One Dimensional Man*, London: Routledge & Kegan Paul.

Marglin, S. (1974) 'What do bosses do? The origins and functions of hierarchy in capitalist production', *Review of Radical Political Economics*, 6(2).

Marsden, D. *et al.* (1985) *The Car Industry: Labour Relations and Industrial Adjustment*, London: Tavistock.

Marshall, G. and Rose, D. (1990) 'Out-classed by our critics?', *Sociology*, 24(2).

Marshall, G. (1983) 'Some remarks on the study of working class consciousness', *Politics and Society*, 12(1).

Marshall, G. (1988) 'Some remarks on the study of working-class consciousness', in D. Rose (ed.) *Social Stratification and Economic Change*, London: Hutchinson.

Marshall, G. *et al.* (1988) *Social Class in Modern Britain*, London: Hutchinson.

Marshall, T. H. (1950) *Citizenship and Social Class*, Cambridge: Cambridge University Press.

Martin, J. and Roberts, C. (1984) *Women and Employment: A Lifetime Perspective*, London: HMSO.

Marx, K. (1963) 'The eighteenth Brumaire of Louis Bonaparte', in K. Marx, *Surveys from Exile*, London: Penguin Books.

Marx, K. (1964) *Capital*, vol. 3, Moscow: International Publishing House.

Marx, K. (1971) *Capital*, vol. 3, London: Penguin Books.

Mason, David (1995) *Race and Ethnicity in Modern Britain*, Oxford: Oxford University Press.

Massey, D. (1994) *Space, Place and Gender*, Oxford: Polity Press.

Maynard, M. (1990) 'The re-shaping of sociology? Trends in the study of gender', *Sociology*, 24(2).

Measham, F. and Allen, S. (1994) 'In defence of home and hearth? Families, friendships and feminism in mining communities', *Journal of Gender Studies*, 3(1): 31–45.

Meiksens-Wood, E. (1986) *The Retreat from Class: A New Socialism*, London: Verso.

Melman, S. (1956) *Dynamic Factors in Industrial Productivity*, Oxford: Basil Blackwell.

Melman, S. (1958) *Decision Making and Productivity*, Oxford: Basil Blackwell.

Mess, H. A. (1928) *Industrial Tyneside*, Bureau of Social Research for Tyneside.

Miles, R. (1993) *Racism after 'Race Relations'*, London: Routledge.

Mingione, E. and Magatti, M. (1994) *Follow-up to the White Paper: The Informal Sector*, Brussels: European Commission, Directorate General V.

Modood, T. (1992) *Not Easy Being British*, Stoke-on-Trent: Trentham Books.

Moore, H. L. (1988) *Feminism and Anthropology*, Cambridge: Polity Press.

Morgan, K. and Sayer, A. (1985) 'A "modern" industry in a "mature" region: the remaking of management–labour relations', *International Journal of Urban and Regional Research*, 9(3).

Morgan, D. and Stanley, L. (eds) (1990) *Debates in Sociology*, Manchester: Manchester University Press.

Morris, J. *et al.* (1993) *Working for the Japanese: The Social and Economic Consequences of Japanese Investment in Wales*, London: Athlone.

Morris, L. (1994) *Dangerous Classes: The Underclass and Social Citizenship*, London: Routledge.

Morris, L. D. (1985) 'Renegotiation of the domestic division of labour in the context of male redundancy', in H. Newby, J. Bujra, P. Littlewood, G. Rees and T. Rees (eds) *Restructuring Capital*, London: Macmillan.

Moser, K. A., Goldblatt, P. O., Fox, J. and Jones, D. R. (1987) 'Unemployment and mortality: comparison of the 1971 and 1981 longitudinal study census samples', *British Medical Journal*, 294, January.

Mosse, C. (1969) *The Ancient World at Work*, London: Chatto & Windus.

Mueller, F. (1992) 'Designing flexible teamwork: comparing German and Japanese approaches', *Employee Relations*, 14(1).

Munck, R. (1988) *The New International Labour Studies*, London: Zed Books.

Murcott, A. (1983) 'It's a pleasure to cook for him: food, mealtimes and gender in some South Wales households', in E. Gamarnikow, D. Morgan, J. Purvis and D. Taylorson (eds) *The Public and the Private*, London: Heinemann.

Murray, F. M. (1985) 'Industrial Restructuring and Class Politics in Postwar Italy', PhD thesis, University of Bristol.

Murukami, T. (1995) 'Teamworking', PhD thesis, University of Warwick.

National Commission on Education (1993) *Learning to Succeed*, London: Heinemann.

National Committee of Inquiry into Higher Education (1997) *Higher Education in the Learning Society* (the Dearing Report), London: HMSO.

Newson, J. and Newson, E. (1963) *Patterns of Infant Care in an Urban Community*, London: Allen & Unwin.

Nichols, T. (1969) *Ownership, Control and Ideology*, London: Allen & Unwin.

Nichols, T. (ed.) (1980) *Capital and Labour: Studies in the Capitalist Labour Process*, Glasgow: Fontana/London: Athlone.

Nichols, T. (1986) *The British Worker Question: A New Look at Workers and Productivity in Manufacturing*, London: Routledge & Kegan Paul.

Nichols, T. (1992) 'Different forms of labour', *Work, Employment and Society*, 6(1) March.

Nichols, T. (1994) 'Industrial accidents as a means of withdrawal from the workplace according to the Tavistock Institute of Human Relations: a re-examination of a classic study', *British Journal of Sociology*, 45(3).

Nichols, T. (1996) '*Social Class – official sociological and Marxist definitions*', in J. Irvine, I. Miles and J. Evans (eds) *Demystifying Social Statistics* (2nd edn), London: Pluto.

Nichols, T. and Armstrong, P. (1977) *Workers Divided*, Glasgow: Fontana.

Nichols, T. and Beynon, H. (1977) *Living with Capitalism: Class Relations in the Modern Factory*, London: Routledge & Kegan Paul.

Nichols, T. (1997) *The Sociology of Industrial Injury*, London: Mansell.

Nolan, P. (1989) 'The productivity miracle?', in Green, F. (ed.) *The Restructuring of the UK Economy*, Brighton: Harvester.

Nolan, P. and O'Donnell, K. (1991) 'Restructuring and the politics of industrial renewal: the limits of Flexible Specialisation', in A. Pollert (ed.) *Farewell to Flexibility?*, Oxford: Blackwell.

Nolan, P. and O'Donnell, K. (1995) 'Industrial relations and productivity', in P. Edwards (ed.) *Industrial Relations: Theory and Practice in Britain*, Oxford: Blackwell.

Nomura, M. (1993) *The End of 'Toyotaism'? Recent Trends in a Japanese Automobile Company*, CRWS Conference on the Lean Workplace, York University, Ontario, 30 Sept.–3 Oct.

Nuss, S. (1991) Personal communication.

O'Connell Davidson, J. (1992) 'The Employment Relation: Degradation and Diversity in the Privatised Water Industry', PhD thesis, University of Bristol.

Office of Health Economics (1993) *The Impact of Unemployment on Health*, Briefing 29, 1993.

OMIRP (Oxford Motor Industry Research Project) (1993) *New Management Techniques: Proceedings of a Workshop*, Oxford: Oxford Brookes University, School of Planning.

Pahl, R. E. (1989) 'Is the emperor naked? Some questions on the adequacy of sociological theory in urban and regional research', *International Journal of Urban and Regional Research*, 13(4).

Pahl, R. E. (1993) 'Does class analysis without class theory have a future? A reply to Goldthorpe and Marshall', *Sociology*, 27(2).

Pahl, R. and Wallace, C. (1988) 'Neither angels in marble nor rebels in red', in D. Rose (ed.) *Social Stratification and Economic Change*, London: Hutchinson.

Palmer, G. (1996) 'Reviving resistance: the Japanese factory floor in Britain', *Industrial Relations Journal*, 27(2).

Paneth, M. (1944) *Branch Street: A Sociological Study*, London: Allen & Unwin.

Papastergiadis, N. (1998) *Dialogues in the Diasporas: Essays and Conversations on Cultural Identity*, London: Rivers Oram Press.

Parkin, F. (1978) 'Social Stratification', in T. Bottomore and R. Nisbet (eds) *A History of Sociological Analysis*, London: Heinemann.

Parsons, T. (1951) *The Social System*, London: Routledge & Kegan Paul.

Pascall, G. and Cox, R. (1993) *Women Returning to Higher Education*, Buckingham: Open University Press.

Patten, J. (1989) *On Being British*, Mimeograph, London: Home Office.

Patterson, S. (1963) *Dark Strangers*, London: Penguin.

Payne, J. and Payne, C. (1993) 'Unemployment and peripheral work', *Work, Employment and Society*, 7(4).

Phillips, A. (1987) *Divided Loyalties: Dilemmas of Sex and Class*, London: Virago.

Phizacklea, A. (ed.) (1983) *One Way Ticket*, London: Routledge & Kegan Paul.

Phizacklea, A. (1995) *Gender, 'Race' and Migration: Casualisation and Organisation*, paper for the European Seminar on Forms of Informal Employment in the European Union, Athens, May 1995.

Pietila, H. and Vickers, J. (1990) *Making Women Matter: The Role of the United Nations*, London: Zed Books.

Piore, M. and Sabel, C. (1984) *The Second Industrial Divide: Possibilities for Prosperity*, New York: Basic Books.

Plowden, B. (1967) *Children and their Primary Schools*, London: HMSO.

Pole, C. J. (1993) *Assessing and Recording Achievement*, Buckingham: Open University Press.

Pollard, A. *et al.* (1994) *Changing English Primary Schools*, London: Cassell.

Pollard, S. (1969) *The Development of the British Economy 1914–1967*, London: Edward Arnold.

Pollert, A. (1996) ' "Team Work" on the assembly-line: contradictions and the dynamics of union resilience', in P. Ackers *et al.* (eds) *The New Workplace and Trade Unionism*, London: Routledge.

Porter, M. (1983) *Home, Work and Class Consciousness*, Manchester: Manchester University Press.

Poster, M. (1978) *Critical Theory of the Family*, London: Pluto Press.

Potts, L. (1990) *The World Labour Market: A History of Migration*, London: Zed Books.

Pugh, D. S., Hickson, D. J. and Hinings, C. R. (1964) *Writers on Organisations*, London: Hutchinson.

Ramazonoglu, C. (1989) *Feminism and the Contradictions of Oppression*, London: Routledge.

Randall, G., Ford, J. and Rennie, S. (1991) *Appraisal of Staff: An Equal Opportunities Approach*, University of Bradford: Work and Gender Research Unit, Occasional Paper, No. 2.

Rattansi, A. (1982) *Marx and the Division of Labour*, London: Macmillan.

Reddy, W. M. (1987) *Money and Liberty in Modern Europe: A Critique of Historical Understanding*, Cambridge: Cambridge University Press.

Reddy, W. M. (1992) 'The Concept of Class', in M. L. Bush (ed.) (1992) *Social Orders and Social Classes in Europe Since 1500*, London: Longman.

Reich, R. (1991) *The Work of Nations*, New York: Knopf.

Rhys, G. (1995) 'The transformation of the motor industry in the UK', in R. Turner (ed.) *The British Economy in Transition: From the Old to the New?*, London: Routledge.

Ritzer, G. (1993) *The Macdonaldisation of Society: An Investigation into the Changing Character of Contemporary Social Life*, Thousand Oaks, Calif.: Pine Forge Press.

Robbins, D. (ed.) with Caldwell, L., Day, G., Jones, K. and Rose, H. (1982) *Rethinking Social Inequality*, London: Gower.

Roberts, B., Finnegan, R. and Gallie, D. (eds) (1985) *New Approaches to Economic Life*, Manchester: Manchester University Press.

Roberts, E. (1984) *A Woman's Place: An Oral History of Working-Class Women*, Oxford: Blackwell.

Roberts, Robert (1971) *A Classic Slum*, Harmondsworth: Penguin.

Robertson, D. and Hillman, J. (1997) *Widening Participation in Education by Students from Lower Socio-Economic Groups and Students with Disabilities* (Report 6 of the Dearing Report on Higher Education), London: HMSO.

Robertson, R. (1992) *Globalisation: Social Theory and Global Culture*, London: Sage.

Robertson, R. (1995) 'Globalisation: time–space and homogeneity–heterogeneity', in M. Featherston, S. Lash and R. Robertson (eds) *Global Modernities*, London: Sage.

Roethlisberger, F. J. and Dickson, W. J. (1939) *Management and the Worker*, Cambridge, Mass.: Harvard University Press.

Roots, P. (1986) *Collective Bargaining: Opportunities for a New Approach*, Warwick Papers in Industrial Relations 5, IRRU, University of Warwick.

Rosaldo, R. (1993) *Culture and Truth. The Remaking of Social Analysis*, London: Routledge.

Rowbotham, S. (1975) *Hidden from History: 300 years of women's oppression and the fight against it*, London: Pluto Press.

Rowntree, B. S. and Lavers, G. R. (1951) *English Life and Leisure: A Social Study*, London: Longmans.

Roy, D. (1952) 'Quota restriction and goldbricking in a machine shop', *American Journal of Sociology*, 57(5).

Roy, D. F. (1953) 'Work satisfaction and social reward in quota achievement', *American Sociological Review*, 18(5).

Roy, D. (1954) 'Efficiency and the "fix": informal social relations in a piece-work machine shop', *American Journal of Sociology*, 60(3).

Roy, D. (1960) 'Banana time. Job satisfaction and informal interaction', *Human Organisation*, 18.

Royal Statistical Society (1995) *Report of the Working Party on the Measurement of Unemployment in the U.K.*, AMSO.

Rubery, J. (1978) 'Structured labour markets, worker organisation and low pay', *Cambridge Journal of Economics*, 2(1).

Runciman, W. G. (1966) *Relative Deprivation and Social Justice: A Study of Attitudes to Social Inequality in Twentieth Century England*, London: Routledge & Kegan Paul.

Salaman, G. (1986) *Working*, London: Tavistock.

Samuelson, P. (1943) 'Full employment after the war', in S. Harris (ed.) *Postwar Economic Problems*, New York: McGraw Hill.

Saunders, P. (1989) 'Left write in sociology', *Network*, 44.

Savage, M. and Miles, A. (1994) *The Remaking of the Working Class*, London: Macmillan.

Sayer, A. and Walker, R. (1992) *The New Social Economy: Reworking the Division of Labour*, Oxford: Blackwell.

Sayles, L. (1958) *Behaviour of Industrial Workgroups*, New York: Wiley.

Sayyid, B. (1994) 'Sign O'Times: Kaffirs and Infidels Fighting the Ninth Crusade', in E. Laclau (ed.) *The Making of Political Identities*, London: Verso.

Scarborough, H. and Terry, M. (1996) *Industrial Relations and the Reorganization of Production in the UK Motor Industry: A Study of the Rover Group*, Warwick Papers in Industrial Relations 58, IRRU, University of Warwick. An abbreviated version of this paper has been published as 'United Kingdom: The reorganisation of production', in T. A. Kochan *et al.* (eds) *After Lean Production: Evolving Employment Practices in the World Auto Industry*, New York: Cornell University Press 1997.

Scase, R. (1992) *Class*, Buckingham: Open University Press.

Scott, A. (1994) *Willing Slaves? British Workers under Human Resource Management*, Cambridge: Cambridge University Press.

Scott, A. M. (1986) 'Industrialisation, gender segregation and stratification theory', in R. Crompton and M. Mann (eds) *Gender and Stratification*, Cambridge: Polity Press.

Scott, D. (1990) *Coursework and Coursework Assessment in the GCSE*, Coventry: University of Warwick.

Scott, M., Roberts, I., Holroyd, G. and Sawbridge, D. (1989) *Management and Industrial Relations in Small Firms*, London: HMSO.

Scott, W. H. *et al.* (1956) *Technical Change and Industrial Relations*, Liverpool: Liverpool University Press.

Scott, W. H. *et al.* (1963) *Coal and Conflict*, Liverpool: Liverpool University Press.

Seabrook, J. (1978) *What Went Wrong?*, London: Gollancz.

Seabrook, J. (1982) *Unemployment*, London: Quartet Books.

Seabrook, J. (1985) *Landscapes of Poverty*, Oxford: London.

Seabrook, J. (1988) *The Race for Riches: the Human Cost of Wealth*, London: Marshall Pickering.

Sear, N. (1962) 'Industrial research in Britain', in A. T. Welford (ed.) *Society: Problems and Methods of Study*, London: Routledge & Kegan Paul.

Searle, C. (1992) 'The gulf between: a school and a war', *Race and Class*, 33(4).

Seed, J. (1992) 'From "middling sort" to middle class in late eighteenth and early nineteenth century England', in M. L. Bush (ed.) *Social Orders and Social Classes in Europe Since 1500*, London: Longman.

Select Committee Report (1989) *Educational Provision for the Under Fives*, London: HMSO.

Sewell, G. and Wilkinson, B. (1992) '"Someone to watch over me": surveillance, discipline and the JIT labour process', *Sociology*, 26(2).

Shanin, T. (1973) *The Awkward Class*, Harmondsworth: Penguin.

Shioma, H. and Wada, K. (eds) (1995) *Fordism Transformed: The Development of Production Methods in the Automobile Industry*, Oxford: Oxford University Press.

Showler, B. and Sinfield, A. (1981) 'A most unequal tax', in B. Showler and A. Sinfield (eds) *The Workless State*, London: Martin Robertson, pp. 215–40.

Silver, H. (1973) *The Sociology of Educational Opportunity*, London: Methuen.

Silverman, D. (1970) *The Theory of Organisations*, London: Heinemann.

Sinfield, A. and Showler, B. (1981) 'Unemployment and the unemployed in 1980', in B. Showler and A. Sinfield (eds) *The Workless State*, London: Martin Robertson.

Sivanandan, A. (1976) 'Race, class and the state: the black experience in Britain', in *Race and Class*, XVII(4).

Skeggs, B. (1997) *Formations of Class and Gender: Becoming Respectable*, London: Sage.

Skellington, Richard (1992) *Race in Britain Today*, London: Sage Publications.

Skinner, W. (1971) 'The Anachronistic Factory', *British Royal Society*, 49.

Skocpol, T. (1979) *States and Revolution*, Cambridge: Cambridge University Press.

Smeeding, T. M. and Rainwater, L. (1991) *Cross National Trends in Income Poverty and Dependency: The Evidence for Young Adults in the Eighties*, paper presented to JCPS Conference on Poverty and Marginality, Washington.

Smith, C. (1991) 'From 1960's automation to flexible specialization: a déjà vu of technological panaceas', in A. Pollert (ed.) *Farewell to Flexibility?* Oxford: Blackwell.

Smith, C. and Elger, T. (1996) *The Local in the Global: Transplant Localisation as a Contested Process*, CLS/IRRU Conference on the Globalization of Production and the Regulation of Labour, University of Warwick, 11–13 Sept.

Smith, C. *et al.* (1990) *Reshaping Work: the Cadbury Experience*, Cambridge: Cambridge University Press.

Smith, D. (1988) 'The Japanese example in south west Birmingham', *Industrial Relations Journal*, 19(1).

Smith, D. E. (1978) 'A peculiar eclipsing: woman's exclusion from man's culture', *Women's Studies International Quarterly*, 1(4).

Smith, D. J. (1992) *Understanding the Underclass*, Policy Studies Institute.

Smith, J. H. (1961) 'The university teaching of social sciences', *Industrial Sociology*, Paris: UNESCO.

Smith, P. and Morton, G. (1993) 'Union exclusion and the decollectivization of industrial relations in contemporary Britain', *British Journal of Industrial Relations*, 31(1).

Snell, K. (1992) 'Deferential bitterness: the social outlook of the rural proletariat in eighteenth and nineteenth century England and Wales', in M. L. Bush (ed.) (1992) *Social Orders and Social Classes in Europe Since 1500*, London: Longman.

Social Trends 28, London: HMSO.

Solomos, John (1992) 'The politics of immigration since 1945', in P. Braham, A. Rattansi and R. Skellington (eds) *Racism and Antiracism: Inequalities, Opportunities and Policies*, London: Sage Publications.

Solomos, John (1993) *Race and Racism in Britain* (2nd edn), London: Macmillan.

Spinley, B. (1953) *The Deprived and the Privileged*, London: Routledge & Kegan Paul.

Stacey, M. (1969) 'The myth of community studies', *British Journal of Sociology*, XX, (2).

Stacey, M. (1981) 'The division of labour revisited or overcoming the two Adams', in P. Abrams, R. Deem, J. Finch and P. Rock (eds) *Practice and Progress: British Sociology 1950–1980*, London: Allen & Unwin.

Stacey, M. (1986) 'Gender and stratification, one central issue or two?', in R. Crompton and M. Mann (eds) *Gender and Stratification*, Cambridge: Polity Press.

Stanley, L. (ed.) (1990) *Feminist Praxis*, London: Routledge.

Stanworth, M. (1984) 'Women and class analysis: a reply to John Goldthorpe', *Sociology*, 18(2).

Starkey, K. and McKinlay, A. (1989) 'Beyond Fordism? Strategic choice and labour relations in Ford UK', *Industrial Relations Journal*, 20(2).

Stationery Office (1997) *The Learning Age*, London: HMSO.

Statistics of Education, London: HMSO, 1997.

Statistics of Education, London: HMSO, 1998.

Stein, Maurice, R. (1960) *The Eclipse of Community*, New York: Harper.

Stephenson, C. (1996) 'The different experience of trade unionism in two Japanese transplants', in P. Ackers *et al.* (eds) *The New Workplace and Trade Unionism*, London: Routledge.

Stewart, R. (1970) *Managers and their Jobs*, London: Macmillan.

Summerfield, P. (1984) *Women Workers in the Second World War*, Beckenham: Croom Helm.

Sylva, K. and Moss, P. (1993) 'Learning before school' in National Commission for Education, *Briefings*, London: Heinemann.

Taylor, B. *et al.* (1994) 'Transplants and emulators: the fate of the Japanese model in British electronics', in T. Elger and C. Smith (eds) *Global Japanization?*, London: Routledge.

Taylor, R. (1982) *Workers and the New Depression*, London: Macmillan.

Thompson, E. P. (1968) *The Making of the English Working Class*, Harmondsworth: Penguin.

Thompson, E. P. (1978) *The Poverty of Theory*, London: Merlin Press.

Thompson, E. P. (1991) *Customs in Common*, London: Merlin Press.

Thompson, P. (1983) *The Nature of Work: An Introduction to Debates on the Labour Process*, London: Macmillan.

Thompson, P. (1990) 'Crawling from the wreckage', in D. Knights and H. Willmott (eds) *Labour Process Theory*, London: Macmillan.

Thompson, P. *et al.* (1995) ' "It ain't what you do, it's the way that you do it": production organisation and skill utilisation in commercial vehicles', *Work Employment and Society*, 5(4).

Titmuss, R. (1962) *Income Distribution and Social Change*, London: Allen & Unwin.

Tolliday, S. and Zeitlin, J. (1986) 'Introduction: between Fordism and flexibility', in S. Tolliday and J. Zeitlin (eds) *The Automobile Industry and its Workers*, Cambridge: Polity Press.

Tomaney, J. (1994) 'A new paradigm of work organisation and technology?', in A. Amin (ed.) *Post-Fordism: a Reader*, Oxford: Blackwell.

Tomlinson, J. (1986) 'Public education, public good', *Oxford Review of Education*, 12(3).

Tomlinson, J. (1993) *The Control of Education*, London: Cassell.

Tönnies, F. (1957) *Gemeinschaft und Gesellschaft*, New York: Harper & Row.

Touraine, A. *et al.* (1965) *Workers' Attitudes to Technical Change*, Paris: OECD.

Townsend, P. (1979) *Poverty in the United Kingdom*, Harmondsworth: Penguin.

Townsend, P. and Davidson, N. (eds) (1982) *Inequalities in Health: The Black Report*, Harmondsworth: Penguin.

Trilling, C. (1993) *Remembering Denny*, New York: Farrar Straus & Giroux.

Trist, E. L. and Bamforth, K. W. (1951) 'Some social and psychological consequences of the longwall method of coal getting', *Human Relations*, 4(1).

Trist, E. L. *et al.* (1963) *Organisational Choice*, London: Tavistock.

Turnbull, P. J. (1986) 'The "Japanisation" of production and industrial relations at Lucas Electrical', *Industrial Relations Journal*, 17(3).

Turnbull, P. J. (1988) 'The limits to "Japanisation" – Just-in-Time, labour relations and the UK automotive industry', *New Technology, Work and Employment*, 3(1).

Turner, B. A. (1971) *Exploring the Industrial Subculture*, London: Macmillan.

Turner, H. A. *et al.* (1967) *Labour Relations in the Motor Industry*, London: Allen & Unwin.

Turner, H. A. (1962) *Trade Union Growth, Structure and Policy*, London: Allen & Unwin.

Tyne and Wear Research and Intelligence Unit (1994) *Economic Activity and Employment, 1991 Census Topic Report.*

Tyne and Wear Research and Intelligence Unit (1994a) *Economy and Labour Market 1994.*

Tyne and Wear Research and Intelligence Unit (1995) *Unemployment Trends 1994.*

UCAS (1996) *Qualified Applicants: Those who did not enter higher education*, Cheltenham: UCAS.

Ullah, P. (1987) 'Unemployed black youths in a northern city', in D. Fryer and P. Ullah (eds) *Unemployed People: Social and Psychological Perspectives*, Milton Keynes: Open University Press.

United Nations (1976) *Report of the World Conference of the International Women's Year*, New York: UN World Plan of Action.

United Nations (1980) *Report of the World Conference of the United Nations Decade for Women*, New York: United Nations.

United Nations (1986) *Report on the World Conference to Review and Appraise the Achievements of the United Nation's Decade for Women, Nairobi*, New York: United Nations.

van Olselen, C. (1976) *Chibaro*, London: Pluto Press.

Wakeford, N. (1993) 'Beyond educating Rita: mature students and access courses', *Oxford Review of Education*, 19(2).

Walby, S. (1986) 'Gender, class and stratification', in R. Crompton and M. Mann (eds) *Gender and Stratification*, Cambridge: Polity Press.

Walby, S. (ed.) (1988) *Gender Segregation at Work*, Milton Keynes: Open University Press.

Walder, A. G. (1986) *Communist Neo Traditionalism: Work and Authority in Chinese Industry*, Berkeley: University of California Press.

Walker, C. R. and Guest, R. H. (1952) *Man on the Assembly Line*, Cambridge, Mass.: Harvard University Press.

Wallerstein, I. (1979) *The Capitalist World Economy*, New York: Cambridge University Press.

Waring, M. (1988) *If Women Counted: A New Feminist Economics*, London: Macmillan.

Warr, P. (1987) *Work, Unemployment and Mental Health*, Oxford: Clarendon Press.

Warwick, D. and Littlejohn, G. M. (1992) *Coal, Capital and Culture*, London: Routledge.

Watson, J. M. (1978) 'The Big Chimney', from J. Common (ed.) *Seven Shifts*, Bradford: EP Publishing.

Weber, M. (1968) *On Charisma and Institution Building*, Chicago: University of Chicago Press.

Wedderburn, D. (ed.) (1974) *Poverty, Inequality and Class Structure*, Cambridge: Cambridge University Press.

West, J. (ed.) (1982) *Work, Women and the Labour Market*, London: Routledge & Kegan Paul.

Westergaard, J. (1977) 'Class, Inequality and "Corporatism"', in A. Hunt (ed.) *Class and Class Structure*, London: Lawrence & Wishart.

Wheelock, J. (1990) *Husbands at Home: The Domestic Economy in a Post Industrial Society*, London: Routledge.

Whitston, K. (1996) 'Scientific Management and Production Management Practice in Britain between the Wars', *Historical Studies in Industrial Relations*, 1.

Whyte, W. F. (1955) *Money and Motivation*, New York: Harper & Row.

Wickens, P. (1987) *The Road to Nissan: Flexibility, Quality, Teamwork*, London: Macmillan.

Wickens, P. (1993) 'Lean production and beyond: the system, its critics and the future', *Human Resource Management Journal*, 3(4).

Wiener, Martin (1985) *English Culture and the Decline of the Industrial Spirit. 1850–1980*, Harmondsworth: Penguin.

Williams, K. *et al.* (1987) 'The end of mass production?', *Economy and Society*, 16(3).

Williams, K. *et al.* (1992) 'Against lean production', *Economy and Society*, 21(3): 321–54.

Williams, K. *et al.* (1993) 'Ford versus "Fordism": the beginning of mass production?', *Work, Employment and Society*, 6(4).

Williams, K. *et al.* (1994) *Cars: Analysis, History, Cases*, Providence: Berghahn.

Williams, R. (1958) *Culture and Society*, Harmondsworth: Penguin.

Williams, R. (1961) *The Long Revolution*, Harmondsworth: Penguin.

Williams, R. (1965) *The Long Revolution*, Harmondsworth: Penguin.

Williamson, W. (1982) *Class, Culture and Community – A Biographical Study of Social Change in Mining*, London: Routledge & Kegan Paul.

Willman, P. and Winch, G. (1985) *Innovation and Management Control: Labour Relations at BL Cars*, Cambridge: Cambridge University Press.

Willmott, H. (1984) 'Images and ideals of management work', *Journal of Management Studies*, 21(3).

Willmott, P. (1963) *The Evolution of a Community*, London: Routledge & Kegan Paul.

Wirth, L. (1928) *The Ghetto*, Chicago: University of Chicago Press.

Womack, J. *et al.* (1990) *The Machine that Changed the World*, New York: Rawson Associates.

Wood, S. (1989) 'The Transformation of Work?', in S. Wood (ed.) *The Transformation of Work?*, London: Unwin Hyman.

Wood, S. (1993) 'The Japanization of Fordism', *Economic and Industrial Democracy*, 14.

Wood, S. (ed.) (1982) *The Degradation of Work? Skill, Deskilling and the Labour Process*, London: Hutchinson.

Woodward, J. (1958) *Management and Technology*, London: HMSO.

Woodward, J. (ed.) (1970) *Industrial Organisations: Behaviour and Control*, Oxford: Oxford University Press.

Wright Mills, C. (1959) *The Sociological Imagination*, Oxford: Oxford University Press.

Young, M. and Willmott, P. (1957) *Family and Kinship in East London*, London: Routledge & Kegan Paul.

Zorbaugh, H. (1929) *The Gold Coast and the Slum*, Chicago: University of Chicago Press.

Zweig, F. (1961) *The Worker in an Affluent Society*, London: Heinemann.

SUBJECT INDEX

All page references in italics refer to tables
All page references in bold refer to footnotes

AUTHOR INDEX